GAME DEVELOPMENT
WITH LUA

GAME DEVELOPMENT
WITH LUA

PAUL SCHUYTEMA

MARK MANYEN

CHARLES RIVER MEDIA, INC.
Hingham, Massachusetts

Publisher: Jenifer Niles
Cover Design: Tyler Creative
Cover Image: © Chris Listello 2005.

CHARLES RIVER MEDIA, INC.
10 Downer Avenue
Hingham, Massachusetts 02043
781-740-0400
781-740-8816 (FAX)
info@charlesriver.com
www.charlesriver.com

This book is printed on acid-free paper.

Paul Schuytema and Mark Manyen. *Game Development with Lua.*
ISBN: 1-58450-404-8

All brand names and product names mentioned in this book are trademarks or service marks of their respective companies. Any omission or misuse (of any kind) of service marks or trademarks should not be regarded as intent to infringe on the property of others. The publisher recognizes and respects all marks used by companies, manufacturers, and developers as a means to distinguish their products.

Library of Congress Cataloging-in-Publication Data
Schuytema, Paul.
  Game development with Lua / Paul Schuytema and Mark Manyen.
     p. cm.
  Includes index.
  ISBN 1-58450-404-8 (pbk. with cd-rom : alk. paper)
  1. Computer games--Programming. 2. Lua (Computer program language) I. Manyen, Mark, 1963- II. Title.
  QA76.76.C672S382 2005
  794.8'1526--dc22
                                  2005013303

Printed in Canada
05 7 6 5 4 3 2 First Edition

CHARLES RIVER MEDIA titles are available for site license or bulk purchase by institutions, user groups, corporations, etc. For additional information, please contact the Special Sales Department at 781-740-0400.

Requests for replacement of a defective CD-ROM must be accompanied by the original disc, your mailing address, telephone number, date of purchase, and purchase price. Please state the nature of the problem, and send the information to CHARLES RIVER MEDIA, INC., 10 Downer Avenue, Hingham, Massachusetts 02043. CRM's sole obligation to the purchaser is to replace the disc, based on defective materials or faulty workmanship, but not on the operation or functionality of the product.

To the Magic Lantern team:
the finest game developers we've had the pleasure to work with!
–Paul Schuytema & Mark Manyen

Contents

Acknowledgments

This book wouldn't have been possible without the fine scripting work of Nick Carlson, who worked with us on the sample game and the various examples in the book—he may be just starting his college career, but he has a great future ahead! Also, a huge thank-you goes out to Chris Listello, for the art in Take Away and the cover illustration. We also have to send out a large thank-you to Roberto Ierusakimschy for the great introduction to this book, and the entire Lua Tecgraf team for creating such a functional and high-performance scripting language in Lua. Finally, thanks to the Charles River team: to Jenifer Niles for her support and for the copy and tech editors that helped us refine our writing, and to the entire production team for helping to create a project we are all very proud of.

Foreword

The concept of scripting is important in any software undertaking, but for game development, it is crucial. Scripting languages allow programmers to separate the "hard parts" of game development from the "soft parts." Hard parts, which usually require sheer computer performance, change little during the development process and can be reused frequently. Graphical engines and artificial intelligence (AI) modules are examples of hard parts. Those modules are best programmed in a language like C or C++, which offer performance at the cost of flexibility. Soft parts control the hard parts in order to create the final shape and quality of a product. These parts are best programmed with a scripting language like Lua, which gives the programmer the flexibility he needs to try, test, and change the game code.

Lua was born as a scripting language for two particular industrial applications, both related to the games industry. We needed both a flexible data-description language and a scripting language to describe simple actions (for example, data validation). These origins specified certain requirements for Lua: portability, small size, and non-limiting. It had to be portable, because our clients' computer base was quite heterogeneous (MS-DOS, Windows 3.0, IBM AIX, as well as several other platforms). It had to be small, both because it could not bloat the applications using it and because several of its target machines were small. At the same time, previous experience had taught us that any language should not restrict programmers, because when users configure applications, they frequently need (and create) elements that we cannot imagine beforehand. Since its first versions were available, Lua presented good performance, mostly as a byproduct of its simplicity. Over time, that simplicity proved to be a valued property, so we added it to the list of Lua's requirements.

Lua was an instant success in Tecgraf. Soon, several other projects were using Lua, so we made it available to the outside world. This proved to be a wise move as making Lua freely available to the public gave us a team of international consultants that has since helped the evolution of the language.

At the end of 1996, Bret Mogilefsky, then working at Lucas Arts, read a paper about Lua on Dr. Dobb's Web site and decided to adopt it for the game he was developing, *Grim Fandango*. A few months later, he spread the word about Lua at the Game Developer's Conference. Soon Lua was being used by several game companies. The growing adoption of Lua came as a surprise for us. We never thought about Lua as a language for game development. It did have numerous uses related to graphics but not necessarily to games. In hindsight, however, the move into game development makes sense.

All of Lua's strong points are important for game development: simplicity, portability, and efficiency, and since then, we have paid more attention to those game programmers. Several features introduced over recent years, such as coroutines, have been geared toward game development. Although the functionality of Lua is by no means restricted to game development, game development does play a key role in the further development of Lua.

This book is a more-than-welcome arrival within the growing list of Lua titles. With its focus on game programming, this book is a must-have for anyone intending to develop serious games. We hope it will help to spread Lua even more in this growing field.

— Roberto Ierusalimschy

Introduction

GAME DEVELOPMENT WITH LUA

Game development is an exciting process—there is nothing more satisfying than creating an interactive playing experience that can provide hours of enjoyment for a player. This process, however, is becoming more complicated. Gone are the days of hit games being created over evenings and weekends in someone's basement— now game-development teams with dozens of members work for months (and years) to create play experiences. Even the simplest "casual games" that you can download from the Web are often created over months of hard work by a team of professional developers.

Given the growing scale of game development, one thing remains constant— the ability to test, change, tweak, and rapidly adjust how a game works. Often, this component is essential to the design and development process. By partnering a scripting language such as Lua with a core low-level language (like C++), you can develop professional games, yet still allow yourself, as a developer and designer, the freedom to experiment.

AUDIENCE

This book is aimed at three primary audiences:

Game Programmer. A programmer is the team member who must implement the connection between Lua and C++, and who is often called on to code some or all of a game's scripts. For the programmer, this book will show how to integrate Lua and LuaGlue functionality into a game-development project. The upshot for the team programmer is that implementing Lua will free him up later in the development process, because many of the game play features can now be implemented by designers and script programmers.

Game Designer. Often, the game designer will use a scripting language like Lua to implement facets of the game design into the runtime environment. For the designer, this book will serve as a primer to the Lua language and provide a solid foundation on which to build up real-world scripting skills. It should also serve as a creative catalyst for the designer: a game developed with Lua empowers the designer with the tools for rapid prototyping, rapid implementation, and true creative experimentation.

The Development Hobbyist. Nothing can be more rewarding and intellectually challenging than learning how to create your own game. The game industry has inspired an army of weekend hobbyists who enjoy learning more about games and game development by working on their own projects, and the industry is much richer for their efforts. This book will show the advanced hobbyist how to implement Lua into his own project. It will also provide a ready-made framework for the less-advanced hobbyist to dive in, learn Lua, and start crafting his own game with no C++ coding at all (a complete console and game "sandbox" is provided).

IN THIS BOOK

In this book, you will find an introduction to Lua, both in historical context and as an introduction to scripting with the language. You will also learn how to link the Lua API into your C++ application so you can create your own LuaGlue functions that allow Lua to extend your C++ functionality.

Once we have built our foundation, this book will take you through the development of a "rapid prototype" game, using the Lua scripting language. This game will provide the context with which to explore the foundational C++ approaches and the Lua scripting approaches to:

- Saving and loading game data
- Building a modular and flexible GUI system
- Managing a game's real-time events through Lua scripts

■ Using Lua to define and control game AI (Artificial Intelligence)

ON THE CD

ON THE CD The CD that accompanies this book will provide a host of useful material that will extend your understanding of Lua in the realm of game development even further. On the CD, you will find:

■ Lua 5.0 distribution
■ Project to build a Lua library
■ Microsoft's DirectX 9 SDK
■ Source code for all of the projects and in-depth examples in the book (both in Lua and in C++)
■ A command-line Lua interpreter (the application and source code)
■ A custom Lua-enhanced shareware version of the Zeus program editor
■ Essential license documents
■ A basic Lua scripting style guide
■ A complete game created in C++ and Lua (the application, source code, and Lua scripts)

1 Diving into Game Development

In This Chapter

■ Growing Complexity
■ A Better Way
■ Why Lua?

Creating your own game can be one of the most exciting undertakings you can imagine. Crafting a play experience that delivers fun, challenge, and the thrill of victory is a rush to anyone involved.

If you are a game hobbyist, you know the thrill the moment you get to play your own game for the first time, as well as that extra-special thrill when you let others play it and you see that glow of fun and excitement wash across their faces.

That feeling isn't alien to seasoned developers, either. We care just as much about our games, and nothing gives a development team a bigger thrill than seeing someone having fun playing a game that was a true labor of love, blood, sweat, and tears.

GROWING COMPLEXITY

Years ago, many games were created in garages and basements, on weekends and after work. Now creating the games carried in the local electronics store requires dozens of specialized team members working together.

This growing complexity has lead to an era of specialization. Artists work in 2D or 3D animation or static models. Programmers are focused on network programming, artificial intelligence (AI), and 3D rendering. In this era of specialization, it's getting harder to get into the dynamic, creative flow of game development that was the norm years ago.

As the size of development teams continues to grow, so does the complexity of the games, and with this increased complexity comes increased dependencies of one game system on another. These dependencies can often create a long, laborious development cycle in which creative ideas go untried, and deadlines cause less opportunity for innovation and inspiration.

Several years ago, I had the opportunity to travel to a well-known development studio as they were wrapping up a third-person adventure/shooter game. The game looked great: the 3D environments were rich, and the interaction with the environments felt very realistic.

I was able to watch the process that brought that game play to life: first, a 3D artist created the game environments in a 3D modeling program. Those models were then exported into an in-house tool in which a designer could set up "trigger areas" that would signal that game events would happen whenever a player character or AI-controlled enemy entered the region. Then, the designer would have to sit down with a programmer and talk through every trigger region and tell him what he wanted to happen. The programmer would jot down notes and work for several days to implement this code. Once finished, the designer could see the result and request any required changes, at which time the process began again.

Although the results were solid, I couldn't help thinking about how painful, time-consuming, and static this process was. I knew there had to be a better way, but at that time, I was unfamiliar with scripting languages.

A BETTER WAY

That "better way" was to implement the project in concert with a midlevel scripting language, which would allow the designer to take on the entire interaction-development cycle, thus freeing the programmer to do the myriad other essential tasks.

From a game developer's perspective, scripting languages are tools that allow immediacy to reenter game development. Although it may take hours to get a clean build of a game project, a script programmer can make changes in seconds and see the results instantly. Game designers can test out ideas independent of programmers. Artists can create interfaces and wire in flow and function.

Scripting languages, which exist in a layer above the compiled code written by software engineers, are often compiled at runtime and are usually simple languages that make data handling and manipulation easy for the programmer or game designer.

Why use a scripting language? This is a valid question for veteran or hobbyist developers alike. From a designer's point of view, developing a game with a scripting language creates a very clear delineation between technology and game-play code. Often, in a script-enabled project, the lower-level nuts and bolts are left to a core language like C++, and the higher-level operations—such as interface handling, data management, artificial intelligence, and event handling—are handled by the scripting language. This separation of duties can give your game more stability and allow for parallel development.

Scripting languages can also engage less-technical members of a development team in the core development process. Interface artists can not only create the interface art but they can also create the script framework so those interfaces work in the game, without programmer intervention. Designers can work on AI or data manipulation, or on scenario scripting directly, without having to work through a programmer to implement their ideas.

Scripting languages are, by their very nature, easier to learn and work with than a low-level language such as C++. A scripting language like Lua doesn't deal with the nuts and bolts of memory management, object rendering, or TCP/IP network connections, and because of this, it's an easy tool to pick up, learn, and be productive with. Scripting doesn't take years to learn—a developer can pick up the syntax and the approach in hours rather than months.

In this book, we'll explore how to use the Lua language in concert with a C++ foundation to create a complete game from the bottom up. Along the way, you'll learn about the language in particular, and how a scripting language can really enhance the development process, whether you are a seasoned developer or a weekend warrior.

Other scripting languages are out there, so why did we choose Lua? If we look at the whole field of scripting languages, we can see Perl, Tcl, Ruby, Forth, Python, Java, and Lua. Although all of these scripting languages have their place in various fields, two scripting languages are well suited to the world of game development (that is, well suited to serve as intermediary languages above a C++ foundation): Python and Lua.

Many commercial games have been developed successfully using both Python and Lua, because they both have a very strong capability to work together with a compiled C++-based technology and can be extended through the use of C++. If you get a chance to frequent any programmers' hangouts, often you'll hear the two languages debated with a passion often reserved for sports (think Cubs versus White Sox, Jets versus Giants, Mets versus Yankees). Truth be told, both languages are great tools for game development.

WHY LUA?

Lua is an excellent choice for games because one of its core design goals is *extensibility*. It is designed from the ground up to be embedded within a larger application. Because this design goal, it is extremely easy to add Lua to an application. The embedded nature of Lua also makes it good at communicating with its parent application. Game programmers want a scripting language that is easy to implement in the technical design of the game. On this point, Lua delivers.

Lua is free, small, fast, and portable. All game developers and publishers love the word *free* when it comes to tools. Usually you get what you pay for, but with Lua you get so much more. The license under which Lua is distributed is exceptional in its flexibility. The source code is remarkably small, and the runtime footprint is exceptionally tight, making it easy on compile times and the runtime memory budget.

The most amazing aspect of Lua, however, may be its speed of execution. With any scripting solution, the first reaction of game programmers is usually: "Scripting is slow—the frame rate will never be good enough." This statement is completely untrue of Lua; in fact, we have not found a place where Lua was used and became a bottleneck. Finally, the game development world is heading for a new round of hardware, which means we are about to learn how to deal with a new set of platforms. Because Lua is portable, at least one aspect of our technology base will not be obsolete when we move to these new machines.

Lua is a very simple language to learn. There are no high-level "programmer" concepts (like objects or inheritance) to learn, so most computer-literate people can pick up the basics of Lua in a short time and start doing meaningful work right away. If team members are familiar with other languages, Lua will be a snap to pick up, making it suitable for non-programmer team members to get into the game and modify (or create) features and art.

In our company, we recently shipped our 13th game using Lua. Our team is small, but it has the standard mix of programmers, artists, and designers. When we get ready to start a new project, we first identify the technology needs of the project (what are the new things that we need to implement that we don't already have?) and work to design the functionality we need. The programmers can, armed with this technical design, hunker down and focus on the issues they know best. Simultaneously, the designers and artists can lay out the flow of the interface and the core functionality of the game—and they can get started, right away. Often the artists (both 2D and 3D) spend some time capturing the needed look and feel of the game. While this process is going on, the three designers, who are all fluent in Lua as well, dive in and begin constructing the foundation of the game, the game data, and the core game systems. They don't even have to wait for the programmers; if there is some functionality they need, they can often "sub it in" in Lua and press on. The end result is that we can develop games much more rapidly because we've got the entire team working full force from the get-go.

One project in particular stands out: while working on an election simulator for the 2004 presidential election, we were able to prototype nearly 100 percent of the game in Lua to test our approaches to AI and game flow, and then later go back and re-engineer the mission-critical components into C++. The ability to prototype allowed a single developer to work through the lion's share of the design and development process, which is a level of efficiency rare in this industry.

SUMMARY

Game development is an exciting enterprise—it's something we want to just dive in and do, right away. Lua gives us this ability: we can rapidly implement core concepts, quickly lay out and test interfaces, and easily manage copious quantities of runtime data—and do all of this without a deep technical background.

In the chapters that follow, we'll learn how to implement Lua into a game project, and we'll learn about the language itself. Then we'll take a journey together and craft an entire game, from start to finish. When we're done, we'll have a solid grasp of this nimble little language and how it can really enhance your games and your game-development experience.

2 What Is a Scripting Language?

In This Chapter

- ■ Introduction to Scripting Languages
- ■ Introduction to Lua

Computers are capable of many things, from generating reports to simulating economic models to recreating the experience of running your own theme park. But computers can't think on their own—they need to be tasked in a very regimented way. Most computer users specify tasks by using applications—tools such as a word processor or spreadsheet program. Software developers use low-level programming languages, such as C++, to task a computer (often to build applications for users). Between the "point and click" world of applications and the "build it from the ground up" world of low-level programming languages, you'll find scripting languages.

INTRODUCTION TO SCRIPTING LANGUAGES

Scripting languages provide easy communication with a computer's native functionality. At the outset, scripting languages were used as batch command tools—vehicles to stream a series of repeated commands into some kind of command processor. Early script languages were often called batch languages or job-control languages.

A familiar example is the old *.bat file of MS-DOS days. These "batch" files were simple text documents that contained a stream of DOS commands that were executed one after the other. The language itself was the DOS command set; it was the file and the extension that made them a pseudo script (see the following example).

```
copy g:\whitehouserun\working\whr.exe
copy g:\whitehouserun\working\whrd.exe
ren *.txt *.lua
copy *.lua g:\luabank\whitehouserun
```

Computer languages are created to facilitate the solution of some sort of problem, from the system-level control of C and C++ to the artificial intelligence processing of a language such as LISP. Scripting languages generally share some commonalities. They are often used for rapid development (at a cost of speed and efficiency) and often employ a text-based syntax that is easier to write and read for nonprogrammers. The idea is that an educated user can write and use scripts without the need for programmer intervention. Scripting languages often excel at linking functionality that was created in some other, lower-level language.

Script files are either interpreted (that is, they are processed at the moment they are called, rather than pre-compiled) or compiled at load time. Lua, for example, is compiled into binary form when the Lua file is loaded and remains compiled until it is released from memory.

In the realm of software development, especially game development, integrating a scripting language with a low-level language can provide a developer greater control over the runtime environment and far greater flexibility to modify and experiment with that environment during the development process.

INTRODUCTION TO LUA

Lua is different from a traditional scripting language in that it is a "glue" language. Whereas old-school scripting languages were created to handle the execution of repetitive tasks, glue languages are tools that allow a user to "glue together" functions and processes of another language. Doing this allows a script programmer to do far more than simply execute commands; the programmer now can use the script to create new commands out of the building blocks of lower-level functions. In this book, we'll explore using Lua to glue together C++ functions as they relate to elements of game development: GUI, AI, data, and so on.

Lua, on its own, is a simple yet powerful language that allows a script programmer to perform a great number of processes. The language possesses powerful string and math functions, flexible data types (that do take a while to get used to!), and the ability to define functions. But without some sort of "glue" to connect Lua to some other environment, all that functionality is essentially lost. (True, you can execute Lua and see the results on a Lua command line, but beyond learning the language, command-line output is pretty much useless for game development.) The classic first task one learns in any computer language is how to get the language to call out "Hello world." The Lua version of this task is shown in Listing 1.1.

LISTING 2.1   The age-old "hello world" program in Lua

```
--Lua's "hello world"
myString = "hello world"
print(myString)
```

When Lua is used as a partner for a lower-level, more powerful language, such as C++, it really comes into its own. Lua can allow game developers to prototype game situations or even complete games rapidly. Game developers can craft the entire GUI for a game without any programmer intervention. Lua can also be utilized to manage the saving and loading of saved game files that can be read and debugged easily. Lua, in the world of game development, allows developers to create an environment that maximizes productivity and allows for easy experimentation.

According to the team that created Lua (described later), Lua is a "language engine" that can be embedded within an application. Lua is its own language (syntax and comments that are "pure" Lua), yet it also consists of an API (Application Programming Interface) that allows it to exchange data with an application that you develop. Lua can also be extended by the creation of C++ functions called from within Lua (these are the "glue" functions we mentioned earlier). When used in partnership with an application-development language (such as C++), Lua can be used as a framework for building a unique project-specific language, specially geared toward the task at hand. This extensibility makes Lua so well suited for the game-development environment.

As a stand-alone language (executed through a runtime window) Lua is quite limited and is useful only as a teaching tool. (We'll use a console to learn the language in later chapters.) Lua is meant to be integrated with another language, and it's in this context that it shines. This implementation can be simple, with only a few LuaGlue functions allowing it to communicate with the lower-level language, or it can be extended so greatly that it essentially becomes a new language based on the user-created LuaGlue functions.

Lua's History

Lua, which is Portuguese for "moon," was developed at the Pontifical Catholic University (Brazil) in 1993. The language was developed by a team (Roberto Ierusalimschy, Waldemar Celes, and Luiz Henrique de Figueiredo) from the Computer Graphics Technology Group (Tecgraf), who released it as freeware. One of the goals of the Lua development team was to create a small, efficient programming language that would work very well with the C programming language. In the realm of scripting languages, Lua is one of the fastest and most efficient, making it an ideal candidate for game development. The Lua core is less than 120 K in size (compared to about 860 K for Python and 1.1 MB for Perl), making it a lean environment when compiled and integrated into a game-development system. Lua generally performs much faster than the other leading game-development scripting language, Python; complete benchmarks can be found at the Computer Language Shootout Benchmarks page (*http://shootout.alioth.debian.org/*).

Tecgraf, created in 1987, is charged with developing and maintaining computer graphics and user interface software for use in technical and scientific software. In addition to Lua, the Tecgraf team has created IUP (a system for creating user interfaces), CanvasDraw (a platform-independent graphics library), TWF (a file format for graphics on Web pages), and other systems. You can find out more about Tecgraf by visiting *www.tecgraf.puc-rio.br.*

Lua License

Lua is free, open source software that can be used in both academic and commercial applications for no cost. For more information on the definition of open source software, visit *www.opensource.org.*

For game-development professionals, licensing costs are a huge factor in game-development decisions. Often, game engines can run well past the $500,000 mark for a single project, and often middleware technology (as which a scripting language is categorized) can run from $5,000 to $50,000 per project. For these reasons, open source software can be an attractive option.

Many times, open source software can be hampered by its very nature—because it doesn't exist to generate a profit, the code can often be buggy, quirky, and poorly commented. Also, because no one is being paid to offer technical assistance, support can be shoddy.

Lua avoids many of these pitfalls—it's a small and simple implementation originating (and still being maintained) by a single source, and the implementation is clear and concise. Lua was also developed by a team of computer-engineering professionals, and that same team still oversee its evolution. Unlike many other open source projects that grow and grow, Lua is designed to be extensible at the project level, not at the API level, so the core remains quite stable.

The spirit of the Lua license is that Lua can be used for any purpose for no cost and without requiring you to ask permission of the authors. If you'd like to learn more about the Lua license, you can visit *www.lua.org/license.html.*

ON THE CD The complete Lua 5.0 license follows (this license is also provided on the CD ROM):

Lua 5.0 License

Copyright ©2003-2004 Tecgraf, PUC-Rio.

Permission is hereby granted, free of charge, to any person obtaining a copy of this software and associated documentation files (the "Software"), to deal in the Software without restriction, including without limitation the rights to use, copy, modify, merge, publish, distribute, sublicense, and/or sell copies of the Software, and to permit persons to whom the Software is furnished to do so, subject to the following conditions:

SUMMARY

Scripting languages began as simple tools to provide "power users" a way to batch often-used commands into simple text files. Now multiple scripting languages, such as Python, Ruby, and Lua, offer the power and flexibility of true computer languages. Over recent years, scripting languages have come to the forefront in the game-development industry as viable middleware products that can extend the performance of a development team and the game project itself. Lua, created in Brazil by a team from Tecgraf, is ideally suited for use in game development, due to its small size, speed, and ease of integration with C and C++. The fact that Lua is an open source language that is supported by its creators and a growing faction of loyal users makes it an ideal choice for both professional and hobbyist game development.

3

Lua in the Realm of Game Development

In This Chapter

■ Scripting Languages and Games
■ Lua in a Game Project

Real-world game development is often governed by two conflicting pressures: the need to experiment and test ideas, and the need to develop quickly and on schedule. A scripting language, when properly integrated into the development process, allows veteran programmers to do what they do best: create the systems and building blocks of the game application.

SCRIPTING LANGUAGES AND GAMES

A scripting language can allow artists to work directly on the GUI, designers and junior programmers (script programming is a great way to bring junior programmers "into the fold" of game development) to work directly on the game flow and logic, and level designers to directly control their environments and the play experience.

Scripting languages are not high performance—they do not run at the speed of native code; therefore, they are not the best tools for writing performance-heavy operations. But a glue language—one that can be extended by writing accessible functions in the core language, such as Lua—can be used as the controlling mechanism for calling high-performance native code functions and processes. (Lua is one of the fastest scripting languages out there, so most speed concerns are mitigated.) C functions can be written to take advantage of that language's performance advantages and then "glued" to Lua so that a script programmer can utilize those functions.

An example of this process is the ability to place a 3D object in the game world. The rendering system is purely C++, but Lua calls the C++ to create an object of a specific model type and indicates its placement in the world. Lua is then used to indicate animations for the 3D entity. Lua does not handle any of the complex math required to transform the object in real time, but it does tell the lower-level rendering functions what to do and when. In the next example (see Listing 3.1), `AddEnvironmentObject()` is a LuaGlue function—it directly interacts with a C++ method and allows Lua to be the controlling mechanism for a lower-level 3D function. A function like this would be written by a C++ programmer to expose lower-level functionality to the script programmer or designer.

LISTING 3.1   Lua script used to place 3D objects into a scene

```
--Lua script to add room, table, and human models
--to a 3D runtime environment
envmID = AddEnvironmentObject("casino_02.mlg",0,0,0,0,0,0)
tableID = AddEnvironmentObject("poker_table_normal_02_5card.mlg",-
2,0,1.5,0,0,0)
if bodyID1 ~= nil or headID1 ~= nil then
    PositionChildEntity(tableID, bodyID1, "anchor_0")
end
-- This sets the color of the Ambient light in the scene
AddLight(LIGHT_AMBIENT, 30, 30, 30)
-- This Adds a directional light source to the scene
AddLight(LIGHT_DIRECTIONAL,  1.0, -1.0, 1.0, 255, 255, 255)
-- set initial camera look at
StartCamera(0,0,.556, 0,3,-5, 0.03,1.5,3,20,.5,2,0.001)
```

LUA IN A GAME PROJECT

The integration of a scripting language into a game-development project can enhance team productivity and truly extend the capabilities of a native compiled language. Lua excels in a number of essential game-development areas.

In a game-development team, you may have several team members all using Lua to perform their jobs. The team's programmers are responsible for integrating Lua into the game-development environment; often, they may be called on to script some Lua code. Game designers are usually the primary users of a scripting language, because they have the most direct and intimate relationship with the higher-level game concepts and data. Often, artists use Lua as well, either to lay out, design, and "wire together" a user interface or to lay out and assemble a 3D scene of component objects.

Lua is a powerful tool that can be used to perform the following tasks:

- Author a game's user interface
- Define, store, and manage essential game data
- Manage real-time game events
- Create and maintain a developer-friendly save/load game system
- Author a game's artificial intelligence system
- Prototype functions for later porting into a high-performance language

User Interface

The user interface is the medium through which a player interacts with your game. It is one of the most essential elements of your game, because it governs all of the interactions of your player. Because of its importance, the GUI is an aspect of your game that needs to be up and running quickly and tested and improved constantly to maximize the player's experience.

Lua can allow GUI artists to quickly set up all major interface elements—to place them on the screen, to manage user input, and to output game data. With a small set of core GUI components and control functions created by the game's programmers, an artist can author not only the art but the interaction of the game as well. This frees up programmer time and allows for maximum creative control for the artist as well as maximum testing time for your GUI design. Listing 3.2 shows an example of Lua used to create a text GUI item.

LISTING 3.2   Example of Lua used to create a text GUI item

```
--Text object example
CreateItem(200,"TextField")
SetItemPosition(200, 300, 20, 200, 28)
SetFont(200, "Arial", 16)
ItemCommand(200, "SetColor", 255,255,255,255)
ItemCommand(200, "SetString", "I am a text object")
```

Managing Game Data

Managing game data is always a challenge for game developers. The game data defines the parameters and characteristics of all the objects in the game world, from how much a pulse-gun upgrade costs to how fast a hover cart can move. For a data-intensive game, developers often utilize a spreadsheet program for entering and saving the data and then create a tool that parses the data into some sort of game-readable format. This method can often be seen in data-intensive games, such as role-playing games (RPGs) (in which an NPC's, or a non-player character's, stats are stored in tabular form) or strategy games (in which unit stats are stored in the data table).

Lua can make this system easier by having the storage medium (the Lua file) be the same data that is used by the program. By creating a simple data-management system, variables and types can be defined in Lua and then loaded by simply loading in the file. An entire processing step is eliminated, which allows designers to alter, expand, or collapse game data as needed with no programmer intervention. The nature of Lua's syntax, plus the ability to insert comments in the scripts, makes the files very readable. If an intermediary tool is needed, it is very easy to write the functions needed to export the Lua data into a Lua file that can be later loaded during runtime.

By itself, Lua does not have any capabilities to access data within an external database (such as mySQL or the Jet database engine), but access functions can be created in C++ and attached to the LuaGlue function to facilitate such control.

In the next example, shown in Listing 3.3, we see an example of a Lua file being used to house the game data directly, in this case, via the use of LuaGlue functions that insert the data into an internal data format managed within the core code. The output of this listing is show in Figure 3.1.

LISTING 3.3 Lua used to save data for a presidential-election game

```lua
-- Auto-generated LUA campaign data file
-- File created on: 07/28/04 12:02:08
AddCampaign( newID)
SetCash( newID, 38000000)
AddPerson( newID, CANDIDATE, "John Kerry", 70, 85, 100, SELF)
AddPerson( newID, RUNNING_MATE, "John Edwards", 65, 80, 100,
RUNNING_MATE)
SetCampaignData( newID, "Portrait", "ui_kerry.bmp")
SetCampaignData( newID, "RunningMatePortrait", "ui_edwards.bmp")
SetCampaignData( newID, "Name", "Democratic Party")
SetPersonLocation( newID, CANDIDATE, 22)
SetPersonLocation( newID, RUNNING_MATE, 34)
SetPersonHomeState( newID, CANDIDATE, 22)
SetPersonHomeState( newID, RUNNING_MATE, 34)
SetPersonFatigueValue( newID, CANDIDATE, 1)
SetCampaignColor( newID, 0, 200, 0, 255)
SetCampaignData( newID, "ColorName", "blue")
SetCampaignThinkTime( newID, 2)
SetCampaignData( newID, "LastAction", "Rest")
SetCampaignData( newID, "UniOrg", "3")
SetUniversalOrgLevel( newID, 3)
```

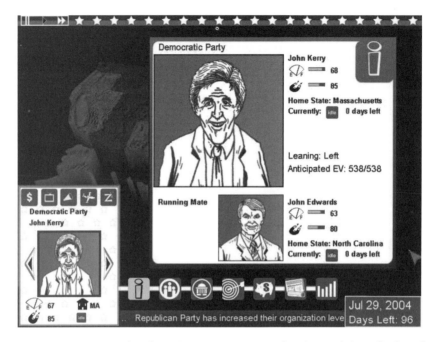

FIGURE 3.1 Screenshot from *Frontrunner* game, showing real-time display of Lua data.

Event Handling

Often, many of the most important processes in a game are triggered by events, either from the player or from the agents within the game world interacting with each other. This event can be as simple as the player tapping the W key on the keyboard or as complex as two game entities arriving at a third game entity at the same time.

Event-driven programming is nothing new to those familiar with Windows programming—events are the foundation on which Windows GUI operations are built. By crafting an event system in C++ and then using Lua to receive and process those events, you can create a very straightforward feedback loop between the inner workings of your game and higher-level Lua functions and user input. A simple example is capturing a keyboard input and sending your Lua event processor that event, plus a value that indicates which key was pressed. This concept will appear throughout this book—an event returns an ID of the event type plus an ID of what item triggered that event, as shown in Listing 3.4.

LISTING 3.4 Example of capturing a button event

```
SetEventHandler("MainMenuEvent")
function MainMenuEvent(id, eventCode)
```

```
        if eventCode == GUI_EVENT_BUTTON_UP then
            if ID == OK_BUTTON then
                AddTextToConsole("OK button pressed")
                PlaySound("button_click.wav")
            end
        end
    end
```

Saving and Loading a Game State

One of the most challenging aspects of a game-development project is the means by which the game saves and loads the game state for the player. Players will need to leave your game from time to time, and they'll need a way to save their progress. Players also like to save a game's state before trying something new and challenging, with the ability to restore the game should the player fail. Also, during game development and testing, developers will frequently need to load in a certain game state to test program functionality or to confirm that a bug has been fixed.

If you utilize Lua to save your core game data, you can also use Lua as the mechanism to save and load the data that constitutes a current game state. A save-game file in Lua is simply a text file of executable Lua code. A programmer or designer can then look at the save-game file to interpret the state of the game world (as well as edit the file). Loading in the game state is as simple as executing the Lua file. Using Lua's standard input/output functions, writing a function to save out an executable Lua file that reconstructs game data is a straightforward task. The advantage of this system is that it can allow a designer to edit and modify the save function (there is no need for a special load function) as game data grows or contracts during development. During the final stages of deployment, the save function can be coupled with a script compile function to make the save data encrypted from the player.

Artificial Intelligence

Artificial intelligence is key in today's games—the player wants a wily, challenging adversary that plays and "feels" human. Game developers know that real-world AI isn't about simulating how a human plays and acts but rather creating that appearance for the player. For years, game developers have argued over the merits and disadvantages of computer opponent "cheating" (computer opponents who have access to more world data than the player). That argument is best saved for another time and another place; however, nearly all developers can agree that player perception of AI behavior is far more important than AI simulation.

Lua can be utilized as a very effective tool from which to construct AI decision making. Certain components of artificial intelligence, such as pathfinding, are best left to the lower-level code world. Pathfinding (how a computer-controlled entity finds its way in a virtual world) is a very math-intensive operation, and the computer tests and retests potential paths for the shortest or most direct approach. (Pathfinding would probably be wired into a higher-level LuaGlue function that would control the pathfinding parameters, but we will also explore a Lua implementation of pathfinding in a later chapter.) Another example would be move-searching using a min-max approach, such as that used by computer chess programs that look many moves ahead and attempt to calculate the best possible move. In general, any "thinking functions" that require a lot of mathematical calculating, tree navigation, or trial-and-error computing is best left to the lower-level code. Artificial intelligence that relies on more limited data sets and is parameter based (such as how a poker player might bet during a hand of Texas Hold 'Em, or a campaign manager might choose to spend advertising dollars) is more in the "sweet spot" of Lua scripting. The advantage of using Lua is that the designer can "sculpt" the AI design by trial and error and rapid testing and iteration without tying up programming resources. Using Lua effectively in AI implementation means carefully designing the functions (the C functions, that is) that allow the Lua script programmer to access and react to the world state. (If the world state is kept largely in Lua data, these functions may be implemented in Lua as well.) Using Lua as an event-management system also allows the AI designer to react to changes in the game world and create an active, reactionary AI system.

In the next example, shown in Listing 3.5, you can see that Lua is being utilized (with a number of LuaGlue functions) to evaluate potential travel destinations for a campaign based on the number of electoral votes in a state and the support for a campaign in that state.

LISTING 3.5 Example of LUA AI function to determine to which state a simulated presidential candidate should travel

```
--AI candidate travel
StateTravTable = {}
stateCount = 1
--build a set of potential "travel to" states
while stateCount < 6 do
    pickState = math.random(1,51)
    --make sure there are enough electoral votes to make it worthwhile
    if GetStateData(pickState,"ElectoralVotes") > 12 then
        StateTravTable[stateCount] = pickState
        stateCount = stateCount + 1
    end
end
--pick the state out of the list with the lowest support
```

```
    lowSupport = 100
    targetState = 1
    for indx = 1,5 do
        if TalleySupport(StateTravTable[indx], Campaign) < lowSupport then
            lowSupport = TalleySupport(StateTravTable[indx], Campaign)
            targetState =  StateTravTable[indx]
        end
    end
    --issue the travel order
    Travel(Campaign, Person, targetState)
    SetCampaignData(Campaign, "LastAction", "Travel")
```

Rapid Prototyping

A commercial game must present a high-performance experience to the player—frame-rate hits and processing lags are not tolerated in today's competitive market. Profiling function calls is a tried and true methodology to locate slower performing functions, but this assumes all functions are written and performing their required tasks. Prototyping and performance enhancement are often mutually exclusive.

Lua is an excellent tool with which to prototype core game functions for later porting into the game's native language. Given the way that Lua "glues" itself to native language functions, porting a single function from Lua to C++ means that any dependent Lua code can operate without change. This tool allows a designer to prototype functionality—this function, if deemed to require higher performance, can be passed off to a programmer, who already has the algorithmic structure from which to work. The result is a C function and a LuaGlue call that is both high performance and seamlessly integratable into the project.

SUMMARY

Lua, when used in conjunction with C++, is a powerful partner with which to author game software. The areas in which Lua excels—such as GUI development, event management, data storage and retrieval, game-state saving and loading, and AI development—are the areas of game development that need rapid prototyping, testing, and a "design and iteration" cycle. Rapid changes to the core-language code base of a project can often destabilize a project and drive a programmer off of mission-critical tasks. By breaking those tasks out into the Lua environment, both programmers and designers can work with the scripts to design, test, and implement functionality rapidly and safely.

4 Introduction to Lua

In This Chapter

- Using the Lua Console
- Lua Basics
- Variables
- Operators
- Control Structures

This chapter will introduce you to the console, a small program that will allow you to experiment with the Lua scripting language immediately (as well as using it to run larger script files). With the console in hand, you'll begin to work through the core elements of the Lua scripting language (which will be very familiar to those of you with some programming experience) to learn how to utilize this tool in the realm of game development.

USING THE LUA CONSOLE

ON THE CD

The Lua console application included on the CD-ROM allows you to enter Lua commands at a prompt for immediate processing. It also allows you to load and execute Lua script files. You will learn how to create this console in the next chapter, but in this chapter, we'll use it as a tool as we explore the language of Lua.

The console is a simple application that looks very similar to the MS-DOS command prompt application you find in Microsoft® Windows®. Whereas the command prompt application processes DOS commands (or runs batch files, the DOS version of scripting), the console application processes Lua commands.

Lua commands are simple statements that can be processed immediately by the Lua environment. Examples of simple Lua commands follow:

```
myValue = 7
print("hello")
myTable = {1,2,3,4}
```

The Lua environment can process these commands immediately. Take a few moments to open the Lua console and type in these commands. Press the Enter key after each. You'll see that some, such as the `print` command, produce output, whereas others are simply processed.

In the console, you can copy text to the clipboard by using the standard command-prompt convention of clicking and dragging to select text, and then pressing the Enter key to copy it. You can paste text by right-clicking.

A Lua script is simply a file (a text file, generally with the extension .lua) that contains a series of Lua commands, one after the other. Lua really doesn't care about formatting, tabs, carriage returns, or anything like that—those are simply conventions we use to make our script files more readable (though Lua does need spaces between commands so that it won't confuse a variable name with a function call).

The short Lua script

```
for indx = 1,4 do
    Print("line: ", indx)
end
```

is just as valid as the Lua commands

```
for indx=1,4 do print("line: ",indx) end
```

The formatted script is obviously easier to read, but the formatting doesn't affect the Lua environment.

The Lua name for a single command or a stream of commands (what we call a script file) is a "chunk." Chunks can be small (such as a single print command) or multiple megabytes in size (in the case of a large save-game or data definition script).

Although you can use single-command or single-line entry in the Lua console, it's generally easier to start thinking about running Lua script files. We'll work through an example of running a Lua script file in the console, and then we'll move on to learning the syntax and key commands of the language.

ON THE CD

If you look on the CD-ROM, you'll find the script file shown in Listing 4.1 as the first file for this chapter:

LISTING 4.1   ch4_1.lua

```
-- Game Development with Lua
-- by Paul Schuytema and Mark Manyen
-- Published by Charles River Media
-- Lua script example
-- Listing 4.1
-- Hello World
myString = "Hello World"
print(myString)
```

To run this file from the console, copy it into a local folder on your hard drive. (It is a good idea to create a folder for all of your scripts that you will be working with as you read through this book—for our examples, we use c:\lua_scripts.)

FIGURE 4.1   Running a script file from the console.

To execute the following command from the console, see the image shown in Figure 4.1.

The `dofile` command will run a Lua script file immediately. The parameter to this command is a string that indicates the name and path of the file. We use "\\" instead of a single backslash, because the backslash character is the trigger to let the Lua environment know that a special character is coming (such as double quotes, a carriage return, and so on).

By using the `dofile` command, you can run any of the scripts you create (at least those that do not use any specialized LuaGlue functions written in C++) from the console. If you run a script with an error, the Lua environment will report an error message that will help you debug the script.

For this and the next chapter, it would be a good idea to create one or more script files so that you can work through the short Lua examples that follow. Use the same `dofile` approach to run the scripts (this will be easier than trying to enter them into the console manually).

LUA BASICS

Lua is a simple language—its strength comes from the way that it can be extended when used in partnership with C++—but it's still good to start at the beginning. In this section, we'll explore the basic syntax of the language.

Language Semantics

In Lua, you have a lot of flexibility with identifiers (variable and function names), but you can't begin an identifier with a number. Also avoid using an underscore (_) followed by capital letters, because that format is reserved for Lua itself, such as _Start.

Lua's Reserved Words

Lua also has a small set of reserved words that cannot be used as identifiers, shown in Table 4.1.

TABLE 4.1 Lua reserved words

and	local
break	nil
do	not
else	or
elseif	repeat
end	return
false	then
for	true
function	until
if	while
in	

In Chapter 9, "Designing a Lua Implementation," we'll discuss using a Lua style guide to make your scripting easier to read and more consistent, but for now, we recommend using the following format for naming variables, constants, and function names:

- All caps with underscores for constants, for example, MY_CONSTANT
- Initial lowercase for variable names, for example, myVariable
- Initial lowercase g to indicate a global variable, for example, gMyGlobal
- First word caps for function names, for example, function MyFunction()

In Lua, you can add a comment to a piece of text by adding two dashes (--) before the text (a line feed will end the comment). You can also create block comments as well, as shown in the following example:

```
-- this is a comment in Lua that is on its own line
myValue = 7  --you can also add a comment to a line of script
--[[

function Counting()
    for indx = 1,50000 do
        print(indx, "+", indx + 1, "=", indx + (indx + 1))
    end
end
--]]
```

VARIABLES

In Lua, you don't need to declare a variable before you use it, which sends up cheers from some camps and groans from others. Because you don't have to declare a variable—a variable is created the first time you use it—it's very easy to just drop in a variable when you need it. Formalists will say that this leads to sloppy programming—you may lose track of a variable because it isn't declared explicitly, or you may use a same-named variable in another function and corrupt your data. The bottom line is that we do have to be careful and keep track of our variables—the language won't do it for us. You also don't need to specify a type for the variable (string, number, and so forth)—the type is inferred from the value you assign to the variable. This method has the advantage of great flexibility, but it also has the disadvantage of creating a real debugging challenge if you aren't careful in your variable use.

To create, classify, and assign a value to a variable, simply use it within Lua, as follows:
```
myValue = 7
```

This code creates a variable names `myValue` and assigns it the number value of 7. You can use the `type` function to see the type of a variable. Try the following code in the console:

```
Ready> myValue = 7
Ready> print(type(myValue))
number
Ready> myValue = "hello"
```

```
Ready> print(type(myValue))
string
```

You'll notice that the type of a variable can change simply by assigning it a value of another type. Five variable types are available in Lua: Nil, Boolean, String, Number, and Table.

Nil

Nil is simply a single value type that is used to represent that a variable has no value yet assigned to it (see the following example). If you assign nil to a variable, you are actually deleting that variable.

```
myValue = nil   --this deletes the variable
local myValue   --this creates a local variable with an initial nil
value
```

Boolean

Boolean variables can have only two values: true and false. Boolean variables are useful in conditional statements, as shown in the following example:

```
myValue = true  --creates a boolean variable with a value of true
```

String

Strings in Lua are relatively straightforward, but Lua does have a number of very powerful string-manipulation functions that we'll explore in the next chapter (in fact, fast string manipulation is one of the great strengths of Lua). Lua strings can be as small as a single character or can contain more than a million characters.

```
myValue = "hello world"  --a string variable
```

Special String Characters
Strings can also contain special characters, and Lua provides the sequences (similar to C) shown in Table 4.2.

TABLE 4.2   Lua sequences

\a	bell	\v	vertical tab	
\b	back space	\\	backslash	$\rightarrow$

\f	form feed	\"	double quotation mark
\n	newline	\'	single quotation mark
\r	carriage return	\[	left square bracket
\t	horizontal tab	\]	right square bracket

It should be noted that Lua will attempt to convert between numbers and strings if it makes sense within the context of a statement. Try the following code in the console:

```
Ready> print("8" + 8)
16
Ready> print("8 + 8")
8 + 8
Ready> print("hello world" + 8)
ERROR:[string "?"]:1: attempt to perform arithmetic on a string value
```

Number

Numbers in Lua are double-precision floating-point values. Lua does not contain an integer type (for values below 1e14 there are no rounding errors, so the integer type is not needed). Numbers can be represented in the following ways:

- `myNumber = 7`
- `myNumber = 0.765`
- `myNumber = 7.65e8` (This mean 7.65×10 to the 8th power, or 765,000,000.)
- `myNumber = 7.65e-2` (This means 7.65×10 to the −2 power, or .0765.)

Table

Tables in Lua are one of the language's most powerful and confusing aspects. We'll discuss tables in greater detail and use tables in our scripts in later chapters, but for now, let's begin with a rather inaccurate definition: tables are like arrays.

Try the following code on the console:

```
Ready> myTable = {2,4,6,8,10}
Ready> print(myTable[3])
6
Ready> myTable[6] = 12
Ready> print(myTable[6])
12
```

In this context, the table functions just like a simple array to store a series of values. We use the square brackets to provide the index to get the value back out of the table. Later we'll look at tables more closely and paint a more accurate picture.

Local and Global Variables

By default, all Lua variables are global in nature—that is, they keep their value intact throughout the entire session until the script changes them. Although this stability is convenient for the script programmer, it can also lead to confusion when you are working on a game with a myriad of Lua scripts and functions.

It's generally a good idea to use the g character (see the "Language Semantics" section) as the first character of a variable name if the value is indeed meant to be global (this will make your scripts easier to debug later). It's also a good idea to use local variables whenever possible.

Local variables are variables that are destroyed when the block of script in which they were defined is finished executing. This block can be within either a control structure or a function, depending on where you define the variable.

To define a local variable you can declare it either with no value or with an initial value, as shown in the following example:

```
local myValue  -- the variable is declared and has a value of nil
local myValue2 = 3  --the variable has an initial value of 3
```

The scope of the variable (the realm in which it exists) is determined by the position of the declaration. See the following examples:

```
function MyFunction()
local myX = 7  --this will be destroyed when the function is done
if myX < 10 then
    local myY = "hello world"  --this will be destroyed
    --when this code block is done
    print(myY)  -- prints "hello world"
end
print(myY) --print nil, because the variable above is destroyed
end
```

Local variables will help keep your code more constrained as your project grows to include more and more script files (so you won't have to go tracking down a global variable that was set incorrectly in some other portion of your game project). Local variables are perfect for those "use all the time" variables that control counters within control structures (see "Control Structures," later in this chapter) such as for loops.

OPERATORS

Operators are the special symbols that allow you to have two values (such as variables) interact with each other. Arithmetic operators will produce an arithmetic result, whereas relational operators will produce a Boolean (`true` or `false`) result.

Arithmetic Operators

Lua supports the following standard mathematical operators:

- addition, for example, a + b = c
- subtractions, for example, a − b = c
- multiplication, for example, a * b = c
- division, for example, a / b = c

Relational Operators

You can also use the following standard relational operators to compare values and/or statements:

```
if a == b then   -- equal to
    print("a is equal to b")
end
if a ~= b then   -- not equal to
    print("a is not equal to b")
end
if a < b then   -- less than
print("a is less than b")
end
if a > b then   -- greater than
    print("a is greater than b")
end
if a <= b then   -- less than or equal to
    print("a is less than or equal to b")
end
if a >= b then   -- greater than or equal to
    print("a is greater than or equal to b")
end
```

If you use relational operators to compare two tables together, you will get the expected results *only* if the tables are the exact same object. Because tables are referred to by the variable you associate with them (as a pointer), you aren't really dealing with the contents of the table directly. For example:

```
tableA = [1, 2, 3]
tableB = [1, 2, 3]
if tableA == tableB then
    print("The tables are the same")
else
    print("The tables are not the same")
end
```

In the previous example, we will see the result "The tables are not the same" because the tables are two separate structures.

```
tableA = [1, 2, 3]
tableB = tableA
if tableA == tableB then
    print("The tables are the same")
else
    print("The tables are not the same")
end
```

In the second example, we get the "The tables are the same" because tableB now points to the very same data as tableA. It's important to note that you can check the values within tables just like you'd expect. If we use the first example and then add the following conditional:

```
if tableA[2] == tableB[2] then
    print("The values are the same")
end
```

we will see that the values within the table are indeed equivalent.

Logical Operators

Logical operators perform a test on two arguments and return a value based on the arguments' relationship. In Lua, the logical operators are always rendered in lower-case characters.

The and operator compares two arguments. If the first argument is false, it will be returned; otherwise, the second argument will be returned.

```
a = 5
b = 10
c = 20
```

```
if (a < 10) and (b < 20) then
    print("this returns true -- which is the value of the second
    argument")
end
if (a > c) and (b < 20) then
    Print("this returns false -- which is the value of the first
    argument")
end
```

The or operator is the opposite of the and operator. It returns the first argument if it is not false. If the first argument is true, then the and operator will return the second argument.

```
a = 5
b = 10
c = 20
if (a < 10) or (b < 20) then
    print("this returns true -- which is the value of the first argument")
end
if (a > c) or (b < 20) then
    print("this returns true -- which is the value of the first argument")
end
if (a > c) or (b < 5) then
    print("this returns false -- which is the value of the second argument")
end
```

The not expression always returns a value of true or false. In Lua, false and nil are the only values considered false by the logical operators—any other value is considered true. The not operator will return the opposite value of the argument (see Figure 4.2)

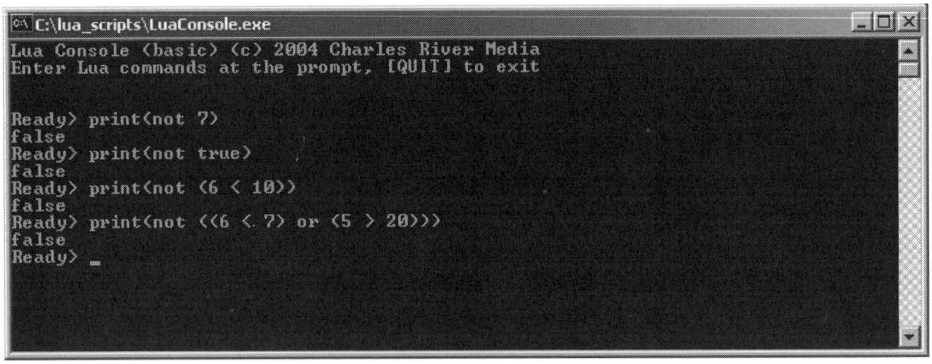

FIGURE 4.2   Some examples of the not operator in the console.

CONTROL STRUCTURES

Lua contains a small set of vital control structures that allows you to handle the lion's share of the decision making within your scripts. All of the control structures end their code blocks with the end terminator.

Although you don't have to indent your control structures for your scripts to function properly, it's generally a good idea to get into the habit of indenting one tab stop (four spaces) for each nested control structure. As you'll see in later chapters, you'll be using a lot of nested control structures in your game scripting, especially when you are writing your artificial intelligence functions.

If

The real workhorse is the ubiquitous if statement—if you are familiar with other programming or scripting languages, you've encountered this before many times. An if statement allows you to evaluate an argument; if it evaluates to true, the script block will be executed. For example:

```
myValue = 7
if myValue < 10 then
    print("myValue is less than ten. ")
end
if (myValue > 5) and (myValue < 10) then
    print("myValue is between five and ten. ")
end
```

You can extend the functionality of the if statement by creating another block of script using the optional else keyword. The script block bracketed by the else-end terminators will be executed when the if argument tests false. For example:

```
myValue = 20
if myValue == 21 then
    print("the value is 21")
else
    print("the value is NOT 21")
end
```

In addition, you can string together a series of conditionals using the elseif keyword. You'll find this keyword very useful during AI scripting, because Lua doesn't have a case-style statement. For example:

```
myValue = 17
if myValue < 6 then
    print("myValue is between zero and five. ")
elseif myValue < 11 then
    print("myValue is between six and ten. ")
elseif myValue < 16 then
    print("myValue is between eleven and fifteen. ")
elseif myValue < 21 then
    print("myValue is between sixteen and twenty. ")
else
    print("myValue is greater than twenty. ")
end
```

While and Repeat

The control structures based on `while` and `repeat` (see the next example) are similar in that they allow a block of script to be executed until some condition is met. The `while` structure evaluates an argument first, and if it evaluates to `true`, the block is executed (which means that it might never be executed). The `repeat` structure tests the argument at the end of the block, guaranteeing at least one cycle through the script block.

The `while` structure utilizes the `do` keyword much in the same way the `if` control structure used the `then` keyword: to define the start of the conditional script block. An example of a `while` structure follows:

```
indx = 1
while indx < 10 do
    print("loop pass: ", indx)
    indx = indx + 1
end
```

In this example, if `indx` begins with a value of ten or greater, the script block will never be executed.

In the `repeat` control structure, the `repeat` keyword begins the script block, which ends with the `until` keyword. The argument to the control structure immediately follows the `until` terminator, for example:

```
indx = 1
repeat
    print("loop pass: ", indx)
    indx = indx + 1
until indx > 10
```

In this example, if `indx` begins with a value of 1,000, it will still move through the script block at least once. As you think through what structure to utilize, you'll need to determine if the code in the block must be run at least once—if that's the case, then you'll want to utilize the `repeat` structure.

You'll need to take special care that your argument will eventually return a `true` evaluation, or you'll find yourself trapped within the script block until you forcefully end your program.

For

Lua provides two types of `for` structures (numeric and generic), but we'll cover just the numeric structure here. We'll touch on the generic structure in the advanced section on tables in the next chapter.

The `for` structure allows you to execute a block of script a finite amount of time, based on the values of the expressions you provide. A simple example follows:

```
for indx = 1,10 do
    print(indx)
end
```

After the `for` keyword, you provide a range of values for a variable you declare. The block of script will iterate once for each value in the range, with your variable changing in value each time through. The `do` keyword is used to begin the block, and `end` is used to terminate it.

You can use an third option to define the "step" value of the looping. For example:

```
for indx = 10,1, -1 do --this counts backwards
    print(indx)
end
for indx = 1,100, 2 do --this counts forwards by 2s
    print(indx)
end
```

You should keep in mind a few points when using the `for` structure. First, the expressions used to determine the parameters of the looping are evaluated only the first time through, so even if they change in the body of the script, the number of iterations of the loop won't be affected. Second, the variable that holds the iteration value is a local variable, which is destroyed as soon as the looping is finished. To save that value outside of the script block, you'll need to store it into some other global or higher-level local variable.

Break

The `break` statement allows you to force-exit from a looping control structure. You can't use this statement outside of a loop, and it must be the last statement of a block of script (often an `if-then` statement). Review the following example:

```
for indx = 1,100 do
    if indx == 52 then
        print("52--ouch! ")
        break  --the last line of the block, breaks the for loop
    end
    print("the value is ", indx)
end
print("this is the line that will be executed after the break")
```

SUMMARY

Lua is a simple, straightforward scripting language that utilizes many of the structures and conventions found in other programming languages, so if you are familiar with programming at all, scripting in Lua will come quite easily.

The Lua console is a great tool for experimenting with short Lua chunks and statements, but it can be also used to run Lua script files on their own. (Later, you will run Lua scripts from within the context of your game project.)

In this chapter, we explored the basic syntax of the language and the core statements. In the next chapter, we'll build on this knowledge and dive deeper into Lua, and then we'll be ready to use the scripting language in a real game project.

5 Deeper into Lua

In This Chapter

- Functions
- Standard Libraries
- More on Strings
- More on Tables
- Basic I/O

In the previous chapter, you got your feet wet with the Lua syntax and worked through some simple examples in the Lua console. This chapter will finish laying the groundwork for your basic understanding of the Lua language. You'll learn more advanced techniques and standard functions that will become part of your toolbox as you ready yourself for entering the exciting world of Lua game development.

FUNCTIONS

Functions are the primary tools for organizing the behavior of your game-development scripts. Functions are blocks of Lua code that are called from a single identifier (actually a variable), and they can perform a process, return a value, or both.

A simple function definition follows:

```
function Wow()
    print(" ")
    print("Wow, that was awesome!")
    print(" ")
end
```

ON THE CD

All of the functions for this chapter can be found in the ch5_1.lua script file on the CD-ROM. If you run this file from the console, you can simply execute the functions from the command line (see Figure 5.1).

To begin a function definition, you use the `function` statement, followed by the name of the function, and then a list of arguments that can be passed into the function. In this sample function, there are no arguments that can be passed into the function, but we still need to use the `()` to indicate an empty list. The block that defines a function is concluded by the `end` terminator.

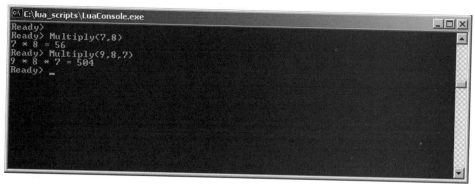

FIGURE 5.1   The console allows you to load a file that contains function definitions and then execute those functions from the command line.

Functions in script files are not executed when that file is loaded (as with the `dofile` command) but are loaded into memory and associated with the function name variable.

Single Arguments

Now let's look at a function that takes a single variable as a parameter, as shown in the next example:

```
function SetName(myString)
    print(" ")
    print("Your name is:", myString)
    print(" ")
end
```

In this function, `myString` is the argument that is passed into the function, and it used within the function. In functions, these arguments are created as local variables that are discarded when the function completes executing.

Multiple Arguments

You can also pass multiple arguments into a function, separating them with a comma, as follows:

```
function MyInfo(myName, myAge)
    print(" ")
    print("Your name is:", myName)
    print("Your age is:", myAge)
    print(" ")
end
```

Lua also provides a powerful tool that allows you to define functions that will accept a variable number of parameters. You use three dots (...) in place of the variable list of arguments. Lua will then create a local table called arg that contains all of the variables, plus it provides you with the number of variables (via the arg.n value). You'll want to make sure that you call out this element clearly in the comments that introduce a function, because the script may change hands during the development of a game, and it is easy to forget how many arguments a function is looking for. A sample consult output from the HowMany() function is shown in the following example:

```lua
function HowMany(...)
    if arg.n > 0 then
        for indx = 1, arg.n do
            local myString = string.format("%s%d", "Argument ", indx,
            ":")
            print(myString, arg[indx])
        end
    else
      print("No variables entered.")
    end
end
```

In this function, we can pass in as many legal arguments as we like. The arg table holds all of the values, and the arg.n field holds the number of values in that table. Usually, you use this variable argument approach in concert with some expected variables, making some mandatory and some optional, as in the following function:

```lua
function Multiply(val1, val2, ...)
    --the default is one
    local myString
    if arg.n == 0 then
      myString = string.format("%d%s%d%s%d", val1, " * ", val2, " = ",
      val1 * val2)
    else
        local val3 = val1 * val2 * arg[1]
        myString = string.format("%d%s%d%s%d%s%d", val1, " * ", val2, " *
        ", arg[1], " = ", val3)
    end
    print(myString)
end
```

In this function, the first two arguments are required; the function will simply multiply together the numbers. If a third argument is passed in, it will also become a multiplier. If any additional arguments are passed into the function, they are simply ignored.

Returning Values

In addition to utilizing functions to perform isolated processes, functions can return values back to the calling script. To return a value, a function uses the `return` statement, followed by the value (often a variable name) to return. A simple example follows:

```
function TimesTwo(myValue)
    myValue = myValue * 2
    return myValue
end
```

You can use a function that returns a value as an argument in a statement, for example:

```
a = 24 + TimesTwo(12)
print(a)
```

You can also have a function return multiple arguments, simply by separating them by a comma. The following example, also shown in Figure 5.2, shows the output of the `ThreeDice()` function in the console.

```
function ThreeDice()
    d1 = math.random(1,6)
    d2 = math.random(1,6)
    d3 = math.random(1,6)
    myTotal = d1 + d2 + d3
    return d1, d2, d3, myTotal

end
```

Another interesting capability that Lua possesses is the ability to use the `return` statement to call another function. What's interesting about this (rather than just calling another function in the body of a function) is that Lua interprets the use of a `return` statement as the physical end of the processing in that function, and it's then removed from the stack.

```
C:\lua_scripts\LuaConsole.exe                                    _ □ X
Ready>
Ready> print(ThreeDice())
1       1       3       5
Ready> print(ThreeDice())
1       1       6       8
Ready> print(ThreeDice())
3       1       1       5
Ready> print(ThreeDice())
1       3       4       8
Ready> a,b,c,d = ThreeDice()
Ready> print(a,b,c,d)
4       4       4       12
Ready> print(c)
4
Ready> _
```

FIGURE 5.2 The output of the `ThreeDice()` function in the console.

This capability allows you to string together a series of function calls without running the risk of a Lua stack-overflow error. Under the hood, Lua maintains a "stack" of values, variables, and such, so that when it returns from a function, it can "pop" the variables and other data off the stack and pick up where it left off. If you have a clean way to exit a function and build up function call on function call, you'll fill up this limited data space and cause the Lua command interpreter to crash. For an example, perform a `dofile` call on the "ch5_2.lua" file and run the example by entering `ExploreMaze()` into the console.

ON THE CD

In this old-school dungeon romp shown in Figure 5.3, we use the functions themselves as the various locations in the maze and use `return` to send the player into new realms. Because each function is cleared away from the stack when `return` sends the game flow to a new location, we never run the risk of any kind of data overflow or becoming trapped in an endless set of nested function calls, which will fill the Lua stack and crash the program.

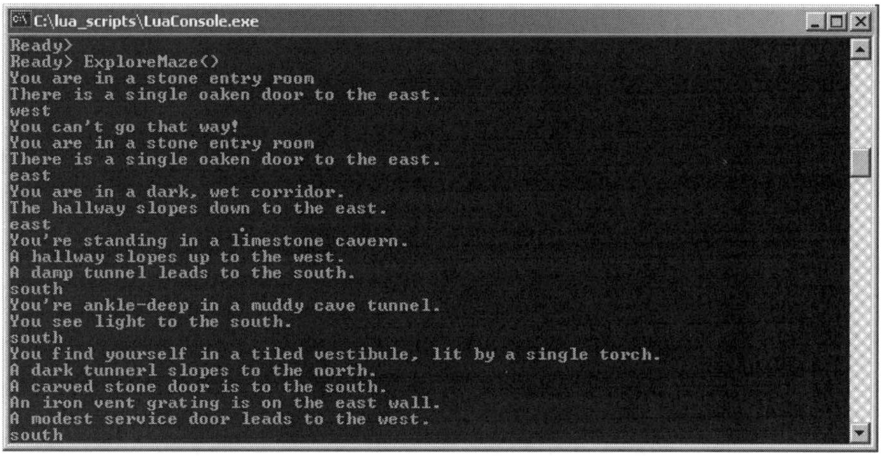

FIGURE 5.3   Output of an old-school text dungeon romp.

STANDARD LIBRARIES

Lua provides access to a number of standard function libraries that can allow you to perform some quite sophisticated tasks without the need for additional scripting. Full details of the standard libraries included within the 5.0 version of Lua can be found in the language's online manual at *www.lua.org/manual/5.0/*.

Through the rest of the chapter, we'll touch on useful standard functions that will make your life easier in the realm of game development.

assert (myValue)()

The `assert` function allows you to run a chunk of compiled Lua script as a process function. You pass in the variable that points to the compiled script, and it is executed immediately. You can load in and compile the script by using either the `loadstring` or `loadfile` function.

In game development, `loadfile` isn't really all that useful (because we can already load Lua files in a more straightforward fashion), but using `loadstring` in partnership with the `assert` function can come in quite handy. With this function, you can build a small Lua chunk into a string and then simply run that string using `assert`.

You can also run a chunk by just using the `loadstring` function, as shown in Figure 5.4, by itself—it does not provide the error reporting that `assert` provides, but it's a good "quick and dirty" way to run a small chunk, as shown in the following example:

```
myString = "math.max(7,8,9,10)"
loadstring(myString)()
```

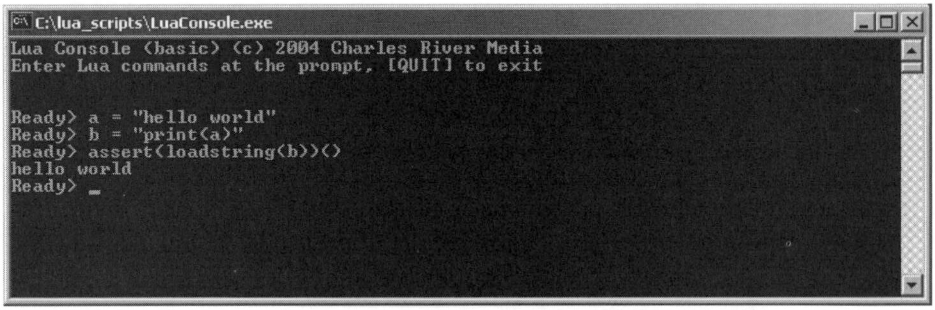

FIGURE 5.4 Here is an example of placing Lua into a string and using `loadstring` and `assert` to run the code.

dofile (filename)

We've been using this function already; it loads a Lua script file and processes it immediately. Generally, we use this function to load a file of function definitions that we can call on later, but we can also use it to load a data file (such as a save-game file, which we'll look at in a later chapter) or Lua code that we'd like to run immediately, as shown in the next example:

```
dofile("scripts/runtime_functions.lua");
```

Generally, a game project has several subfolders to hold the game's assets (such as textures, scripts, sounds, and so on). The `dofile` function sees your program executable's directory as the current directory level, so to run a file in the scripts folder, you'll need to add a `scrpts/` to the start of the filename string.

In later chapters, we'll learn about two custom functions: `RunGUI()`, which runs a user-interface Lua file, and `RunScript()`, which is similar to `dofile`, but it can run already compiled Lua binary files as well.

Math Functions

Lua provides function-level access to the standard C library of math functions. The vast majority of these are simply LuaGlue interfaces to the corresponding functions in the C library. The functions are actually stored in a tabled called "math" that you can access with the identifiers shown in Table 5.1.

TABLE 5.1   Identifiers

math.abs	math.max
math.acos	math.min
math.asin	math.mod
math.atan	math.pow
math.atan2	math.rad
math.ceil	math.sin
math.cos	math.sqrt
math.deg	math.tan
math.exp	math.frexp
math.floor	math.ldexp
math.log	math.random
math.log10	math.randomseed

The table also contains `math.pi`, which is a variable that holds the value of pi.

A few functions of special interest to us in the realm of game development are outlined in the next sections.

math.floor()

The `floor` function rounds down a number to a whole value (remember, in Lua, there is no concept of floating point or integer). This function simply drops the decimal value. If you'd like to use this function to round a number, simply add .5 to the number first, as shown in the following example:

```
a = 5.125
b = 5.75
a = a + 0.5
```

```
b = b + 0.5
a = math.floor(a) -- a will equal 5
b = math.floor(b) -- b will equal 6
```

math.random()

In the realm of game development, random numbers are everywhere. The Lua `math.random()` function generates a pseudo random number between 0 and 1 (like most other languages' random functions). What makes this Lua function work especially well for games is its ability to pass in minimum and maximum values. The function will then generate whole number values between those arguments, as shown in the next example:

```
-- 6-sided dice
myDie = math.random(1,6)
```

When you start your program, it's a good idea to seed the random-number generator with a unique value, so you'll get the most random-seeming results. This process is often done in the StartGui.lua file that initializes the game environment, on the script side of things (see Chapter 7, "Communication between Lua and C++"). The easiest way to do this is by using the `os.date` function, so that you get a unique time value for the seed, as follows:

```
\math.randomseed(os.date("%d%H%M%S"))
```

For debugging, you might want to set the random seed to an integer value—this will ensure that you'll get the same series of pseudo random numbers each time you run the game.

math.min()

During game development, it's often necessary to determine the lowest or highest value in a set of values (such as the highest stat of a hero character, or the state with the most electoral votes). The `math.min` and `math.max` functions will do this for you. Each function can take an arbitrary number of parameters and return either the lowest value in the set (`math.min`) or the highest value in the set (`math.max`).

In Lua, much of our data will be in the form of tables, which poses a bit of a challenge for using these functions, because you need to add each element of the table to the function call. Fortunately, we can "build" a Lua string and use the `loadstring` function to perform the operation, as shown in the following example:

```
function GetMin(theTable)
    myString = "myValue = math.min("
    for index,value in ipairs(theTable) do
```

```
            myString = string.format("%s%d%s", myString, value, ",")
        end
        --remove final comma
        myString = string.sub (myString, 1, string.len(myString) - 1)
        --add final )
        myString = string.format("%s%s", myString, ")")
        --run the chunk
        loadstring(myString)()
        return myValue
    end
```

This function and the partner function, `GetMax(myTable)` are found in ch5_3.lua on the CD-ROM. These functions will take tables as their arguments and return the smallest or largest values in those tables.

MORE ON STRINGS

One of Lua's great strengths is its robust string-handling capabilities. Lua has extensive pattern-matching capabilities, as well as a set of solid string manipulation functions. In this section of the chapter, we'll explore some of the most relevant string functions as they relate to game development. More information about all the Lua string manipulation functions can be found in the Lua online manual.

The short examples that follow are all located in the ch5_small_examples.lua file on the CD-ROM.

Type Conversion

Often, you'll find the need to convert a number into a string and vice versa. To convert a string into a number, use the `tonumber()` function, as follows:

```
myString = "1234"
myNumber = tonumber(myString)
print(myNumber + 2) -- this will display 1236
```

You can also convert a number to a string using the `tostring()` function:

```
myNumber = 1234
myString = tostring(myNumber)
print(type(myString)) -- you will see "string"
```

string.char(n1, n2, ..)

This function returns a string based on the ASCII values of the numerical arguments passed in. This function isn't used often, but it's useful to insert a line feed in a Lua save-game file, to make the file more readable to human eyes. For example:

```
myFile:write(string.char (10)) -- writes out a linefeed to the open
file
```

string.len(myString)

Often, it's helpful to know the length of a string you want to manipulate; the string.len function provides that information. It returns a number that represents the number of characters in the string that was passed as an argument. For example:

```
myString = "1234"
print(string.len(myString)) -- will print 4
```

string.sub(myString, start, end)

This function returns a portion of the indicated string. The start value is the location in the string where you want to start grabbing characters, and the end value is where the grab will stop. For example:

```
myString = "hello world"
newString = string.sub(myString, 1, 5)
print(newString) -- this will print "hello"
```

You can use negative values for start and end—in that case, the positioning is based on the end of the string, rather than the beginning (–5 for a start value will position the start five characters from the end of the string). For example:

```
myString = "hello world"
newString = string.sub(myString, -5, 10)
print(newString) -- this will print "world"
```

You can also leave off the end value altogether. In this case, the function will read to the end of the string. In this way, you can grab a suffix of the desired string, as follows:

```
myString = "hello world"
newString = string.sub(myString, -5)
print(newString) -- this will print "world"
```

string.format()

The `string.format` function allows you to format and build strings. You'll find yourself using this function constantly when you are outputting game text to a GUI text object. The first use of this function, as shown in the previous example, is to use it to append values to a string (because Lua doesn't allow you to simply add together two strings together), as shown in the next example :

```
string1 = "hello"
string2 = "world"
for index = 1, 3 do
    string1 = string.format("%s%s", string1, string2)
end
print(string1) -- prints "helloworldworldworld"
```

In the preceding example, the first argument to the `string.format` function sets up the form that the new string will take. The `%s` item means a string (`%d` means a digit), so the `%s%s` means that the string will be constructed of two string components.

The second primary use of `string.format` is to build a complex string out of component parts (many of which probably come from variables). For example:

```
myName = "Fred"
myStr = 16
myString = string.format("%s%s%d%s", myName, "'s strength is ", myStr, ".")
print(myString)
```

In this example, the pattern `%s%s%d%s` tell the function where to put in the component parts, so we get the result "Fred's strength is 16." In this approach, the arguments that follow the pattern simply fill out the pattern to create the result. We can also change the `string.format` approach to get the same results, as shown in the next example:

```
myString = string.format("%s's strength is %d.", myName, myStr)
```

In this case, we place the pattern and the fixed-string elements together, and the variables at the end. Both work equally as well.

Another use for `string.format` is to set up the display of digits to a desired number of significant figures. Review the next example:

```
myHealth = 17.34556
myString = string.format("%.2f%s", myHealth, "% of health remaining.")
print(myHealth) -- prints "17.34556"
print(myString) -- prints "17.35% of health remaining. "
```

In this example, the %.2f tells string.format to round the myHealth value to two decimal places.

string.find(sourceString, findString)

The string.find function will search a source string for the first occurrence of another string. If it finds that string, it will return the start and end positions. If it does not find the target string, it will return nil. For example:

```
myString = "My name is John Smith."
sStart, sEnd = string.find(myString, "John")
print(sStart, sEnd) -- prints "12  15"
```

Strings and Patterns

Lua's most powerful string functions make use of the concept of patterns. We saw an initial use of patterns in the string.format function shown earlier—a pattern is a template that allows Lua to filter out meaningful results from a string. A simple example follows:

```
myString = "The price is $17.50."
filter = "$%d%d.%d%d"
print(string.sub(myString, string.find(myString, filter)))
```

In this example, the filter sets up the format of what we're looking for. The filter expects the dollar sign and the decimal point to be in the right spot, but the numbers can be any digits. The result of this example is "$17.50."

You can create the opposite pattern by using an uppercase letter; %d means all digits, %D means everything that's *not* a digit.

The % sign, preceding any special character (such as ( ) . % + _ * ? [^ $) will enable you to user that character in the pattern, so that %% means the pattern for the percentage sign.

Lua understands the following characters for pattern construction:

.	all characters
%a	letters
%c	control characters
%d	digits
%l	lowercase letters

$\rightarrow$

%p	punctuation characters
%s	space characters
%u	uppercase letters
%w	alphanumeric characters
%x	hexidecimal digits
%z	the character that is represented by 0

string.gsub(sourceString, pattern, replacementString)

This function returns a string that modifies the source string but replaces any characters that fit the pattern with the replacement string. A simple example follows:

```
myString = "My name is John Smith. My phone is 555-3257."
newString = string.gsub (myString, "%d", "*")
print(newString) -- returns "My name is John Smith. My phone is ***-
****."
```

Using this pattern approach, you could update an area code in a phone record, for example:

```
custData = "(309) 555-1234"
custData = string.gsub(custData, "%(%d%d%d%)", "(781)")
print(custData) -- prints "(781) 555-1234"
```

You can add an optional last parameter that limits how many replacements are made. For example:

```
myString = "happy, hello, home, hot, hudson"
myString = string.gsub(myString, "h%a+", "An H word!", 2)
print(myString)
```

In this case, we are searching the string for a pattern that begins with h. The %a+ says to look for an arbitrary amount of letters, which will stop if it finds a space or punctuation character. The number 2 says to replace only the first two matches.

string.gfind(sourceString, pattern)

This function iterates, one match at a time, over a string and return the substring that matches the parent. Review the following example:

```
myString = "This is my rather long string."
print(myString)
counter = 1
for myWord in string.gfind(myString, "%a+") do
    print(string.format("Word #%d: %s", counter, myWord))
    counter = counter + 1
end
```

This example uses a for control structure to step through the source string. The %a+ pattern captures individual words (which can be very useful when parsing game data). See Figure 5.5.

FIGURE 5.5   The console output of the previous string.gfind example.

MORE ON TABLES

As we saw in our previous chapter, tables are very functional and can be used in many ways. The most simple way, of course, is to use tables much like the arrays we find in other languages. Look at the following example:

```
myTable = {}
for index = 1,100 do
    myTable[index] = math.random(1,1000)
end
```

In this example, we've used a for control structure to create a 100-element table. Each element is then set to a random value between one and 1,000. We can access any element in the table by simply using myTable[X], where X is the index of the value we want.

table.getn(myTable)

Lua has some simple but very powerful built-in functions that allow you to perform operations on a table. The first, `table.getn()`, returns the number of elements in a table. If we run it on the example

```
print(table.getn(myTable))
```

we'll get the number 100. Often, when using tables to store game data, you won't know how many elements are in the table. By using `table.getn()`, you can get that value and use it to walk through each value in the table, as shown in the next example:

```
for index = 1, table.getn(myTable) do
    print(myTable[index])
end
table.sort(myTable)
```

This simple function walks through your table and re-indexes the values from lowest to highest. You can also add another parameter to this function call—a name of a function that you have written that will return a `true` or `false` value as it compares table values. See the following examples:

```
function Sort(theTable, direction)
    if direction ~= 1 then
        table.sort(theTable)
    else
        function Reverse(a, b)
            if a < b then
                return false
            else
                return true
            end
        end
        table.sort(theTable, Reverse)
    end
end
```

ON THE CD

This function is in the ch5_3.lua file.

This function will take a table as a parameter and sort just like `table.sort()`. If you add an optional second parameter 1, then the table will sort in the opposite (descending) order.

table.insert(myTable, position, value)

The `table.insert()` function will insert a new item into a table. The position value is optional—if it is not included, the function simply appends the value to the end of the table. If the position value is provided, the function will re-index the other items in the table accordingly.

The following example inserts the value `hello` into the 25th index of the table and will re-index the table.

```
table.insert(myTable, 25, "hello")
```

table.remove(myTable, position)

This function removes and returns an element from the specified table, re-indexing as needed. If you do not supply the optional position value, it will remove the last item from the table. For example:

```
print(table.remove(myTable, 25))
```

If we run this code on the table from the previous examples, it will remove `hello` and drop the table back down to 100 elements. Because the function returns the value, it will print `hello` to the console.

Table Reference

Remember that tables do not have to be referenced only by numerical index values. Tables can use any value as an index key. See the next example:

```
myData = {}
myData.name = "Thardwick"
myData.class = "Barbarian"
myData.str = math.random(3,18)
myData.dex = math.random(3,18)
```

In this example, we use named values instead of index values. These are the keys that allow you to access the values in a table. This table can also have numerical indexes as well. We can add the following data:

```
myData[1] = 17
myData[2] = 34
myData[3] = 24
```

This approach gives us the flexibility to have a table that not only is constructed of fields but also contains an array that we can walk through and index.

Multidimensional Tables

You can create multidimensional tables quite easily in Lua. In fact, in an upcoming chapter, you're going to learn how to save and load game data to and from these sorts of tables. Think of multidimensional tables as tables within tables that you can access by multiple key values. An example follows:

```
widget = {}
widget.name = {}
widget.cost = {}
widget.name[1] = "Can opener"
widget.cost[1] = "$12.75"
widget.name[2] = "Scissors"
widget.cost[2] = "$8.99"
```

In this example, we created an empty table called widget. We then created two keys, name and cost that are also empty tables. Now that we have the structure defined, we can start adding data to the table. When we refer to widget.cost[1], we are referring to the cost key, which references a table, and the index is an index into that table. If we run the function table.getn(widget.cost), we'll receive the value 2, indicating that the table is two elements long.

pairs()

The pairs() function allows you to walk through a table, item by item. Look at the following example:

```
myNames = {"Fred", "Ethel", "Lucy", "Ricky", "Rockey", "Betsy", "Bill"}
for index, value in pairs(myNames) do
    print(index, value)
end
```

In this for control structure, pairs() iterates over the table (which can be of unknown length) and gives you the index value and the data value of each table item (see Figure 5.6).

In the following example, you can also accomplish the same task with a more traditional for loop approach, even if you don't know the size of the table:

```
for index = 1, table.getn(myNames) do
    print(index, myNames[index])
end
```

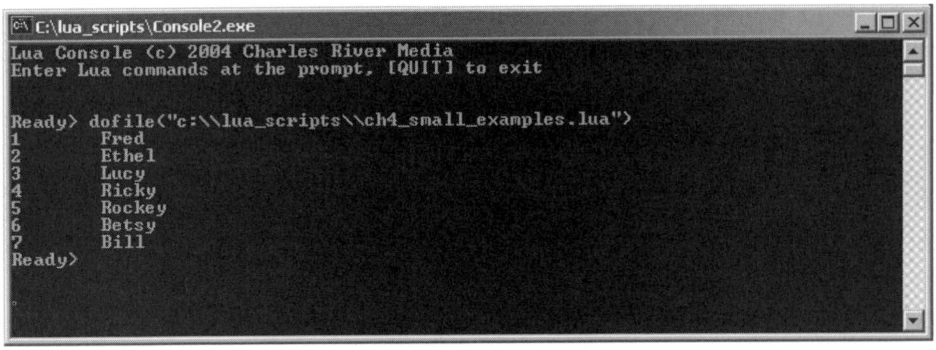

FIGURE 5.6   Console output of the `pairs()` example.

The `pairs()` function, though, is useful when you are trying to move through a table with non-numerical keys, as in the next example:

```
myData = {}
myData.name = "Billy"
myData.interest = "Wind surfing"
myData.quote = "Cold out, eh?"
myData.shoesize = 11
for index, value in pairs(myData) do
    print(index, value)
end
```

BASIC I/O

In the context of this book, we are going to use Lua to save and load our vital game information. We'll learn more about this task in a later chapter, but the advantage of using Lua as a save/load system is that you don't have to parse the data at all—we can let Lua do that work for us, because all game data will be represented as valid Lua script files.

That being said, we still need to have a basic idea about writing out data to a file, so we can create those valid Lua files. We'll need to learn a little bit about how Lua handles file writing.

The first thing we have to do is open a file for writing, and we do that with the `io.open()` function, shown next:

```
myFile = io.open("test_data.lua", "w")
```

This function takes two arguments: a string with filename of the file you are going to create, and a string that indicates what sort of control you will have for writing to the file. The w is for write mode—this will create a file if one doesn't exist and will write to the file as if it were new (all previous data will be lost). For our save-game data, this mode is generally what we'll use, because we want to write a complete game state each time we save. We might also want to use a for append mode—this preserves existing data and simply writes new information from the end of the file.

If an error occurs while opening or creating the file, the returned variable (in this case, myFile) will be nil. We can use that result to ensure the file opened successfully before we write anything. Look at the following example, which opens a file and writes out several lines:

```lua
myFile = io.open("test_data.lua", "w")
if myFile ~= nil then
    myFile:write("-- Test lua file")
    myFile:write(string.char (10))
    myFile:write(string.char (10))
    myFile:write(string.format("%s%s", "-- File created on: ",
    os.date()))
    myFile:write(string.char (10))
    myFile:write(string.char (10))
    myFile:write("print(\"hello world!\")")
    io.close(myFile)
end
```

In this example, we open the file and use the write() function to write strings out to the file. The string.char() function writes out linefeeds, so we've got a file that's easy to read. We use the Lua escape character, \, to enable us to insert quotation marks in the hello world line. Finally, we use the io.close function to close our file. If you run this script, you'll see that it will indeed generate a valid Lua file that you can then run from the console using the dofile() command.

SUMMARY

We covered a lot of ground in this chapter, from learning about functions to picking up some advanced string and table understanding. The goal of this chapter was to lay the groundwork so that you are ready to start using Lua in the game-project example we'll be developing over the next few chapters.

We learned how to create functions in Lua and how to pass in arguments to the functions and get data back out of the functions by using the return statement. We then took a closer look at how Lua works with strings and its primary data tool, the table. Finally, we look an initial look at the file I/O capabilities that are built into Lua. All of these aspects of the language will come into play as we work through our sample game in the coming chapters.

Work through the examples in this chapter with the console to get your sea legs; then it'll be time to put on your C++ hat for a time to learn how to actually bolt Lua into a stand-alone application and begin scripting in earnest.

6 Integrating Lua into a C/C++ Program

In This Chapter

- Initial Design Concerns
- Basic Implementation

From the C++ programmer's point of view, Lua is a "black box" that processes commands and calls for some services. Lua often interacts directly with the user of a program or the game player and serves as a top layer, processing and reacting to input before it gets passed down to the core program code. Because Lua sits between the user and the code base, care should be taken in designing the integration and communication between C/C++ and the scripting language.

INITIAL DESIGN CONCERNS

During the initial technical design phase of a game project, the technical staff should take every opportunity to identify places where Lua could be exploited. Identifying these areas early on is a key design goal that will make your life much easier as the project progresses. In fact, it may be better to identify and implement too many places in which to use Lua than too few because these hooks are generally easier to remove than to insert. For example, if a hook was written to allow the Lua coder direct access to the PC speaker, and later the design is modified to make that access unnecessary, it is a simple matter to remove the hook or ignore it. No programmer or designer ever complained that he was given too much control or access.

The Lua Environment

The Lua Environment consists of all the data required by Lua to operate, such as compiled functions, variables, and other working memory. This data is stored in a structure called `lua_State`. Although every Lua-enabled application requires at least one `lua_State` to be opened, an application may have more than one state running if desired (such as to separate the data from two different systems). For our purposes, the Lua Environment is a place to send and receive data to and from Lua. Lua maintains a stack for this purpose (the Lua Stack). The Lua Stack, which is not the system stack, is accessed via Lua API functions.

Lua creates variables at runtime and stores them in the environment. The language supports a number of variable types, but we are going to deal primarily with just three (strings, numbers, and functions) in the C++ code. Dealing with Lua types like tables and user data is very complex and better left to be used exclusively within the Lua scripts.

LuaGlue

Lua allows the programmer to make functions available to the Lua scripts that are written in C++. We call these functions LuaGlue functions because they are the "glue" that binds the C++ world to the Lua Environment. LuaGlue functions look and feel just like functions defined in Lua to the Lua programmer, but they provide access to anything the C++ programmer makes available. They are the primary vehicle for Lua scripts to read and modify C++ data and to issue commands to C++. The Lua API provides functions for C++ code to directly call functions defined in Lua. It also provides a method to pass strings and larger blocks of text to the Lua interpreter for execution; communication between C++ code and Lua scripts is a two-way street (see Figure 6.1).

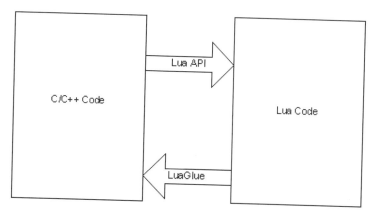

FIGURE 6.1   C/C++ and Lua communication

BASIC IMPLEMENTATION

ON THE CD   One of the strengths of Lua is the ease in which it can be embedded in a program. The designers of Lua provide a simple-to-use interface for powering your application with Lua. An example of this is the console program that reads strings from the keyboard and passes them directly to the Lua Environment. The complete program source (and executable) can be found on the accompanying CD-ROM in the Lua folder. Partial listings follow as the functionality is described, as shown in Listing 6.1.

LISTING 6.1 Partial Lua console

```
// Simple Lua console with limited vocabulary
// include the standard system headers.
#include <stdio.h>
#include <string.h>
/*
** Include the Lua headers.
**     Note that they are "C" language headers.
**     Because we are a C++ program, we need to let the C++
**     compiler know that the referenced prototypes and data
**     will not have C++ namespace processing.
*/
extern "C" {
#include <lua.h>
#include <lualib.h>
#include <lauxlib.h>
}
/*
** This is an example of a LuaGlue function
** The function will be called from the Lua Environment
** Again, since Lua is written in ANSI C, we need to
** turn off the C++ namespace function (extern "C")
*/
extern "C" int _Version(lua_State *L)
{
    puts("This is Version 1.0 of the Console Program");
    puts(LUA_VERSION);
    puts(LUA_COPYRIGHT);
    puts(LUA_AUTHORS);
    return 0;
}
/*
** This is where we hook up our LuaGlue functions.
** The program will register each of the defined functions
** and allow them to be called from Lua.
*/
static luaL_reg ConsoleGlue[] =
{
    {"Version",        _Version},
    {NULL, NULL}
```

```
};
char gpCommandBuffer[254];
const char *GetCommand(void)
{
    printf("Ready> ");
    return gets(gpCommandBuffer);
    puts("\n");
}
```

Creating the Lua Environment

The first task is to create the Lua Environment. This is done using the Lua API call lua_open() (see Listing 6.2).

LISTING 6.2   Lua Environment setup

```
lua_State *pLuaState = lua_open();
luaopen_base(pLuaState);
lua_iolibopen(pLuaState);
lua_strlibopen(pLuaState);
lua_mathlibopen(pLuaState);
lua_dblibopen(pLuaState);
```

The function returns a pointer to a lua_State structure, which represents the Lua Environment. This important pointer is passed to most Lua API functions. After the lua_State structure is created, the Lua libraries that the application requires are initialized. For this example, we started all the libraries that are in the Lua 5.0.2 distribution. This allows Lua scripts access to all the functions shipped with Lua; some applications may not need some libraries, and those unneeded libraries can be omitted.

Adding LuaGlue

Next, the program registers any LuaGlue functions the C++ code wishes to make available to Lua scripts. In the example shown in Listing 6.3, we provide a simple function that prints the version information of the program as well as for the Lua distribution. This is done in a loop and using a simple data structure to centralize groups of LuaGlue functions for easy reference and bug fixing.

LISTING 6.3   LuaGlue setup

```
for(int i=0; ConsoleGlue[i].name; i++)
{
```

```
    lua_register(pLuaState,
        ConsoleGlue[i].name, ConsoleGlue[i].func);
}
```

Processing Commands

All that is left is to loop through the process of getting a string from the keyboard and passing it to the Lua Environment. The Lua API function luaL_loadbuffer, shown in Listing 6.4, loads the passed string into the environment, checks for syntax, and prepares the code for execution. The function will return 0 if it passes all the tests and the code is ready to execute. Once the string is successfully loaded, it can be run with the API function lua_pcall. The return value from this function is 0 if the execution is successful. In the case of an error, Lua returns a string describing the error on the Lua Stack. This string can be read using the API function luaL_checkstring. The example program prints the word ERROR: and then the string from Lua so the user can see what happened.

LISTING 6.4   Console process loop

```
const char *pCommand = GetCommand();
while(stricmp(pCommand, "QUIT") != 0)
{
    // send command to the Lua Environment
    if (luaL_loadbuffer(pLuaState, pCommand,
            strlen(pCommand), NULL) == 0)
    {
        if(!lua_pcall(pLuaState, 0, LUA_MULTRET, 0))
        {
            // error on running the command
            printf("ERROR:%s\n",
                luaL_checkstring(pLuaState, -1));
        }
    }
    else
    {
        //error loading the command
        printf("ERROR:%s\n",
                luaL_checkstring(pLuaState, -1));
    }
    // get next command
    pCommand = GetCommand();
}
```

Ending the Application

When the user enters QUIT, the loop is terminated and the lua_State is released, as shown in the following line:

```
lua_close(pLuaState);
```

This basic example shows the minimum required to get Lua running. For this example, we simply include all of the relevant source code directly into the Visual C++ project and directly access the Lua API. Although this method is perfectly acceptable for small projects, it is much better to abstract the Lua system into a simple library that is C++ friendly and reusable over many projects. To this end, we will now present this library and revise the console program to use it.

The cLua Object and LuaLib

Compiling the Lua distribution into a library makes your project cleaner and allows for a central location for updates and bug fixes in the Lua code without modifying your code or requiring a recompile of all the Lua sources every time you need to do a clean build of your application. Most implementations require a small subset of Lua API functionality, and that functionality can be exposed via a class that also has the benefit of hiding the startup and shutdown procedures required for Lua. The cLua class accomplishes these goals while still allowing the user to get access to the raw API if required. The class definition for cLua is shown in Listing 6.5.

LISTING 6.5 The cLua header

```
struct lua_State;
#define LuaGlue extern "C" int
extern "C" {
typedef int (*LuaFunctionType)(struct lua_State *pLuaState);
};
class cLua
{
public:
    cLua();
    virtual ~cLua();
    bool            RunScript(const char *pFilename);
    bool            RunString(const char *pCommand);
const char *GetErrorString(void);
bool            AddFunction(const char *pFunctionName,
                    LuaFunctionType pFunction);
    const char *GetStringArgument(int num,
    const char *pDefault=NULL);
```

```
    double      GetNumberArgument(int num,
                        double dDefault=0.0);
    void        PushString(const char *pString);
    void        PushNumber(double value);
private:
    lua_State    *m_pScriptContext;
};
```

The constructor handles the opening of the Lua Environment, and the destructor closes it. The code to run strings containing Lua source code and files containing Lua source code are handled by the RunString and RunFile methods of the object The other methods will come in handy as we delve further into LuaGlue functions and passing arguments and returning values in LuaGlue functions.

ON THE CD

We made a library consisting of the required Lua source (from the distribution) and the source to the cLua class. (The project that makes this library is included on the CD-ROM in the C++ Code/Lua folder.) This library allows us to use the same code across many applications as well as provides a central place to update and fix problems in this code that will affect all our linked projects. This is the library we will be using throughout the code samples of this book.

cLua-Enabled Example

The updated console program that uses the cLua object is shown in Listing 6.6. Notice that it is much smaller and easier to follow.

LISTING 6.6   Updated console program

```
// Simple Lua console with limited vocabulary
// Using cLua object and Lua library
// include the standard system headers.
#include <stdio.h>
#include <string.h>
#include <cLua.h>
LuaGlue _Version(lua_State *L)
{
    puts("This is Version 2.0 of the Console Program");
    return 0;
}
char gpCommandBuffer[254];
const char *GetCommand(void)
{
    printf("Ready> ");
    return gets(gpCommandBuffer);
```

```
        puts("\n");
    }
    void main(void)
    {
        // print the banner.
        puts("Lua Console (c) 2004 Charles River Media");
        puts("Enter Lua commands at the prompt");
            puts("\"QUIT\" to exit\n\n");
        cLua *pLua = new cLua;
        pLua->AddFunction("Version", _Version);
        // process commands
        const char *pCommand = GetCommand();
        while(stricmp(pCommand, "QUIT") != 0)
        {
            // pass the string to cLua
            if(!pLua->RunString(pCommand))
            {
                printf("ERROR:%s\n",
                    pLua->GetErrorString());
            }
            // get next command
            pCommand = GetCommand();
        }
        delete pLua;
    }
```

Notice that the example no longer needs the Lua includes (only `cLua.h`) and that the definition of the LuaGlue function `_Version` is shortened by use of the LuaGlue type. The creation of the `cLua` object replaces the code to open and initialize the Lua Environment, and the deletion of that object handles the shutdown of the Lua Environment. The call to `cLua::AddFunction` adds the Version LuaGlue function. For larger lists of functions to register with Lua, it would be better to create the data-driven table approach in the original example. The `cLua::RunString` call replaces the loading and running of the Lua buffer with something that is much more descriptive of the function.

LuaGlue Functions

LuaGlue functions are C++ functions written in a way that allows them to be called directly from Lua scripts. This is the primary method of Lua–script-to-C++-code communication. When the Lua script needs a function written in C++, it calls a LuaGlue function. Lucky for the Lua programmer, LuaGlue functions look exactly like functions defined in Lua. One interesting trick is to write functions in Lua that the Lua programmer needs and then port them to C++ as bottlenecks are identified. Because the calls are exactly the same, the Lua source needs only to remove the original Lua function (or rename it) to start reaping the benefits of the LuaGlue function.

Registering LuaGlue functions (described next) is handled via the AddFunction method. The type LuaGlue is defined for easy definition of LuaGlue type functions and to hide some of the ANSI C/C++ communication problems.

LuaGlue Functions: Parameters and Return Values

One thing that is required to make most LuaGlue functions useful is the ability to send parameters to the function. Lua does this via the Lua Stack. Any type of data supported by Lua can be passed as a parameter to a LuaGlue function. All numbers in Lua are expressed as C++ doubles, and strings are returned as null-terminated strings. Lua tables can also be passed as arguments to LuaGlue functions, but table manipulation using the Lua ANSI C API is very cumbersome and not necessary.

Lua also supports a data type called user data, which we do not use, but this type could also be passed as a parameter. The cLua class has methods for retrieving parameters in a LuaGlue function. The cLua::GetStringArgument method returns a pointer to a null-terminated string or NULL to signify a parameter error. The cLua::GetNumberArgument method returns a double or 0.0 if no argument is available. Both methods take a parameter to specify the number of the parameter to retrieve; the number starts at 1 for the first parameter listed and increases by 1 for each successive parameter.

Return values are also handled using the Lua Stack. To return a value to the caller, simply place the value on the Lua Stack and increment the number of return values in the value returned by the C++ return statement. Notice we said that the number of return values is the value the C++ function returns to the Lua Environment. Lua functions can return *multiple* values to the caller. This feature is very useful and applies to LuaGlue functions as well. It is important that the number of return values agrees with the number of values pushed onto the Lua Stack. Placing values on the Lua Stack is accomplished by calling the cLua::PushString or cLua::PushNumber method.

A best practice is to define a local parameter counter and start its value at 1, and then use and post-increment the counter as you read each parameter from the cLua object. It is also recommended that you always return the same number of return values, even if it means pushing default values as return values. This is due to error handling of accessing nil values in Lua. We will discuss error handling in a later chapter. See the example shown in Listing 6.7.

LISTING 6.7   Examples of retrieving and returning values

```
extern cLua *pLua;
LuaGlue _SwapExt(lua_State *L)
{
    int argNum = 1;
    const char *fileName =
            pLua->GetStringArgument(argNum++);
    const char *newExt =
            pLua->GetStringArgument(argNum++);
    char fname[_MAX_FNAME];
    char ext[_MAX_EXT];
    _splitpath(fileName, NULL, NULL, fname, ext);
    std::string sRet = fname;
    if(newExt[0] != '\0')
    {
        sRet += ".";
        sRet += newExt;
    }
    lua->PushString(sRet.c_str());
    return 1;
}
```

The first thing the function does is collect its parameters from the Lua Environment. In this case the parameters are two `char` strings, which are accessed by `cLua::GetStringArgument`. After it does the string manipulation, it returns the resulting string by calling `cLua::PushString` and returning 1 (the number of return values).

SUMMARY

The designers of Lua have created a very flexible and portable system to embed the language into C programs. The examples in this chapter show how to embed Lua into C++ programs while hiding some of the more complex, difficult-to-read-and-maintain code required by Lua. This is just the first step into the larger world of game programming in Lua.

In the next chapter, we'll explore the technical design of a C++ Lua project, plus look at some coding styles to make Lua scripts more readable.

7 Communication between Lua and C++

In This Chapter

- LuaGlue Functions Revisited
- Communication from C++ Code to Lua
- Event-Driven Scripting
- Error Handling

Lua by itself is a very rich environment. But without a way for Lua scripts and C++ code to communicate, no real work gets done. In this chapter we build on the basic framework presented in Chapter 6 and start the implementation of a system where Lua and C++ code can interact.

LUAGLUE FUNCTIONS REVISITED

In Chapter 6, we touched briefly on the LuaGlue concept. This important topic is fundamental in creating a robust communication system. LuaGlue functions are the gateway for Lua scripts to access C++ code functions. The API that the C++ programmer creates for the Lua programmer is what drives the power of the scripting language. The C++ programmer can make all kinds of data and functionality available to the Lua programmer while containing the interface to some simple-to-debug functions. The trade-offs between control and access are easy to mitigate in this system.

The fact that LuaGlue functions look and feel to the Lua programmer just like regular functions written in Lua is a key property that we will exploit. One way to do this is to develop functions in Lua and have them recoded as LuaGlue functions and comment out the Lua function. Key processes can be tested and perfected in the rapid development environment of Lua and then be moved to the more efficient environment of C++.

It's also important to note that LuaGlue functions need to be documented more carefully than standard Lua functions. The script programmer can refer back to the script itself to see what arguments need to be passed into a Lua function, but he has no direct way of knowing this information about a LuaGlue function.

It's often a good idea to create a document that lists all of the LuaGlue functions, their arguments, and even examples of use for each project that you work on. This document will become a vital reference tool for the script programmers when they need to utilize a LuaGlue function that they haven't worked with for several weeks.

COMMUNICATION FROM C++ CODE TO LUA

LuaGlue functions provide a way for Lua to call C++ code, but how does the C++ code call Lua? Lua provides a system for C code to directly call Lua functions, but the code is somewhat cumbersome, it relies on specific names in the Lua script to be defined, and it is not very flexible. The examples in this book will use an event-driven model to communicate with the Lua code. This sort of system lends itself to easy modification and expansion and provides a central location where all communication to Lua is handled. Some examples of how Lua can be used to handle events follow:

- Key presses and mouse events
- Specific game events (triggers pressed, player dies)
- GUI-based events (button pressed)
- Timer expired

EVENT-DRIVEN SCRIPTING

To use an event-driven system to communicate with Lua, the C code needs to be told which Lua function to call to pass an event to Lua. We provide a LuaGlue function to set the name of the Lua event handler, and Lua calls it to start the events flowing. This way, the Lua programmer controls the name and location of the event-handling function. This approach also lends itself to easy expandability—both sides agree on event codes, and the system is then extended.

Sample Event

To illustrate this concept, consider the following example:

```
EVENT_SAMPLE = 1000
RegisterEvent("EventHandler")
function EventHandler(id, ...)
    if id == EVENT_SAMPLE then
        print("Sample Event!")
    end
end
```

If the preceding script is run, the C++ code can then send an event to the code and have it handled by Lua. The function RegisterEvent, a LuaGlue function provided by the C++ code, stores the name of the event handler for later use. The C++ code for this function is shown in Listing 7.1.

LISTING 7.1   Sample `RegisterEvent` and `FireEvent` functions

```
#define EVENT_SAMPLE 1000
std::string g_strEventHandler = "";
extern "C" int _RegisterEvent(lua_State *L)
{
    g_strEventHandler = g_pLua->GetStringArgument(1, "");
}
void FireEvent(int id)
{
    if(g_strEventHandler != "")
    {
        char buf[254];
        sprintf(buf, "%s(%d)", g_strEventHandler, id);
        lua_dostring(buf);
    }
}
```

Notice that we bypass the Lua system for a simpler method that creates a tiny script and executes it on the fly. This method is fine for now, but later we will want to trap errors and make the system more robust.

Passing Parameters to Events

To make events more generalized, we can pass parameters that are customized for each event to the event handlers using Lua's variable argument system. Notice in the previous example the Lua function `EventHandler` takes the event id as the first parameter and ... as the second parameter. This code tells Lua to put any parameters starting with ... into a local array called `args`. Take for example the following Lua code:

```
EVENT_SAMPLE = 1000
function EventHandler(id, …)
    print(string.format("id = %d\n", id))
    for i = 1,arg.n do
        print(string.format("arg[%d] = ", i)
        print(arg[i])
        print("\n");
    end
    if id == EVENT_SAMPLE then
        print("Sample Event!")
    end
end
EventHandler(EVENT_SAMPLE, 100, "next arg", "lastarg")
```

If this script were run in the console program, the output would look something like that shown in the next example:

```
id = 1000
arg[1] = 100
arg[2] = "next arg"
arg[3] = "lastarg"
```

The C++ function to send the event will also need to be modified to take a string that contains the parameter list. See Listing 7.2.

LISTING 7.2 Variable argument passing example, C++

```cpp
void FireEvent(int id, const char *args)
{
    if(g_strEventHandler != "")
    {
        char buf[254];
        if(args)
            sprintf(buf, "%s(%d,%s)", g_strEventHandler, id, args);
        else
            sprintf(buf, "%s(%d)", g_strEventHandler, id);
        lua_dostring(buf);
    }
}
```

The main complication to this system is making sure that the Lua code and C++ code agree on the value of the event ids and meaning of the passed arguments. This complication is a small price to pay for simplicity.

ERROR HANDLING

During development, scripting errors will be commonplace. Without some tools to let the Lua programmer know what caused the program to stop, finishing the project would be nearly impossible.

The standard Lua error-handling system prints an error message in the console. (Try it in the console program; type something that will cause Lua to error and see what it tells you.) This approach leaves something to be desired when you are not working in a text console environment (like a game). One solution is to provide a console in the game that can be used to view error messages. This method is also a great way to allow the user to use the console to print out variables or run functions. The downside is that this workaround is not acceptable for end-user use.

We will add this functionality in later chapters and expose the debug console only in debug builds. We choose to handle errors by trapping them from Lua and throwing a C++ exception. The exception handler opens a standard dialog box with the message that Lua provides and then closes the application. Any time Lua is called from C, it uses a "protected call" to Lua as apposed to `lua_dostring`-type calls that were used in the previous examples. Lua will not use its normal error-handling system and return a code and string to the calling function instead. The class of the error object is shown in the next example:

```
class CError
{
public:
                CError();
    virtual      ~CError();
    void        AppendLocation(const char *fileName, int lineNum);
    void        AppendMessage(const char *formatString, ...);
    void        Report();
private:
    std::list<std::string>    m_lstMessages;
};
```

When Lua returns any error, a `CError` object is created, and the returned error string is appended with the some information about where the error occurred. The main program is inside a large "try...catch" block where the catch block calls the `CError` `Report` method (the dialog box) and then ends the program. This method effectively catches all Lua errors (or other errors that you want to throw) and reports them.

SUMMARY

In this chapter, we expanded on the LuaGlue concepts presented in Chapter 6 and began work on an event-driven foundation to let the C++ code communicate back the Lua scripting environment. This two-way communication is essential for game development, because user interaction (such as a player using the mouse, interacting with buttons, or entering text) is fundamental to a game-play experience.

Learning how to create our own LuaGlue functions allows us to attack game development from different angles and to match our approach with the problems we need to solve. LuaGlue allows us to write functions in C++ that we can call within Lua, yet have the speed benefit of being compiled into native machine code. Lua itself allows us to write functions at the script level and allows for easy editing, testing, or modification. We can also use Lua to prototype functions that we later want to translate into C++ functions that we access via a LuaGlue function call.

Using the concepts from this chapter, we will build a robust system where Lua code can drive a game including interface, graphics, sound, and game data.

8 Building the Foundation

In This Chapter

■ The Visual C++ 6.0 Workspace
■ DirectX Foundation
■ Introduction to LuaGUI
■ Debugging Window
■ Windows Registry

L ua is an embedded language, which means that for it to be useful, it needs a program around it to provide context and a framework. This chapter will discuss the framework, or shell, that we will use for all examples in this book as well as for the samples we will be developing over the next few chapters.

THE VISUAL C++ 6.0 WORKSPACE

All of the code examples in this book are contained in a Visual C++ 6.0 Workspace. Figure 8.1 shows a quick screenshot of the workspace for reference.

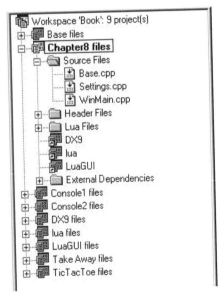

FIGURE 8.1 Visual C++ 6.0 Workspace

The workspace contains projects for all examples as well as all the libraries used. The Base project is the game foundation for all future chapters. The Chapter8 project is the project that we will be discussing in this chapter. The source to the two console examples is in Console1 files and Console2 files. The DX9 library contains all the code that is DirectX specific and provides all the DirectX functionality that the other examples require. The lua project contains the Lua 5.0.2 distribution files (from *www.lua.org*) and the cLua class files. The LuaGUI, Take Away, and TicTac-Toe projects are examples that we cover in later chapters.

DIRECTX FOUNDATION

DirectX is a set of APIs developed by Microsoft that enables programmers to write programs to access the hardware features of a computer, without knowing exactly what hardware will be installed on the machine on which the program (such as video cards, game controllers, or sound cards) eventually runs. DirectX achieves this feat by creating an intermediate layer that translates generic hardware commands into specific commands for particular pieces of hardware.

For our purposes, DirectX lets game programmers write to a standard platform and lets the hardware details be handled by the drivers supplied by external parties (such as the video card manufacturer). A deep understanding of DirectX is not needed for our examples. If you would like to learn more about DirectX, you can find documentation, tutorials, and examples on the Internet. Start with The Microsoft DirectX Developer Center at *www.msdn.microsoft.com/directx/*.

This chapter's example is a basic shell used to implement DirectX functionality and provide a Lua environment and the beginnings of a Lua-based GUI system. Our shell starts up DirectX Graphics and DirectX Audio. It uses standard Windows mouse and keyboard messages for input; to support joysticks and other input devices, DirectX Input could be implemented. The DX9 library is a good start to any DirectX project.

Building the DirectX Shell

ON THE CD

Our first example, shown in Listing 8.1, will build a simple game shell using the DirectX library, the cLua library, and the LuaGUI library. This basic shell will be the building block for all further examples in the book. The C++ code for this shell can be found on the CD in the "Chapter8" project. The specific code referenced is in the file Base.cpp and the function CBase::Init.

LISTING 8.1 Shell initialization

```cpp
bool CBase::Init(HINSTANCE hInstance, const char *szClass,
          const char *szCaption, WNDPROC WindowProc)
{

    m_lpDX=new DXContext(hInstance,szClass,szCaption,WindowProc);
    if (!m_lpDX->Init(800,600,16,2,TRUE)) {
        delete m_lpDX;
        return false;
    }
    m_pSettings = new Settings;
    m_pSettings->Init("Chapter8");
    for(int i=0; MyGlue[i].name; i++)
    {
        m_lua.AddFunction(MyGlue[i].name, MyGlue[i].func);
    }
    m_hConsole = CWinConsole::StartConsole(hInstance, &m_lua);
    if(m_hConsole)
    {
        int x = m_pSettings->GetInteger("DebugWinX");
        int y = m_pSettings->GetInteger("DebugWinY");
        int w = m_pSettings->GetInteger("DebugWinW");
        int h = m_pSettings->GetInteger("DebugWinH");
        if(w == 0 || h == 0)
        {
            RECT r;
            GetWindowRect(m_hConsole, &r);
            w = r.right - r.left;
            h = r.bottom - r.top;
        }

        SetWindowPos(m_hConsole, HWND_BOTTOM, x, y, w, h, 0);
    }
    m_pGUIManager = new CGUIManager;
    m_pGUIManager->Init(&m_lua);
    return true;
}
```

This function performs the following tasks:

- Creates a new DXContext (DX9 Library)
- Sets DirectX Graphics to 800×600×16 with two back buffers
- Creates a Settings interface

- Registers any application-specific LuaGlue functions
- Starts up the debug window
- Starts the LuaGUI system

Start the DirectX Shell Components

The shell initialization begins by starting the DirectX Graphics component for display. The call for this is in `Base.cpp`, but the actual code is found in the DX9 project in the workspace. This code in the DX9 project, a modified Microsoft sample, allows the application to be in a window or full screen in various screen sizes. The DirectX Audio component is also started to give us access to the audio portions of the DirectX API. The Windows messaging system provides mouse and keyboard functionality. A future expansion could be to start DirectX input to support joysticks and other input devices. Our DirectX abstraction provides two objects that are required for the GUI system: sprites and fonts. Both of these objects have roots in Microsoft examples.

Create the Settings Interface

Create a `CSettings` object and tell it where in the Windows registry to store its values. For more on `CSettings` and the Windows registry, see the section "Windows Registry," later in this chapter.

Initialize the Lua Environment

The Lua Environment is started using the `cLua` object as shown in the previous console examples. It is important to start Lua and register any game-specific LuaGlue functions before starting the GUI system because the `cLua` object is required for the GUI system to function properly and the GUI could run code that requires the game-specific functions. The code for the `cLua` object can be found in the file `cLua.cpp` in the Lua project. This project also contains the Lua distribution (5.0.2) that is used throughout the book.

ON THE CD

Create the Lua Debug Window

The debug window is simply the previous console examples migrated to a window. We open it here. The position and size of the window is recorded in the Windows Registry via the `CSettings` object created earlier. See the next section for further details on this window.

Start up the GUI System

The GUI system, which defines all the LuaGlue functions required for GUI operation, is started. During this process the startup Lua scripts will be run. (See Chapter 11 for further details on the full LuaGUI system.) Once this process is complete, the GUI system is ready for action. The GUI library is in the project LuaGUI. We will cover this project much more completely in a later chapter.

Shutting Down

When the program terminates, it must shut down the systems that it started in `CBase::Init`. This step is done in the CBase destructor. The following code closes the debug console window and closes all the DirectX systems:

```
CWinConsole::StopConsole();
if(m_lpDX)
{
    m_lpDX->Cleanup();
    delete m_lpDX;
}
```

INTRODUCTION TO LUAGUI

All examples are built from the DirectX foundation. This foundation contains support for the LuaGUI library, which is the heart of the game system. To introduce the basics of LuaGUI, we will start out with support for sprites and a single event `GUI_EVENT_KEYPRESS`.

Starting the GUI

ON THE CD

The main program starts the GUI system by creating a `CGUIManager` object and calling its `Init` method to give it access to the `cLua` object. `CGUIManager` is defined in the workspace of the LuaGUI project. The file `GUIManager.h` contains the class definition; this file is found on the CD-ROM under "C++ Code/includes". This method sets up all the LuaGlue functions for the GUI and runs a special script called `StartGUI.Lua`. This script should do any initialization required on the Lua side and is a good place to define any constant values or define any Lua base utility functions that you need. It should also call the LuaGlue function `RunGUI` to start up the first interface displayed to the user. `RunGUI` is a big part of the GUI and is how the program moves from interface to interface. `RegisterEvent` tells the GUI system the name of the event handler Lua function and starts the flow of events. The internals of the GUI system remember every interface created during a single run of the program and re-runs any interface called for by `RunGUI` instead of re-running the script.

An Interface

Throughout our discussion of the GUI system, you will find reference to "the interface" or "the interface object." These terms mean any interface that is started with the RunGUI command. There is a one-to-one relationship between an interface and an interface script/event handler. It may be best to think of an interface as a screen in a game. Once an interface is created it can be re-run without having its assets reloaded. In the C++ code, an interface is defined as a CuserInterface object. See the LuaGUI project file UserInterface.h for the class definition.

Interface Items

GUI items—the visible objects that make up the interface (such as a button)—are predefined objects in the C++ code that the Lua code can create and use however it sees fit. In later chapters we will be defining a number of GUI items. We cannot cover all the possible items because there are no limits to what you can create. Common items include buttons, sprites, and list boxes, all of which and more can be added to this system.

GUI items are all built from the CGUIObject class, which you can find in the LuaGUI project. Because all items are based on CGUIObject, they all have certain basic functionality. They all have a sprite and a font associated with them that can be used, depending on the item. Sprites are the simplest example because the base class itself does everything necessary to display a sprite on screen. Text objects can have a sprite as a background and display text in the base class's font. This implementation of CGUIObject relies on the DirectX abstraction's sprite and font classes. If the underlying graphics shell changes, the new system must supply these classes for the GUI code to work.

Events

In Chapter 7, we discussed the concept of event-driven programming and systems. This GUI system we are building will be the first system to rely on these concepts. The C++ code will fire events that the Lua code can react to or ignore. In this chapter's example, the event handler will react to only one event, GUI_KEY_PRESS. The script will call the LuaGlue function QuitProgram when this event is triggered. The scripts for this chapter's example are shown in Listing 8.2

LISTING 8.2   Sample Lua script

```
StartGUI.lua:
-- define constant values for all scripts
-- Standard LuaGUI event codes
GUI_KEY_PRESS = 4
```

```
RunGUI("MainMenu.lua")
-- END of StartGUI.lua

MainMenu.lua:
RegisterEvent("EventHandler")
function EventHandler(id, ...)
    if id == GUI_KEY_PRESS then
        QuitProgram()
    end
end
-- END of MainMenu.lua
```

The file StartGUI.Lua is the entry point for the GUI scripting system. We use it to define a variable that contains the event code for GUI_KEY_PRESS. This code allows the Lua coder to use a "human-friendly" name in the code and also allows us to change the value for the event easily if the C++ code changes it for some reason (it should not). It then instructs the GUI system to run the script MainMenu.lua. This script creates a simple interface that responds to only event (GUI_KEY_PRESS), which ends the program.

LuaGlue Functions

We now introduce the first LuaGlue functions related to the GUI system. This list will grow as we cover more functionality of the GUI system.

RunGUI ("interface.lua")

This function instructs the GUI system to create a new interface, or re-run a previously run interface by running the passed Lua code file. This interface becomes the current or live interface. This Lua file should define and register an event handler via the LuaGlue function RegisterEvent.

RegisterEvent ("eventFunction")

This function tells the GUI system what Lua function to call in order to handle GUI events for the current interface. Every interface requires an event handler to do anything interesting.

Expanding the Shell

The foundation was designed to be expandable. One example of this expandability is the loop in CBase::Init (see Listing 8.1) that registers application-specific LuaGlue functions. Any functions that are added to the MyGlue array will be registered automatically with Lua. For this chapter's example, we have only one new LuaGlue function, but it is an important one.

QuitProgram()

This function instructs the program to close. Defining this function in the main program instead of in the LuaGlue library allows each program to handle the exit function on a case-by-case basis. The code for `QuitProgram`, found in `Base.cpp`, sends Windows a message to end the program. This message is handled in `WinMain.cpp`.

Expansion Ideas

The foundation can be expanded in many ways, including the following:

3D functionality
More LuaGUI objects
DirectInput function to support joysticks
A resource-caching system
Ability to switch between full-screen and windowed graphics mode
Animation systems
Particle effect systems
Physics engine
Lots of game-specific expansions

DEBUGGING WINDOW

In Chapter 7, we mentioned that it would be a good idea to allow the user to access the Lua console. In creating the base game shell, this debugging console will be included so that it will be available to all debug versions of any game we build from the shell. The main difference between the text console applications presented in previous chapters and the debug console is that the console applications are text based and the debug console is a true window with the input and output areas separated. The debug window is available only in debug builds; we do not want to allow users to access this powerful feature.

The debug window, implemented as a stand-alone window, is very much like a "mini-application": it has its own window, message handler, and controls. The user can even close it by clicking the close button. The main program creates this window by instantiating a `CWinConsole` object. The debug window is connected directly to the main program only by the use of the common Lua context, a CWinConsole method that allows the main program to insert text into the window, and the implementation of the print LuaGlue function. A single control for input is located at the bottom of the window. The rest of the window is devoted to text output from Lua and the C++ code. When the edit control detects that the Enter key is pressed, it signals the window to send the command found in the control to Lua. The output section contains the output of Lua as well as any text that the main application passes to the object. Notice that the console handles errors differently than the main C++ code. Errors will not generate a C++ exception; they simply display Lua's error text in the output window.

The usefulness of the debug window is pretty clear in the ability to view Lua values, but another powerful feature is that the user can call Lua functions to print variables or even dump them to files using the Lua file I/O libraries. One simple debugging method involves using print statements in tricky code to mark progress. The strings generated by the print statement in the Lua code will appear in the debugging window, if it is open. A user could even redefine a Lua function or change a Lua value on the fly to see what changes in the main program will be affected.

ON THE CD

The code to implement the debug window can be found in the DX9 project in the file WinConsole.cpp.

WINDOWS REGISTRY

Windows provides a central repository for storing program-specific data that must be saved between runs of the program. Microsoft calls it the "registry." In our basic shell, we want to have a simple way to access data in this registry. The registry stores data based on a "key" string. A program can read from or write to a key. Each program creates its own space in the registry where its keys are stored. The provided API from Microsoft is not very hard, but it is always a good practice to centralize and standardize access to data. To this end we will create a class called CSettings to handle all the registry bookkeeping for us. For simplicity, CSettings will support only two of the many methods of storing data in the registry. We will support strings and integers. See Listing 8.3.

LISTING 8.3 CSettings class

```
class Settings
{
public:
                Settings();
    virtual     ~Settings();
```

```
    void            Init(const char *baseKey);

    int             GetInteger(const char *key);
    std::string       GetString(const char *key);

    void            SetInteger(const char *key, int value);
    void            SetString(const char *key, const char *value);

protected:
    std::string       m_baseKey;
};
```

When creating the CSettings object, the Init method must be called to tell the object where in the Windows registry the keys are stored. After the object is initialized, calls to the Get key and Set key methods can be called to retrieve and store data. The complete code for the CSettings class can be found in the "Chapter8" project in the file Settings.cpp.

SUMMARY

In this chapter, we built our first DirectX-based example program in which Lua is an integral part. The foundation is built on the Microsoft DirectX APIs, the Windows registry, a GUI system, a debugging console, and, of course, Lua. This foundation is used for all examples and is a great starting point for your own projects. The DX9 library was shown to hide the DirectX internals, which simplifies their use. We introduced some important concepts of the LuaGUI library, which sets the table for the full-featured LuaGUI discussion to come. The text-based console program from previous chapters has transformed into a debugging console that not only displays error messages but also allows manipulation of the code on the fly. A way to store settings in the Windows registry was covered as well.

9

Designing a Lua Implementation

In This Chapter

■ Game Design 101
■ Setting the Foundation
■ The Design Document
■ A Lua Style Guide

Before we get too deep into the nuts and bolts of scripting our game, we need to lay a solid foundation. We need to understand what sort of game project we are striving to create and then use that knowledge to determine what files and scripts we need to author during the development process. From that foundation, we can flesh out our design document and have in hand a true blueprint for the development of our first game using the Lua scripting language.

GAME DESIGN 101

Before we do any thinking about the nuts and bolts of scripting our game, we need to think about games in general for a moment. A "game" is a play experience that guides a player forward (via rules and activities) toward some ending conclusion (usually a win, lose, or draw).

Taken alone, a game doesn't have to be fun (think of the war games practiced by military units to prepare them for combat), but in our context (as game developers) we truly want our players to enjoy the experience of playing our game.

What Is a Game?

Let's take a moment to look at a more formalized definition of a game, which we've developed over the last ten years of developing games:

A game is a play activity comprising a series of actions, constrained by rules, moving toward an end condition. The rules exist to provide the framework and context for a player's actions. The rules also exist to create interesting situations to challenge and oppose the player. The player's actions, decisions, choices, and chances all make up the flow of play, or the player's "journey" through the game. It is the quality, challenge, excitement, and fun of the player's journey, and not simply the attainment of the end condition, that determines the success of the game.

Let's deconstruct this definition a bit further. A player plays a game by performing actions—this can be moving a joystick to dodge an enemy tank or by rolling the dice and moving the little shoe across the board in *Monopoly*™. These actions are controlled by the rules of the game. In *Monopoly*, I can't simply move my shoe to Boardwalk—I must follow the rules and roll the dice.

It's the rules of a game that direct and control a player's actions: they are the mechanism by which we can create an imaginary world and make the player a participant of that world. The rules carry much of the burden in making a game feel whole and fun. The rules need to make sense within the game itself, and the rules need to create a situation in which the player can, to some degree at least, control his own destiny in the game.

Here we touch on the main point: a player, in an interactive game, needs to be able to control his progress as he progresses through the game. He needs to know that what he does—whether shooting an alien, moving left to dodge a tackle, or moving a game piece—matters and makes a difference.

When we create a game, we must always remember that our game is designed to have an audience: our players. It is their experience that matters the most, not how cool our tank model looks or how realistic our explosions are. Everything we do in the games we create should play to that audience. In fact, everything we present to a player in the game should be essential to his enjoyment of the game and his progress toward the end of the game. No opportunity should be wasted by just presenting him with something to look at or listen to that does not have relevance to the player's journey through the game.

Get in Their Heads

When defining rules for a game and challenges for a player to face, it's important to know a little about player psychology. Let's touch on this quickly: first and foremost, players do not like to lose; they like to win. But truth be told, they like to win by a narrow margin rather than by a huge margin—they enjoy the fact that victory was grabbed from the jaws of defeat. This feeling is just a component of our natural desire to succeed but also to be excited and entertained while we succeed.

So, part of our role when creating the rules for any game is to craft the rules and the situations such that players will be tested and challenged and that their efforts will allow them to eek out an exciting victory.

As an interesting aside (which will be key for our own game project here), in the early days of arcade-game development, the developers at Atari® created a set of "crown jewels" of game design—those components of their games that made them so addictive to quarter-dropping players. One such component was the idea of the endless game (think of *Asteroids*®): a game that never ended until you lost.

On the surface, this seems like a rather silly idea, but the real key here was that the designers needed to create the perception in the player that, if he had been only a little bit better, had only done something a little differently, he could go further next time. It was this perception that kept the players dropping quarters into these endless games that they could never win.

Another key component of player psychology is the fact that players like lots of indications of success along the way—they enjoy a string of smaller-scale victories rather than just one single payoff at the end of the experience. This point fits well into the journey metaphor: players don't play games just for the destination, they play games to enjoy the ride along the way (often more than the destination itself).

With this in mind, we want to craft a play experience that provides the player with the chance to enjoy multiple victories on his way to the ultimate victory or ultimate high score. You can think of these as "nested games," if you'd like. Consider the venerable arcade game, *Star Wars*® (one of the first arcade games to use digitized speech). In that game, you played a series of mini-games: fight the TIE fighters, battle the turrets, make the trench run, and finally destroy the Death Star. Each step possessed encapsulated challenges and mini-victories, but they all worked toward the larger goal of trying to save the Rebellion. In a PC game, consider an action game played through a series of levels: surviving and beating one level is its own mini-victory that adds to and propels the player toward the ultimate victory.

Finally, it's important to remember that the player will employ only a few of his senses when playing your game. The entire play experience must be conveyed through what the eyes see and what the ears hear. Being aware of this sensory limitation will allow you to design visuals for your game and audio (sound effects and music) that will enhance the player's experience, rather than confuse or overwhelm him.

When you think of designing your game, you want to put the player at the center of the experience and use that as the measuring stick with which to measure your design. But you also need to be aware of the technical issues for your game: your target platform, your schedule, the makeup of your team, and which aspects of your game are best suited for C++ development and which will fare better in the world of Lua scripting.

SETTING THE FOUNDATION

One of the first steps when we dive into a Lua-enabled game project is to lay down some boundaries: what will be handled by Lua and what will be handled by traditional C++ programming?

Starting this questioning process can be pretty straightforward, because C++ can do some things very well that Lua can't do at all, such as rendering to the screen. But before we can walk too far down this path, we need to have a fairly solid idea of our goal.

For this, we need a scope document: a short document that covers the basic capabilities of the game we are getting ready to develop. From this document, we'll derive the answers to the previous questions, plus create a design document that will serve as a blueprint as we roll up our sleeves and begin scripting.

For this book, we're going to create an action-shooter arcade game, somewhat derived from the old vector arcade game called *Rip Off*. We'll call our game *Take Away* (Figure 9.1). We'll start with a "high concept"—a sentence or two describing the essence of our game:

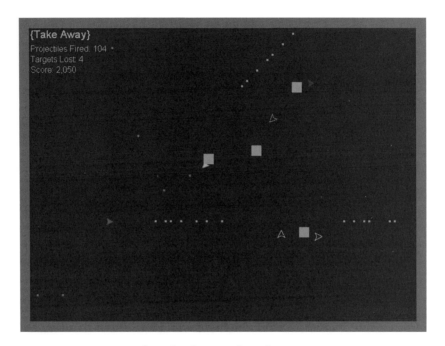

FIGURE 9.1   A screen-shot of *Take Away* in action.

Take Away will pit the player, who controls a small ship, against an endless horde of enemies who are intent on stealing his supply crates. The player can fly and blast and must survive as long as possible—when his last crate is stolen, the game is over.

This high concept gives us the initial idea of the game, plus it outlines the fundamental play metric: blast at things and survive. From the high concept, we can work to create a scope document. Obviously, for a game as simple as this one, the scope is quite straightforward. For a larger, commercial-quality game, you might need three or four pages to outline the full scope of your game. Anything longer than that, however, and you're probably getting too detailed for a scope document.

The scope document for our sample game is shown in Table 9.1.

TABLE 9.1   Scope document for *Take Away*

Title	*Take Away*
Platform	PC
Players	Single-player only
Genre	Action/arcade
High Concept	*Take Away* will pit the player, who controls a small ship, against an endless horde of enemies who are intent on stealing his supply crates. The player can fly and blast and must survive as long as possible—when his last crate is stolen, the game is over.
Goal	The goal is to accumulate as many points as possible. The player must protect eight supply crates from being dragged off screen by the enemy. When the last one is dragged off, the game ends.
Features	The game world is the screen area; the player cannot move out of the screen area. The player controls a ship—he can accelerate, turn, and shoot (there is no "gravity" in this game, so movement continues after a player thrusts). The game ends when the last crate is dragged off screen. The player earns points for each enemy he destroys. The enemies will try to steal the crates and shoot the player and may try to ram the player. The game will speed up through time. The player can save his game at any time.

From this scope document, we can now start making some decisions on how we will be implementing Lua. Often, it's a good idea to start with the experience from a player's point of view, and to begin thinking through your needs in terms of interface and what will be visible on the screen.

Often, game programs will begin with a loading or splash screen. This screen lets the player know what game he is loading and provides some eye candy for the player while the game loads. In our example game, the loading of the game will be almost instantaneous, but we'll still want to have a loading screen to anchor the player.

It's a good idea to lay out your interface screens in some sort of table, so you can see what you need at a glance. An example of how such a table might look with our single screen is shown in Table 9.2.

TABLE 9.2 Interface screens for *Take Away*

Lua file	Called From	Leads To	Description
StartGUI.lua	executable	GUI_Loading.lua	This is the start up file that will initialize the game, set up the constants, and call the loading file.
LuaSupport.lua	StartGui.lua	n/a	This file holds all game-specific (not interface) functions.
GUI_Loading.lua	StartGUI.lua	GUI_MainMenu.lua	This loading splash screen will display the game logo for a few seconds and then open the main menu.

You'll notice a file called StartGUI.lua—we were introduced to that file in the previous chapter. This is the startup file called by the program executable that initializes the game world and allows the Lua scripter to begin the program flow.

The tail end of StartGUI.lua is shown in the following example:

```
-- This initializes the game at startup.
math.randomseed(os.date("%d%H%M%S"))

-- Load in the support functions
dofile("Scripts\\LuaSupport.Lua")

--Start in the ingame screen
RunGUI("Loading.lua")
```

First, we can see that we use the os.date() function to initialize the random-number generator, so that we get a fresh series of pseudo random numbers at the start of our file. We then load in the LuaSupport.lua file, which contains the game's non-interface-specific function definitions, and finally we use the RunGUI LuaGlue function we learned about in Chapter 8 to run the first user interface file.

The other file listed in our table is LuaSupport.lua—this file is used as a repository of all of the functions that we use in the game that aren't directly linked to an interface (those we'll keep in the individual interface files). Often, your LuaSupport.lua file will grow into the largest script file in your game, and when you load it, you are compiling the Lua chunks into memory so that the functions can be called quickly from within your game. As your project grows in size, you may find that it's a good idea to break this file into smaller files, such as AI_functions.lua, Save_game.lua, and so on.

So, from the start we know we've got three Lua files in our project, but as we look over our scope, we can start to flesh out what additional Lua scripts we'll need to construct during the development of the game. After all, we've got quite a bit of information we need to present to the player and keep track of, such as the following items:

- Starting up the game
- Displaying the actual game sprites
- Displaying the high score
- Managing the projectiles
- Controlling the enemy ships
- Managing the storage containers
- Keeping track of the game data
- Saving the game

From this list, we can create a workable table for our Lua scripts that will allow us to manage our game quite effectively. See Table 9.3 for the scripts. Figure 9.2 shows the anticipated flow through the various GUI and support Lua files that make up the *Take Away* game.

TABLE 9.3 Lua scripts used in *Take Away*

Lua file	Called From	Leads To	Description
StartGUI.lua	executable	GUI_Loading.lua	This is the startup file that initializes the game, sets up the constants, and calls the loading file.
LuaSupport.lua	StartGui.lua	n/a	This function performs the following actions: rendering ships controlling ships managing the game world saving the game
GUI_Loading.lua	StartGUI.lua	GUI_MainMenu.lua	This loading splash screen displays the game logo for a few seconds and then opens the main menu.
GUI_MainMenu.lua	GUI_Loading.lua	GUI_InGame.lua	Windows desktop This main menu displays top scores, allows the player to $\longrightarrow$

			start the game, and exits the game. The player can also load a saved game from here.
GUI_InGame.lua	GUI_MainMenu.lua	GUI_EndGame.lua/ GUI_Escape.lua	The InGame interface is displayed when the game is being played. The player can bring up the Escape menu by pressing the Esc key. The player will be taken to the End Game screen when the game is over. This interface also displays the player's current score.
GUI_EndGame.lua	GUI_InGame.lua	GUI_InGame.lua	This screen lets the player know the game is over, shows the final score, and then takes the player back to the main menu.
GUI_Escape.lua	GUI_InGame.lua	GUI_InGame.lua	This screen pauses the game and allows the player to resume, quit, or save the game.
GUI_KeySelect.lua	GUI_MainMenu.lua	GUI_MainMenu.lua	This screen allows the player to "map" the control keys.
Text.lua	StartGui.lua	n/a	This file holds the text strings used in the project.

One thing that you'll notice, after you've put some thought into a scope and a script table for your own project, is that you've already come a long way in designing your game. Obviously, larger games will require many, many more Lua files and quite substantial design documents, but for our current game project, *Take Away*, we have all we need to create our game design document.

Ideally, a design document should be a blueprint for crafting a game from start to finish. The design document should be aware of the technical platform of your game, and it should outline the play dynamics within the game.

When putting together the design for a game, keep several things in mind. First, who is the audience of the document? Odds are, it's either yourself or a game-development team—either way, it's a practical audience made up of the folks who will actually use the document to craft a game. It's *not* a sales pitch document, so

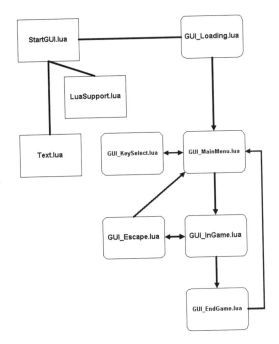

FIGURE 9.2 This chart shows the anticipated flow through the various GUI and support Lua files that make up the *Take Away* game.

don't waste your time with overly long prose, useless images, or anything else that takes away from the goal of the document: to help your game get made.

With all of that in mind, we can now put together the game-design document for our Lua game. This document is simple and straightforward; there is nothing extra here, but it covers all aspects of the game and gives us a clear blueprint of what the game should do.

It's important to note that the design document doesn't describe how to do the myriad tasks in the game; it merely describes the function of the game from all angles. It's up to the programmers, designers, and artists to use their creative abilities to determine the best ways to implement the layout of an interface, a ship sprite, an AI function, or a save-game capability.

THE DESIGN DOCUMENT

ON THE CD Take a few moments to read over the design document (also provided on the CD-ROM in Chapters/Chapter9/takeawaydesign.doc) to get an idea of the blueprint we'll be working with over the next chapters as we work to develop our very first Lua-powered game. We will look at sections of the document as we go through it.

```
Design Document — Take Away

document last modified: 02/14/05
author: Paul Schuytema
I. High Concept
Take Away will pit the player, who controls a small ship, against an
endless horde of enemies who are intent on stealing his supply crates.
The player can fly and blast and must survive as long as possible—when
his last crate is stolen, the game is over.

II. Milieu
Take Away will look and feel like a retro arcade game featuring early
raster graphics. The colors will be bold against a black background.
```

The High Concept section was taken directly from the scope document—this is our short and sweet description of the game as a whole. The Milieu section allows us to describe the visual tone of the game. For more complex games, this section will be more detailed, but for *Take Away*, we just want to hit on the key points: an early raster look and bold colors.

```
III. Technical Specifications
Take Away will be PC based, using a simple DirectX 9 renderer. The GUI
and sprite objects will be custom-coded (via C++), and the main control
mechanism will be Lua.
C++: rendering, sound, input, Lua implementation, LuaGlue functions,
basic GUI objects.
Lua: event handling, GUI design, sprite control, game data, save/load
game, game play, scoring, AI.
The game will utilize 2D sprites for action objects (such as ships) and
interface elements. All art will be 24-bit BMP files.
GUI/control objects needed: draw/position sprite, draw/position text,
text field input, button, timer, keyboard input, mouse input.
```

In the Technical Specifications section, we want to address all of the relevant technical issues for the game, so we know what language will handle what task, what our target system is, and what sorts of inputs we need to process. This section provides a common foundation for all technical members of the team and allows the person responsible for managing the project to assign the right developers to the right tasks.

```
IV. General Play
The game begins with eight "crates" at the center of the screen. The
player's ship appears at the exact center of the screen.
```

```
The player must protect his crates as enemy ships enter and try to tug
them off. When the last crate is pulled off screen, the game is over.
The player can rotate his ship and apply thrust. There is no "gravity"
in our game world, so the ship will continue to move until either it
bounces off of the edge of the game world or the player rotates his
ship and applies counter thrust.
Enemies will come in from off screen random locations (there will be
several types of enemies) and move toward either the player or the
crates. The player can fire on an enemy—a single "hit" will destroy the
enemy. Enemies can also fire at the player.
If an enemy and the player collide, both ships are destroyed.
When the player is destroyed, he will respawn at the center of the
screen.
The player will earn points for each enemy he destroys (either by
shooting or collision).
As time progresses, the enemy ships will move faster and faster, making
play more challenging.
When the game ends, the player sees his score. If the score is high
enough, it's recorded in the top-ten scores.
```

In the General Play section, we outline the play of the game. You'll notice that we don't address the GUI interfaces or menu screens—the real "game," or what happens after the player clicks the Start button. For some games, this section may be dozens of pages long. This is the blueprint for the player's experience, and it's what the Lua scripter will work from when implementing the game play and what the technical team will refer to to understand the context of their tasks.

```
V. Player Controls
The player controls can be mapped to any keys via the KeySelect inter-
face (see below). The player controls are utilized when the game is
being played within the InGame interface.
Player ship turn left (default [): player's ship rotates left 45
degrees.
Player ship turn right (default [): player's ship rotates right 45
degrees.
Player ship thrust (default space): player's ship applies thrust value
to current vector.
Player ship fire (default p): player's ship fires a projectile.
Esc menu (Esc): calls up GUI_Escape.
```

The Player Controls section outlines everything the player can do to interact with the game directly once play is underway. The script programmer will use this information to capture the correct keyboard, controller, or button events and write the proper control handlers.

VI. Game Objects
The game should support an initialization function that sets up all
game parameters, such as speed, scores, bitmap names, and such. This
will make the game parameters easy to tweak and adjust.
All ship objects (the player ship and the four enemy types) are based
off of a 64x64-base bitmap. Each ship has eight rotation variations.
Player ship: (light blue) Responds to player control.
Enemy Alpha: (dark blue) Ignores player and tries for the crate. When
it moves over a box, it will grab it and tow it off screen or until the
enemy is destroyed (the box stays put). Same max-speed as player. 50
points.
Enemy Beta: (light green) Moves toward and shoots at player. Same
max-speed as player. 100 points.
Enemy Gamma: (red) Moves toward player and attempts to ram (does not
shoot). Max speed is greater than player. 200 points.
Enemy Delta: (yellow) Moves toward player or crate (whichever is
closer), can shoot at player, and can tow crate. Same max-speed as
player. 300 points.
Crate: 16x16 solid-color bitmap. Eight in the world to start. When a
towing enemy is killed, the crate stays where it was dropped.

Projectile: 16x16 solid-color bitmap. Projectiles fire at a constant
velocity along the heading of the shooter at the moment of shooting.
They are destroyed when they leave the game world.

In the Game objects section of the design document, we outline every unique
object in the game and describe the object's behavior. This vital section of the document can often exceed 100 pages for a large role-playing game or simulation. The
goal in this section is to describe in enough detail every object so that there is no
ambiguity when it's time to code that object into existence.

VII. Interfaces
Loading: Game logo displays for a set time; progress bar indicates
loading; launches Main interface.
Main: Shows top-ten scores, exits to Windows, sets up key mapping
(KeySelect), plays game (InGame), or loads the save game. The Load
button appears only when there is a save-game file (it shows the date
of the last save of the file). Only one saved game exists at a time.
KeySelect: Allows the player to map the four function keys to any
keyboard keys he wants; the functions keys can also be reset to the
default keys; when done, the player can return to the Main screen.
InGame: This is the actual game; the player can view his score at all
times; pressing Esc calls up the Escape interface; losing game calls
EndGame interface.
Escape: This interface pauses the game and allows the player to save
a game in progress, resume the game, or exit to Main screen.

```
EndGame: This interface reports the player score and lets him know if
it is a top-ten-qualifying score. Takes the player back to Main screen.
```

The Interfaces section is where we cover the functionality of each screen, interface, and subinterface the player may see. Sometimes this section is broken out into a separate document called a "functional specification." Here, we want to provide enough detail to allow the script programmer to accurately create each screen for the game.

Think of the design document for your game as the blueprint for your own construction crew, whether it's just you or a whole team of developers. This document may change during the course of development, but you'll want to create one that covers all aspects of your game before you start making your game in earnest—this is your foundation.

It's important to remember that this is a "working document"—it should contain only what is vital and no extraneous verbiage. This is not a "pitch document" to show a publisher—this is a tool to allow a development team to collaborate effectively to create a single compelling game experience.

A LUA STYLE GUIDE

Because Lua is such a flexible language, it's very easy to just dive in and start scripting. That's great for getting your feet wet, but as your scripts grow in complexity, you need to maintain a sense of order to your scripts.

ON THE CD
Lua can be edited with any simple text editor, or you can use a programmer's editor, such as Zeus, shown in Figure 9.3 (a version of Zeus is found on the CD ROM). Using a programmer's editor will give you more control over the formatting and structure of your Lua files, but it's still up to you to make sure the scripts are easy to read and understand. This is especially true when you must revisit a script after several weeks or months—if your initial scripting was sloppy and careless and you didn't include many comments, it'll be wasted time as you try to figure out just what is going on in a particular function.

The first remedy to this situation is to get yourself in the habit of commenting your scripts liberally. Add a header to each function that explains what's going on, and use comments whenever you are creating a new variable, returning a result, or performing a somewhat cryptic process. Commenting your scripts now can save you hours of time later when you are tracking down a bug.

The best plan of attack is to author your scripts with a consistent style. If you are consistent from script to script, function to function, and project to project, you'll be able to read and review past scripts quickly and with confidence. Working from some sort of standardized style template is also essential if you are scripting in a team environment, because it will force Lua scripters with different approaches to at least adhere to the same sort of naming and structure conventions.

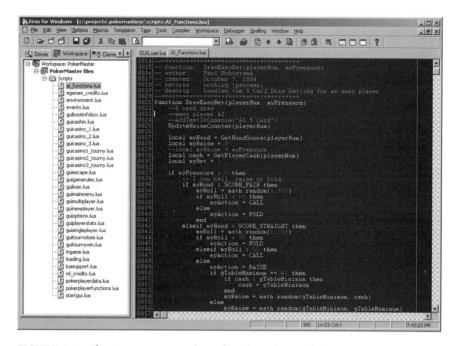

FIGURE 9.3 The Zeus programming editor in action with Lua.

ON THE CD

To get you started, we've included a Lua style guide document (in HTML) on the CD-ROM in Chapters/Chapter9/Lua_style.htm. You can use this document as is for your own Lua coding or as a starting point to modify and create your own in-house style guide. We'll now spend some time exploring some of the main concepts in the style guide.

In our earlier chapters, we spent some time talking about naming conventions with variables. Now we'll look at some other handy conventions. First, you'll want to include a header comment at the top of each script file, providing some information about the file, such as the following:

```
--=======================================
-- (c) copyright 2005, Lantern Learning, LLC
-- All Rights Reserved.  U.S.A.
--=======================================
-- filename:  GUI_Esape.lua
-- author:    Chris Listello
-- created:   April 4, 2004
```

```
-- descrip:   Escape key InGame menu
--=========================================
```

This information will serve as an introduction to the file should you wonder what it's for at a later date or if you have to turn the file over to another developer for more script coding. Following in the same vein, it's a great idea to create a similar standardized comment for the beginning of each function you create, like the following example:

```
--=========================================
-- function:  CreateMultText
-- author:    Paul Schuytema
-- created:   April 1, 2004
-- descrip:   Creates a multiline text object
-- returns:   nothing (process)
--=========================================
function CreateMultiText(localID, x, y, lines, charWIDTH)
```

You'll be surprised at how quickly you can forget what a function does, no matter how cleverly you think you named it. This formalized piece of information will often spark your memory. It's also a great tool for breaking up the visual flow of a large script file—your eye will naturally travel from comment block to comment block as you scan the file quickly.

In Chapter 10, we'll look more closely at the style guide as it applies to the interfaces in our game project. For now, just take a quick read through the style guide on the CD-ROM to familiarize yourself with the various standards we'll work to adhere to in our scripts, and give some thinking as to how you might customize the guide to take into account your own preferences or scripting style.

ON THE CD

The CD-ROM contains a folder for this chapter, and in it, we've put placeholder Lua scripts for all of the scripts we've identified for the design process. Along the way, we've laid a great foundation for a solid Lua implementation in our *Take Away* game.

SUMMARY

In this chapter, we reviewed some core design assumptions before we began thinking about our game project. From there, we laid out just what Lua files we'd need to create to implement our *Take Away* game project. This process allowed us to flesh out and finish our game design document, which will serve as our blueprint for our scripting work.

In the next chapter, we'll look at using Lua to manage and save our runtime game data.

10 Using Lua for Game Data

In This Chapter

■ Simple Game Data
■ Large Data Sets
■ Using Lua to Save Game Data

One of the great strengths of Lua in a game-development environment is its ability to be utilized as the primary tool and approach to store, save, and load vital game data. All games are reliant on their game data, and moving this data into the scripting level means that designers and script coders have immediate access to all game data and can design data storage that fits the needs of the game project, independent of the game's core low-level code. Lua can also be used as the mechanism to save the game data as well as load it into the game at the start of runtime or when a player loads a saved game.

In this chapter, we'll explore using Lua variables and tables to hold our runtime data and how we can write this data to save a game's "world state."

SIMPLE GAME DATA

Nearly all games have a strong data component. Some simpler old-school games, like *Space Invaders*™ or *Asteroids*™, had very little data to keep track of at runtime, but the data was still essential. More modern games, such as *Doom 3*® or *Neverwinter Nights*®, track a huge amount of data during runtime.

Some data is clearly within the realm of the C++ world. Consider a 3D first-person shooter type of game. During every frame of drawing, calculations determine what part of the visual world are drawn to the screen as well as the data that represents the dynamic objects in the world, such as the monster you are fighting or your 3D avatar. These objects are made up of hundreds of vertices and triangles, and that's all data that your game will need to process, transform, and act on.

This type of data—the world, the 3D objects, the rendering of a bitmap onto a section of display memory—is all information that is best managed in your primary development language by your rendering code, which can be modified by the team's programmers. But if we think back to our first-person example of your avatar fighting a monster in a 3D world, some runtime data is ideally suited for the Lua environment. You avatar has certain parameters of performance, such as speed, the amount of ammo left in the gun, what gun is being used, and what armor is being worn. All of this data is just as vital for the game experience, but it's of a "higher level"–closer to the player's experience rather than the nuts and bolts of drawing the scene of the screen. This type of data is exactly what you want to move into your Lua Environment and manage via scripting.

Space Ship Example

Let's get back to our earlier examples for a while and consider the venerable *Asteroids* game. I hope you remember that classic. You controlled a small ship that you could fly around the screen. Your goal was to shoot projectiles to blow up and destroy asteroids that were floating past your part of the infinite void. See Figure 10.1.

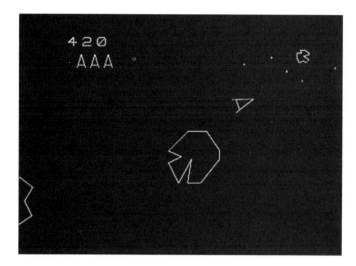

FIGURE 10.1 Screen shot from a game similar to the classic *Asteroids.*

We need to keep track of some essential runtime data regarding our ship: position, rotation, and movement. The position is fairly straightforward—in the game's 2D world, an xy-coordinate tells us where to draw the ship the next time we update the screen. The rotation can simply be a value that represents the facing of the ship (in degrees). If you think of the ship in our *Take Away* game, we limited its facing to simply eight positions, at 45-degree increments. So, for our own game, rotation can be a simple number from one to eight.

The movement data is a little trickier, and we'll need to think about it a bit (especially because our ship in *Take Away* will use a similar movement system to that in *Asteroids*). In *Asteroids*, you pressed a thrust button, which would apply a thrust from the rear of your ship. In the world of *Asteroids*, there is no gravity or friction, so if you applied a thrust in a direction, you'd simply move in that direction forever (or at least until you hit an asteroid). The game world would "wrap" so if you moved off the edge of the screen, you'd appear from the opposite side.

In *Asteroids*, each time your ship was updated on the screen, there was a chance you were moving in some direction, regardless if you were applying thrust or not, and regardless of your rotation. We can think of this movement as an xy-value, just like the position, except that it is the change applied to the positional xy each time the ship is drawn.

ON THE CD Also, thinking about drawing the ship, we've got one more piece of data to keep track of: drawing the little thrust flame off the back of the ship. So, with all of that in mind, if we were setting up the ship's data in Lua, it might look something like the following code (see file ch10_1.lua on the CD-ROM):

```
myShip = {}
myShip.Xposition = 100
myShip.Yposition = 100
myShip.Rotation = 0
myShip.Xthrust = 0
myShip.Ythrust = 0
myShip.ShowThrust = false
```

We begin by creating the myShip table, because we will be using it to store multiple values. We then set up and initialize the keys for that table and set them to initial values (for our example, let's assume a 200×200 world, and we're placing the ship in the middle of the world). We now have a simple yet powerful structure in our Lua Environment that will serve as the container for the ship's data. We could then have a function like that shown in the next example that would handle the movement data and drawing of the ship:

```
function: UpdateShip(theShip)
    theShip.Xposition = theShip.Xposition + myShip.Xthrust
    theShip.Yposition = theShip.Yposition + myShip.Ythrust
    DrawShip(theShip.Xposition, theShip.Yposition)
    if myShip.ShowThrust then
        DrawThurstImage()
    end
end
```

In this example, we use the thrust data to modify the position values, and then we draw the ship at its new location. We then check to see if the thrusters are currently on, and if so, we'll draw the thrust graphic (like a little flame out of the back of the ship).

In this very simple way, we've created a system to hold and manage the data associated with our ship. We'd probably also have events that would modify the Xthrust and Ythrust values, based on the rotation of the ship, whenever the thrust button was pressed.

Think through this example for a moment, and determine if you wanted to keep track of several ships—perhaps you have a fleet or perhaps some are enemies. How would you do that in Lua?

Look over the following script:

```
myShip = {}
yValue = 60
for index = 1,5 do
    myShip[index] = {}
    myShip[index].Xposition = 100
    myShip[index].Yposition = yValue
    yValue = yValue + 20
    myShip[index].Rotation = 0
    myShip[index].Xthrust = 0
    myShip[index].Ythrust = 0
    myShip[index].ShowThrust = false
end
```

In this example, we are initializing five ships by using Lua's ability to nest tables. In the for loop, we offset the starting position of each ship so we'll get a nice row (the yValue). We can then easily use the exact function we created before to update the drawing of the ship, but we just change how we pass in the table as follows:

```
UpdateShip(myShip[2])
```

With this call, we pass in the entire table of the second ship in our group of five, and the specific key references we laid out in our function still work the same way.

If we use a structure like this to hold the data of similar entities in the game, we can take advantage of Lua's standard table functions to manage our population of objects. Say that in our group of five ships (let's imagine they are enemy ships for now), the third ship is destroyed. We can then use the following standard call to remove it:

```
table.remove(myShip, 3)
```

This call will remove that entire subtable for the third ship and re-index the master myShip table accordingly.

If we want to add a ship to the table, we can use the table.insert() function, but we need to make sure we are inserting the right type of item, because each element of the myShip table is actually another table. To do this properly, we need to insert a table as the value field for this function, such as the following:

```
table.insert(myShip, {})
```

This call will insert an empty table into the end of the myShip table. We'd then have to initialize that table with the proper values, as follows:

```
lastEntry = table.getn(myShip)
myShip[lastEntry].Xposition = 100
myShip[lastEntry].Yposition = 100
myShip[lastEntry].Rotation = 0
myShip[lastEntry].Xthrust = 100
myShip[lastEntry].Ythrust = 0
myShip[lastEntry].ShowThrust = false
```

Alternately, you could do something like the following:

```
table.insert(myShip, {Xposition = 100, Yposition = 100})
```

Of course, you'd want to fill out the whole table, but this approach, although less readable, gets the task done in one function call.

TAKE AWAY PLAYER SHIP

Now that we've explored real-time game data with our *Asteroids* example, let's turn our attention to our own *Take Away* game. In this game, we control a single ship that we fly around in much the same way that the *Asteroids* ship moves. When the game begins, we need to initialize the core data for the player's ship, and we do this with the InitialSetUp() function within the game's LuaSupport.lua file. A partial listing of that function is shown in Listing 10.1.

LISTING 10.1 The InitialSetUp() function

```
function InitialSetUp()
    --Sets up key data for the game
    --Initial player values
    myRotation = 1 --Player's rotation (#)
    myX = 390       --Player's x coordinate (#)
    myY = 290       --Player's y coordinate (#)
    myXThrust = 0  --Player's thrust along the x-axis (#)
    myYThrust = 0  --Player's thrust along the y-axis (#)
    alive = "yes"  --Player's life status ("yes" or "no")
    --Initial limits
    respawnInterval = 20  --Number respawnCounter must reach to respawn
    player (#)
    --Initial setting of counters
    respawnCounter = 0    --Player's death period (#)
```

```
        score = 0                --Player's score (#)
        timeCounter = 0          --Passage of time (#)
        targetDoneCounter = 0 --Targets stolen by enemies (#)
        --Preferred game speed
        refreshRate = .1 --Seconds between timer expirations (#)
        --Initial GUI setup goes here
        --
        --
    end
```

In this function, we have decided to simply use regular variables to hold the player's ship data (as opposed to a table). We set up these variables with the default values at the start of this function. We also walk through and set up the other master data variables that are needed in the game.

In the world of Lua scripting, it's often a great idea to set up some sort of initialize function like this that you'll call at the start of a game session. Setting up all of your core data values in a single function enables you to simply call that function when you want to reset the game world to a starting state, and it also gives you "one-stop shopping" when you want to go in and adjust the values to test out different performance parameters.

The final section of this function isn't yet filled in—we'll do that in the next chapter, after we become familiar with the various GUI objects and can draw things to the screen.

Enemy Data

Now that we have the core data set up for our ship, we need to set up the data for the enemies that we'll be battling, as well as the storage crates that we'll be protecting. Because the enemies are all variations on a theme, it makes sense to pack their values into a table and use them like we did in the previous example of enemy ships.

We'll begin with an initialization function that sets up the basic framework for the enemies, shown in the next example:

```
function EnemyInit()

    enemyCount = 5 --Number of enemies in the game
    myEnemies = {} --Creates myEnemies table
    --Creates table, one entry per potential enemy
    for indx = 1,enemyCount do
        --creates a table to hold the data for each enemy
        myEnemies[indx] = {}
        --now initialize the enemy
        EnemyRespawn(indx)
```

```
        end
    end
```

This function sets up how many enemies you'll have active in the world and initializes a nested table to hold their data—it doesn't fill in the data at all but rather calls EnemyRespawn() to fill in the data.

The EnemyRespawn() function fills in the enemy data—we separate this out, because it allows us to call a respawn on the enemies (resetting them all) without reinitializing the tables. We can also simply reinitialize a single enemy at a time (to replace one that was destroyed, for example) by using this function-based approach. This function is shown in Listing 10.2.

LISTING 10.2   The EnemyRespawn() function

```lua
function EnemyRespawn(indx)
--Fills/refills myEnemies table according to indx
--indx is the myEnemies table index assigned to the enemy
    --Initial values
    myEnemies[indx].XTHRUST = 0
    myEnemies[indx].YTHRUST = 0
    myEnemies[indx].ROT = math.random(1,8)
    myEnemies[indx].ID = 14+indx --Starts IDs at 15
    myEnemies[indx].E_TOW = "no"
    myEnemies[indx].FIRE = 0
    --Randomly selects side of screen to enter from
    entrySide = math.random(1,4)
    if entrySide == 1 then        --Left
        myEnemies[indx].EX = math.random(-40,-20)
        myEnemies[indx].EY = math.random(-40,620)
    elseif entrySide == 2 then    --Right
        myEnemies[indx].EX = math.random(800,820)
        myEnemies[indx].EY = math.random(-40,620)
    elseif entrySide == 3 then    --Top
        myEnemies[indx].EX = math.random(-40,820)
        myEnemies[indx].EY = math.random(-40,-20)
    else                          --Bottom
        myEnemies[indx].EX = math.random(-40,820)
        myEnemies[indx].EY = math.random(600,620)
    end
    --Determines enemy's thrust, reaction, and firing abilities based on
    time
    --Reaction time decreases as REACT decreases (must be at least 1)
    --Maximum thrust increases as MAX increases
    --enemyFireInterval (#) compared to FIRE to determine enemy shooting
```

```
            (see EnemyFacing(indx) function)
            if (timeCounter >= 0) and (timeCounter < 100) then
                myEnemies[indx].REACT = 5
                myEnemies[indx].MAX = 5
                enemyFireInterval = 9
            elseif (timeCounter >= 100) and (timeCounter < 200) then
                myEnemies[indx].REACT = 4
                myEnemies[indx].MAX = 6
                enemyFireInterval = 8
            elseif (timeCounter >= 200) and (timeCounter < 300) then
                myEnemies[indx].REACT = 3
                myEnemies[indx].MAX = 7
                enemyFireInterval = 7
            elseif (timeCounter >= 300) and (timeCounter < 400) then
                myEnemies[indx].REACT = 2
                myEnemies[indx].MAX = 8
                enemyFireInterval = 6
            elseif (timeCounter >= 400) then
                myEnemies[indx].REACT = 1
                myEnemies[indx].MAX = 9
                enemyFireInterval = 5
            end
            --Randomly selects the AI type
            myEnemies[indx].TYPE = math.random(1,4)
            --create the sprite and place here
            --
            --
        end
```

We begin by setting up the basic values for the enemy and selecting a random rotation. The ID key is used by the game's GUI system (you'll learn more about this in the next chapter); it's the unique ID key that allows us to address and manipulate the sprite that will represent a particular enemy.

Our next step in initializing an enemy is to determine from which side of the game world it will appear. Our game world is a 600×800-pixel screen space; we simply spawn the enemies outside of this visible frame and allow them to enter the playing field based on their own behavior. We pick a side of the world randomly and then assign a random range of x- and y-coordinates to them so that they will appear (or not appear, if they are off screen) during the next drawing update.

We then set up some behavioral parameters, which we'll go into more deeply in Chapter 12. The short take is that as the time progresses in the game, the enemies increase in difficulty. This function sets up their basic performance parameters based on how deep into the game the player is.

Finally, as per the design document, our game contains four types of enemies. We randomly select which type of enemy we are creating. After this, we'll initialize the GUI sprite that will display the enemy, but we'll tackle that in Chapter 11.

Storage Crate Data

The last piece of data we need to set up is our selection of storage crates that we must protect. We'll want to create eight crates that begin in a ring at the center of the screen (the player will spawn in the center). We can fill in that data by using the function shown in Listing 10.3.

LISTING 10.3   Function for creating storage crates

```lua
function TargetInit()
--Creates and fills myTargets table
    myTargets = {}
    targetCount = 8 --Number of targets in the game
    startID = 2000
    startX = 360
    startY = 260
    --Creates/fills table with initial values
    for indx = 1, targetCount + 1 do
        myTargets[indx] = {}
        myTargets[indx].T_ID = startID
        startID = startID + 1
        myTargets[indx].T_TOW = "no"
        myTargets[indx].T_X = startX
        startX = startX + 30
        if startX > 430 then
            startX = 360
        end
        myTargets[indx].T_Y = startY
        if indx > 3 then
            if indx < 7 then
                startY = 290
            else
                startY = 320
            end
        end
    end

    --now delete the middle target, so the player can spawn in
    table.remove(myTargets, 5)
```

```
      --Creates targets (as sprites) and places them
      --
      --
   end
```

In this function, we begin by setting up the basic data for the crates. Then we use a pair of `if` conditional statements to set up the x- and y-coordinates so that we align the crates in a three-by-three pattern. You'll notice that we create the data for nine boxes, because this is the easiest way to step through the numbers in a neat way. When we're done, we simply delete table element five (the center box), so we've got a nice ring. We can spawn the player ship in the direct center of the screen. See Figure 10.2.

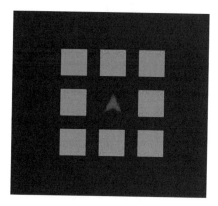

FIGURE 10.2   The storage crates at startup in *Take Away*.

LARGE DATA SETS

Now we see how we can use the simple data structures available in Lua to hold our runtime game data. The approach is quite basic for a simple game such as *Take Away*, but how does Lua work for holding larger amounts of game data? Often, full-featured games such as tycoon games or RPG games require large amounts of data to be loaded and available. In this case as well, Lua shines as a game-development tool.

Spreadsheet-based Data

Often, larger data sets require game developers to utilize some external tool, such as a Microsoft Excel spreadsheet, to hold the data. Imagine trying to track the name and characters stats for 1,000 NPC characters—in this case, it's easy to see how a spreadsheet is a powerful tool with which to hold and manage the data. With this approach, programmers will often create a tool to parse the Excel file in some way and load the data into the game.

We can take this same approach with Lua. If we save our spreadsheet as a CSV file (a file of comma-separated values), we can parse it into Lua and into tables that we can use easily. Consider the example spreadsheet shown in Figure 10.3.

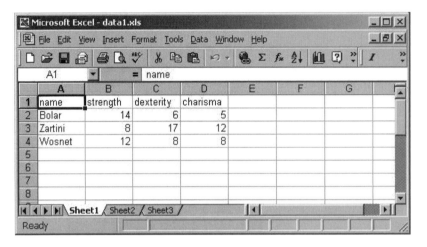

FIGURE 10.3   A simple character spreadsheet matrix in Excel.

ON THE CD

In this example, the first row contains the field names and the following rows contain the data. We can create the following simple function in Lua that will load in this CSV file into a table (see file ch10_2.lua):

```
function GetLines(fileName)
    indx = 0
    myLines = {}
    for line in io.lines(string.format("%s%s", "c:/lua_scripts/",
    fileName)) do
        indx = indx + 1
        myLines[indx] = line
    end
    return indx, myLines --returns number of lines and line table
end
```

We pass in the filename (you'll notice that I hard-coded the path as per our previous examples—you can handle this however you'd like). The function will return the number of lines in the file and a table in which each index is a string that has the entire line.

We can then create a function that will parse an individual line and build a table of the individual values found in that line, as shown in the next example:

```
function GetValues(myString)
    num = 0
    values = {}
    if myString ~= nil then
        while string.find(myString,",") ~= nil do
            i,j = string.find(myString,",")
            num = num + 1
            values[num] = string.sub(myString,1, j-1)
            myString = string.sub(myString, j+1, string.len(myString))
        end
        num = num + 1
        values[num] = myString
    end
    return num, values
end
```

In this function, we pass in a string (which can be one of the lines we just loaded). We use the `string.find()` function to locate the next comma in the line and then use the `string.sub()` function to grab the value before the comma. We then remove the value *and* the comma from the string and continue until there are no more values to parse. The function will then return the number of arguments it retrieved and a table that contains those arguments. This simple two-step process will allow you to parse nearly any CSV file, no matter how simple or complex, if it follows the standard rule of row one holding the value keys and the following rows holding the data.

To finish this example, the following function uses the tools we've just created to load the spreadsheet shown earlier to populate a two-dimensional table and print the results. You can try this right in the console—load the file (via `dofile()`) ch10_2.lua and run the function `LoadCharacters()`.

```
function LoadCharacters()
    myCharacters = {}
    numLines, allLines = GetLines("data1.csv")
    --load labels (the first line)
    count, myLabels = GetValues(allLines[1])
    --ignore line 1, it's got the labels
    for indx = 2, numLines do
        count, charHold = GetValues(allLines[indx])
        myCharacters[indx-1] = {}
        for indx2 = 1, count do
            myCharacters[indx-1][indx2] = charHold[indx2]
```

```
            end
        end
        --now print them
        for indx = 1, 3 do
            for indx2 = 1, table.getn(myLabels) do
                print(myLabels[indx2], myCharacters[indx][indx2])
            end
        end
    end
```

This function loads the labels into one table and the values into another two-dimensional table. Finally, it prints out each character and their corresponding stats. If you spend a little time thinking about this approach, you'll begin to see how easy it is to use Lua in conjunction with a spreadsheet program to save, load, and manage your data.

You can use this approach in two ways, depending on if you want more readable scripts or more flexible data. Method one is to pull the column headers off of the first row of the spreadsheet, as we did in the preceding example, and then create a numerically indexed table with the field key being the same for the label table and for the data table. This approach allows you to set up the breadth and scope of the data in the spreadsheet; Lua simply builds the tables according to the data you have. You'll then have to reference certain values in the code numerically (such as a character's strength by something like `myCharacters[charNum][fieldNum]`, where you know that a `fieldNum` of 4 refers to strength). This method gives you the most flexibility but makes the code harder to read.

The other approach is to hard-code the keys in Lua. This method will limit how easily you can change the structure of the data, but it will make your scripts much easier to read and debug. In this case, we'd address a character's strength by using something like `myCharacters[charNum].strength`.

We've seen how we can use an external tool, such as a spreadsheet, as a place to hold large quantities of data. We can then load that data into Lua tables within our game and use it at runtime. This approach is good when you've got a lot of data to manage and the data is relative—that is, when we want to see all of the data together so that we can work on it en masse. We can use the spreadsheet's ability to sort and to perform bulk operations and formulas on the data. If we're dealing with 800-plus NPCs, this approach might be the one we want to take, because we can easily sort and adjust the values.

Lua-based Data Files

Sometimes, data doesn't really need to be relative to other data elements; it is better viewed by itself (for example, if you are setting up the parameters of objects to purchase in a tycoon game). In this case, entering the data directly into a Lua file, rather than using an intermediary tool, is the way to go. By using Lua as the format for initial data storage, it's easy to see what you have right away, and you don't have to manage any kind of parsing or subsidiary file manipulation. Consider the next example:

```
pokerPlayers = {}
index = 1
pokerPlayers[index] = {}
pokerPlayers[index].Name =          "Ralph Hollywood"
pokerPlayers[index].Gender =        "Male"
pokerPlayers[index].Model =         "poker_player_02.mlm"
pokerPlayers[index].Skin =          "poker_player_02_blue.bmp"
pokerPlayers[index].Anim =          "sit_idle_male"
pokerPlayers[index].CurCash =       550
pokerPlayers[index].Aggressive =    1
```

In this example, we've created a table called `pokerPlayers`, which will hold the data associated with poker players in a Texas Hold 'Em tournament game. We then set an index value to 1, and begin by creating a table with the statement `pokerPlayers[index] = {}`.

This statement creates a subtable for an individual entry. We can then use easy-to-read text keys to fill out the values in the table for this particular player. As you can see from the data, we really don't gain anything if this type of data was first in a spreadsheet, because the values really aren't relative to each other—they are more text based and indicate the character name, the model, the idle animation, and such. Creating and working with this data right in a Lua file is the easiest way to go—we can simply run the file when we need to load the data.

By loading the data in this way, we can simply edit the values directly at runtime, as shown in the following statement that removes the current bet from their cash:

```
pokerPlayers[curPlayer].CurCash = pokerPlayers[curPlayer].CurCash —
curBet
```

If we want to reset the data (such as at the start of a new game session), all we have to do is simply reload the Lua script. If you create a large set of data using this approach, you can use the `ipairs` iterator function to walk through the data set, as shown in the following example:

```
function PrintAll(t)
    for i,v in ipairs(t) do
        print("Player #:", i)
        print(v.Name)
```

```
            print(v.Gender)
            print(v.Model)
            print(v.Skin)
            print(v.Anim)
        end
    end
```

If you pass the two-dimensional pokerPlayers table into this function, it will walk through all of the elements of the primary table and will return an index (i) and the value (v) at that index. In this case, the value is itself another table that we can refer to using our text keys.

USING LUA TO SAVE GAME DATA

The next logical step beyond using Lua to store and modify your game data is to use Lua as a tool to manage the saving and loading of your game. Actually, with Lua, you get the loading for free if you follow this simple rule: save the data as a valid Lua file.

Often, game developers will save data in an internal data format and then load that data back in directly. If we use this approach with the low-level data access we have in C++, this can work quite well, but often, we want the save data that is somewhat readable by human eyes (at least during the development process). In this case, programmers will often write a parser that will handle the loading of the files, but this, once again, ties a process to programmer time. If we change the game data, we need to pull a programmer off of another task to modify the save and load functionality.

Because we are Lua scripters, we can use Lua's built-in I/O functions to handle writing the data. We just need to ensure the data is exported in proper Lua syntax, so that we can use Lua itself to load it by calling dofile().

The following example is a simple modification of the I/O example you saw in Chapter 5.

```
myFile = io.open("c:\\lua_scripts\\test_savegame.lua", "w")
if myFile ~= nil then
    myFile:write("-- Test Lua SaveGame file")
    myFile:write(string.char (10))
    myFile:write(string.char (10))
    myFile:write(string.format("%s%s", "-- File created on: ",
    os.date()))
    myFile:write(string.char (10))
    myFile:write(string.char (10))
    myFile:write("myValue = 10")
    io.close(myFile)
```

```
end
```

If we run this script, we'll create a Lua file that will look like the next example:

```
-- Test Lua SaveGame file

-- File created on: 02/23/05 15:06:27

myValue = 10
```

While the file is simple, it is, in fact, a valid Lua file that we can load via the `dofile()` function. What we need to do to make this file useful, however, is to capture the values of our game variables at runtime. Let's turn our attention back to the variables we used to define our ship on our *Take Away* game. The initialization of these variables looked like the following lines:

```
--Initial player values
myRotation = 1
myX = 390        --Player's x-coordinate (#)
myY = 290        --Player's y-coordinate (#)
myXThrust = 0   --Player's thrust along the x-axis (#)
myYThrust = 0   --Player's thrust along the y-axis (#)
alive = "yes"   --Player's life status ("yes" or "no")
```

If we, for the moment, consider these variables as representing our game universe, then we can write a fairly simple function that will save these values at any given time to a valid Lua file. That function would look like example shown in Listing 10.4.

LISTING 10.4 Function to save values to a valid Lua file

```
function WorldSave()
    myFile = io.open("c:\\lua_scripts\\sample_savegame.lua", "w")
    if myFile ~= nil then
        myFile:write("-- Lua SaveGame file for limited Take Away data")
        myFile:write(string.char (10))
        myFile:write(string.char (10))
        myFile:write(string.format("%s%s", "-- File created on: ",
        os.date()))
        myFile:write(string.char (10))
        myFile:write(string.char (10))
        myFile:write("-- ship data values")
        myFile:write(string.char (10))
        myString = string.format("%s%d", "myRotation = ", myRotation)
```

```
            myFile:write(myString)
            myFile:write(string.char (10))
            myString = string.format("%s%d", "myX = ", myX)
            myFile:write(myString)
            myFile:write(string.char (10))
            myString = string.format("%s%d", "myY = ", myY)
            myFile:write(myString)
            myFile:write(string.char (10))
            myString = string.format("%s%d", "myXThrust = ", myXThrust)
            myFile:write(myString)
            myFile:write(string.char (10))
            myString = string.format("%s%d", "myYThrust = ", myYThrust)
            myFile:write(myString)
            myFile:write(string.char (10))
            myString = string.format("%s%s%s", "alive = \"", alive, "\"")
            myFile:write(myString)
            myFile:write(string.char (10))
            io.close(myFile)
        end
    end
```

The function is quite straightforward—it simply walks through the values you want to capture and writes them to a file. The keystone of this approach is building a string that is a valid Lua statement that captures the value of your variables at the moment of execution. We use the `string.format()` function for this. If you look near the end of the function, you can see where we are capturing a string value. Because we want the output to be valid Lua, we need to surround the string by quotation marks, and we use the escape character (\) to allow us to place quotation marks in the string.

The output of this function looks like the next example:

```
-- Lua SaveGame file for limited Take Away data

-- File created on: 02/24/05 16:30:58

-- ship data values
myRotation = 1
myX = 390
myY = 290
myXThrust = 0
myYThrust = 0
alive = "yes"
```

When you run this file with the `dofile()` function, it sets the variables to the values specified in the file, just as if you were running an initialization function. With this approach, you can see how easy it is to read as well as to edit your save-game file to test any specific game situations you want to explore.

Now let's take this knowledge and use it to create a save-game function that saves all of our data in *Take Away*. The function (see Listing 10.5 through List 10.9) is rather long, so we'll look at it in smaller sections.

In the first section of this function, we initialize the file and write some session information (so it's readable to a human user and has a data stamp). After that, we walk through the non-table data that defines the current state of the game world and simply write these variables. We do this by first assigning the value we want to write to a reusable `myValue` variable and then use that variable in a `string.format()` operation as part of a `write` command.

LISTING 10.5 Save-game function, part one

```
function SaveGame()
--Saves the current game
    gSavedGameDate = os.date("%m/%d/%Y %I:%M%p")
    --Creates the pathway for the file
    local fileName = "Take_Away_Saved_Game"
    --Writes the current game to the specified location
    myFile = io.open(string.format("%s%s%s", "SaveGames\\", fileName,
    ".lua"), "w")
    if myFile ~= nil then --File exists
        myFile:write("-- Take Away save game file");
        myFile:write(string.char (10))
        myFile:write(string.char (10))
        myFile:write(string.format("%s%s", "-- File created on: ",
        os.date()));
        myFile:write(string.char (10))
        myFile:write(string.char (10))
        myFile:write("--Initial player constants")
        myFile:write(string.char (10))
        myValue = myRotation
        myFile:write(string.format("%s%d", "myRotation = ",myValue))
        myFile:write(string.char (10))
        myValue = myX
        myFile:write(string.format("%s%d", "myX = ",myValue))
        myFile:write(string.char (10))
        myValue = myY
        myFile:write(string.format("%s%d", "myY = ",myValue))
        myFile:write(string.char (10))
```

```
myValue = myXThrust
myFile:write(string.format("%s%d", "myXThrust = ",myValue))
myFile:write(string.char (10))
myValue = myYThrust
myFile:write(string.format("%s%d", "myYThrust = ",myValue))
myFile:write(string.char (10))
myValue = alive
myFile:write(string.format("%s%s%s%s", "alive = ", string.char
(34), myValue, string.char (34)))
myFile:write(string.char (10))
myFile:write(string.char (10))
myFile:write("--Initial limits")
myFile:write(string.char (10))
myValue = respawnInterval
myFile:write(string.format("%s%d", "respawnInterval = ",myValue))
myFile:write(string.char (10))
myFile:write(string.char (10))
myFile:write("--Initial setting of counters")
myFile:write(string.char (10))
myValue = respawnCounter
myFile:write(string.format("%s%d", "respawnCounter = ",myValue))
myFile:write(string.char (10))
myValue = score
myFile:write(string.format("%s%d", "score = ",myValue))
myFile:write(string.char (10))
myValue = timeCounter
myFile:write(string.format("%s%d", "timeCounter = ",myValue))
myFile:write(string.char (10))
myValue = targetDoneCounter
myFile:write(string.format("%s%d", "targetDoneCounter =
",myValue))
myFile:write(string.char (10))
myFile:write(string.char (10))
myFile:write("--Preferred game speed")
myFile:write(string.char (10))
myValue = refreshRate
myFile:write(string.format("%s%.2f", "refreshRate = ",myValue))
myFile:write(string.char (10))
myFile:write(string.char (10))
```

This next section of the function walks the myEnemies table and builds a Lua script to call out each key and each value for the entire table. This section of the output file will become rather large because we are writing values explicitly, but the file is easily readable.

LISTING 10.6   Save-game function, part two

```lua
myFile:write("--Enemy information")
myFile:write(string.char (10))
myValue = enemyCount
myFile:write(string.format("%s%d", "enemyCount = ",myValue))
myFile:write(string.char (10))
myValue = enemyFireInterval
myFile:write(string.format("%s%d", "enemyFireInterval =
",myValue))
myFile:write(string.char (10))
for indx = 1,enemyCount do
    myValue = myEnemies[indx].ID
    if type(myValue) == "number" then
        myFile:write(string.format("%s%d%s%d", "myEnemies[",
        indx, "].ID = ", myValue))
    elseif type(myValue) == "nil" then
        myFile:write(string.format("%s%d%s", "myEnemies[", indx,
        "].ID = nil"))
    end
    myFile:write(string.char (10))
    myValue = myEnemies[indx].XTHRUST
    if type(myValue) == "number" then
        myFile:write(string.format("%s%d%s%d", "myEnemies[",
        indx, "].XTHRUST = ", myValue))
    elseif type(myValue) == "nil" then
        myFile:write(string.format("%s%d%s", "myEnemies[", indx,
        "].XTHRUST = nil"))
    end
    myFile:write(string.char (10))
    myValue = myEnemies[indx].YTHRUST
    if type(myValue) == "number" then
        myFile:write(string.format("%s%d%s%d", "myEnemies[",
        indx, "].YTHRUST = ", myValue))
    elseif type(myValue) == "nil" then
        myFile:write(string.format("%s%d%s", "myEnemies[", indx,
        "].YTHRUST = nil"))
    end
    myFile:write(string.char (10))
    myValue = myEnemies[indx].EX
    if type(myValue) == "number" then
        myFile:write(string.format("%s%d%s%d", "myEnemies[",
        indx, "].EX = ", myValue))
    elseif type(myValue) == "nil" then
```

```
        myFile:write(string.format("%s%d%s", "myEnemies[", indx,
        "].EX = nil"))
    end
    myFile:write(string.char (10))
    myValue = myEnemies[indx].EY
    if type(myValue) == "number" then
        myFile:write(string.format("%s%d%s%d", "myEnemies[",
        indx, "].EY = ", myValue))
    elseif type(myValue) == "nil" then
        myFile:write(string.format("%s%d%s", "myEnemies[", indx,
        "].EY = nil"))
    end
    myFile:write(string.char (10))
    myValue = myEnemies[indx].ROT
    if type(myValue) == "number" then
        myFile:write(string.format("%s%d%s%d", "myEnemies[",
        indx, "].ROT = ", myValue))
    elseif type(myValue) == "nil" then
        myFile:write(string.format("%s%d%s", "myEnemies[", indx,
        "].ROT = nil"))
    end
    myFile:write(string.char (10))
    myValue = myEnemies[indx].FIRE
    if type(myValue) == "number" then
        myFile:write(string.format("%s%d%s%d", "myEnemies[",
        indx, "].FIRE = ", myValue))
    elseif type(myValue) == "nil" then
        myFile:write(string.format("%s%d%s", "myEnemies[", indx,
        "].FIRE = nil"))
    end
    myFile:write(string.char (10))
    myValue = myEnemies[indx].E_TOW
    if type(myValue) == "number" then
        myFile:write(string.format("%s%d%s%d", "myEnemies[",
        indx, "].E_TOW = ", myValue))
    elseif type(myValue) == "string" then
        myFile:write(string.format("%s%d%s%s%s%s",
        "myEnemies[",
        indx, "].E_TOW = ", string.char (34), myValue,
        string.char (34)))
    end
    myFile:write(string.char (10))
    myValue = myEnemies[indx].MAX
    myFile:write(string.format("%s%d%s%d", "myEnemies[", indx,
```

```
                "].MAX = ", myValue))
        myFile:write(string.char (10))
        myValue = myEnemies[indx].REACT
        myFile:write(string.format("%s%d%s%d", "myEnemies[", indx,
                "].REACT = ", myValue))
        myFile:write(string.char (10))
        myValue = myEnemies[indx].TYPE
        myFile:write(string.format("%s%d%s%d", "myEnemies[", indx,
                "].TYPE = ", myValue))
        myFile:write(string.char (10))
    end
    myFile:write(string.char (10))
    myFile:write(string.char (10))
```

This next section of the file uses the same methodology as the enemies section, but here we are writing out all of the relevant data contained in the myTargets table.

LISTING 10.7 Save-game function, part three

```
    myFile:write("--Target information")
    myFile:write(string.char (10))
    myValue = targetCount
    myFile:write(string.format("%s%d", "targetCount = ",myValue))
    myFile:write(string.char (10))
    for indx = 1,targetCount do
        myValue = myTargets[indx].T_ID
        if type(myValue) == "number" then
            myFile:write(string.format("%s%d%s%d", "myTargets[",
                indx, "].T_ID = ", myValue))
        elseif type(myValue) == "nil" then
            myFile:write(string.format("%s%d%s", "myTargets[", indx,
                "].T_ID = nil"))
        end
        myFile:write(string.char (10))
        myValue = myTargets[indx].T_X
        if type(myValue) == "number" then
            myFile:write(string.format("%s%d%s%d", "myTargets[",
                indx, "].T_X = ", myValue))
        elseif type(myValue) == "nil" then
            myFile:write(string.format("%s%d%s", "myTargets[", indx,
                "].T_X = nil"))
        end
        myFile:write(string.char (10))
        myValue = myTargets[indx].T_Y
        if type(myValue) == "number" then
```

```
        myFile:write(string.format("%s%d%s%d", "myTargets[",
            indx, "].T_Y = ", myValue))
    elseif type(myValue) == "nil" then
        myFile:write(string.format("%s%d%s", "myTargets[", indx,
            "].T_Y = nil"))
    end
    myFile:write(string.char (10))
    myValue = myTargets[indx].T_TOW
    if type(myValue) == "number" then
        myFile:write(string.format("%s%d%s%d", "myTargets[",
            indx, "].T_TOW = ", myValue))
    elseif type(myValue) == "string" then
        myFile:write(string.format("%s%d%s%s%s%s",
            "myTargets[",
            indx, "].T_TOW = ", string.char (34), myValue,
            string.char (34)))
    end
    myFile:write(string.char (10))
end
myFile:write(string.char (10))
myFile:write(string.char (10))
```

We now walk through yet another table, this time myProjectiles, to write out all of the keys and values contained in that table at the moment of the save. When you are creating a function like this to handle your own saved data, you can create a master loop for table key/value writing, and copy and paste that loop before filling in the specifics. You could also take it one step further than we have here by creating a generic function to write table values and keys. You would first have to create a mechanism to save the strings that relate to table names and their child keys, much in the same way as we did for the generic function to read in CSV files mentioned earlier.

LISTING 10.8   Save-game function, part four

```
myFile:write("--Projectile information")
myFile:write(string.char (10))
myValue = pCount
myFile:write(string.format("%s%d", "pCount = ",myValue))
myFile:write(string.char (10))
myValue = pIndx
myFile:write(string.format("%s%d", "pIndx = ",myValue))
myFile:write(string.char (10))
myValue = playerProjectiles
```

```
myFile:write(string.format("%s%d", "playerProjectiles =
",myValue))
myFile:write(string.char (10))
for indx = 1,pCount do
    myValue = myProjectiles[indx].PROJ_ID
    if type(myValue) == "number" then
        myFile:write(string.format("%s%d%s%d", "myProjectiles[",
        indx, "].PROJ_ID = ", myValue))
    elseif type(myValue) == "nil" then
        myFile:write(string.format("%s%d%s", "myProjectiles[",
        indx, "].PROJ_ID = nil"))
    end
    myFile:write(string.char (10))
    myValue = myProjectiles[indx].PROJ_XTH
    if type(myValue) == "number" then
        myFile:write(string.format("%s%d%s%d", "myProjectiles[",
        indx, "].PROJ_XTH = ", myValue))
    elseif type(myValue) == "nil" then
        myFile:write(string.format("%s%d%s", "myProjectiles[",
        indx, "].PROJ_XTH = nil"))
    end
    myFile:write(string.char (10))
    myValue = myProjectiles[indx].PROJ_YTH
    if type(myValue) == "number" then
        myFile:write(string.format("%s%d%s%d", "myProjectiles[",
        indx, "].PROJ_YTH = ", myValue))
    elseif type(myValue) == "nil" then
        myFile:write(string.format("%s%d%s", "myProjectiles[",
        indx, "].PROJ_YTH = nil"))
    end
    myFile:write(string.char (10))
    myValue = myProjectiles[indx].PROJ_X
    if type(myValue) == "number" then
        myFile:write(string.format("%s%d%s%d", "myProjectiles[",
        indx, "].PROJ_X = ", myValue))
    elseif type(myValue) == "nil" then
        myFile:write(string.format("%s%d%s", "myProjectiles[",
        indx, "].PROJ_X = nil"))
    end
    myFile:write(string.char (10))
    myValue = myProjectiles[indx].PROJ_Y
    if type(myValue) == "number" then
        myFile:write(string.format("%s%d%s%d", "myProjectiles[",
        indx, "].PROJ_Y = ", myValue))
```

```
        elseif type(myValue) == "nil" then
            myFile:write(string.format("%s%d%s", "myProjectiles[",
            indx, "].PROJ_Y = nil"))
        end
        myFile:write(string.char (10))
        myValue = myProjectiles[indx].PROJ_SHIP
        if type(myValue) == "number" then
            myFile:write(string.format("%s%d%s%d", "myProjectiles[",
            indx, "].PROJ_SHIP = ", myValue))
        elseif type(myValue) == "string" then
            myFile:write(string.format("%s%d%s%s%s%s",
            "myProjectiles[", indx, "].PROJ_SHIP = ", string.char
            (34), myValue, string.char (34)))
        end
        myFile:write(string.char (10))
    end
    myFile:write(string.char (10))
    myFile:write(string.char (10))
```

This last section manages the GUI elements that make up the score and such, so that the display will be proper calibrated to the ongoing game, once it is loaded.

LISTING 10.9 Save-game function, part five

```
    myFile:write("--Initial GUI setup")
    myFile:write(string.char (10))
    myFile:write(string.format("%s%s%s%s%s%s%s%s%s%s%s",
    "ItemCommand(GUI_INGAME + 201, ", string.char (34), "SetString",
    string.char (34), ",", string.char (34), "Projectiles Fired: ",
    CommaFormatBigInteger(playerProjectiles), string.char (34), ")"))
    myFile:write(string.char (10))
    myFile:write(string.format("%s%s%s%s%s%s%s%s%s%s%s",
    "ItemCommand(GUI_INGAME + 202, ", string.char (34),
    "SetString",
    string.char (34), ",", string.char (34), "Targets Lost: ",
    CommaFormatBigInteger(targetDoneCounter), string.char (34), ")"))
    myFile:write(string.char (10))
    myFile:write(string.format("%s%s%s%s%s%s%s%s%s%s%s",
    "ItemCommand(GUI_INGAME + 203, ", string.char (34), "SetString",
    string.char (34), ",", string.char (34), "Score: ",
    CommaFormatBigInteger(score), string.char (34), ")"))
    myFile:write(string.char (10))
    if targetDoneCounter == targetCount then
        myFile:write(string.format("%s%s%s%s%s%s%s%s%s%s%s",
        "ItemCommand(GUI_INGAME + 204, ", string.char (34),
```

```
            "SetString", string.char (34), ",", string.char (34), "Your
            Final Score Is ", CommaFormatBigInteger(score), string.char
            (34), ")"))
    else
        myFile:write(string.format("%s%s%s%s%s%s%s%s%s",
            "ItemCommand(GUI_INGAME + 204, ", string.char (34),
            "SetString", string.char (34), ",", string.char (34),
            string.char (34), ")"))
    end
    myFile:write(string.char (10))
    myFile:write(string.char (10))
    io.close(myFile)
    end
end
```

Although this function is rather large, it's quite simple in its approach and very easy to maintain (if you changed your game data, for example). The file begins much like our simpler functions: by writing out the basic player game data (we also save the current date into a global variable that we'll later use to label the file in the user interface). After we write the player's ship data, we set up a for loop to loop through each enemy in the game and write their values. This process gives us a rather long save-game file, but it is one that is very easy to read. We then walk through all of the game targets and finally through the projectiles in the game (which fills up most of our save-game file).

When this file is loaded with a dofile() call, it will recreate the game world precisely at the moment of the save, down to the position and thrust of each and every projectile.

An added advantage to using this method of saving game data is that you can review your data quickly, and easily see if any values are out of whack with your game world—this can be a great help in the development process.

You can also create specific save-game files (by editing the output Lua of your save-game function) to create game situations that you can load in for testing, thereby assuring that all testers are working with the same game data when they are putting your game through its paces.

You can also use this approach to create starting templates for a scenario within your game—which is then nothing more than a save-game file with a specific set of values that represents the world state at the start of a scenario. When the player chooses to play a particular scenario, you simply load the corresponding templated save-game file.

Case Study 1—*Frontrunner*

When we were working on our *Frontrunner* election simulation game (Figure 10.4), we needed the ability to save a game in progress. All of the primary data in the game was stored in data structures created in C by the programmers. We accessed the data through a series of LuaGlue functions, and it seemed to be working just fine until we were faced with saving the game.

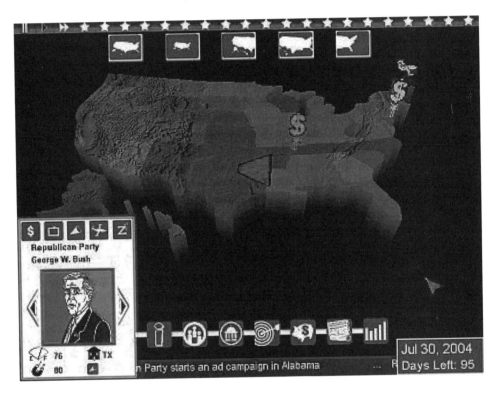

FIGURE 10.4   The *Frontrunner* game in action.

Saving and loading the game was a task for the programmers, because our data was stored in their game-state structures. At first, this system seemed to work fairly well, but we started running into problems as our project grew in complexity. As time went on, we found ourselves with more and more Lua variables that helped to store the state of the game as we went on (such as which campaign was controlled by the human player, how many debates had been run, and so on).

The programming team then had to create a special data type (plus the LuaGlue functions) that allowed us to assign and retrieve values to the Lua variables just before saving and just after loading. What we ended up doing was creating a rather redundant system, and we ended up with a binary save-game file that was impossible for the scripters to debug. When there was an error in saving or loading the game, we'd have to pull the programmers off of their current tasks so they could examine the binary file and help us find the errors.

This very time-consuming approach to debugging an essential game feature caused us to rethink how we saved our game data. We began to look into using Lua itself as our primary save and load mechanism.

Case Study 2–Fitness Tycoon

In our *Health & Fitness Tycoon* game (Figure 10.5), we needed a solid save-game system that would be up and running in the early stages of prototyping the game and could grow as the game grew. We also needed some form of save-game data that made sense to the scripters, so they could examine the data and be able to quickly determine any problems in the system. Early on (and based on our *Frontrunner* experience), we decided to make the save-game system Lua based.

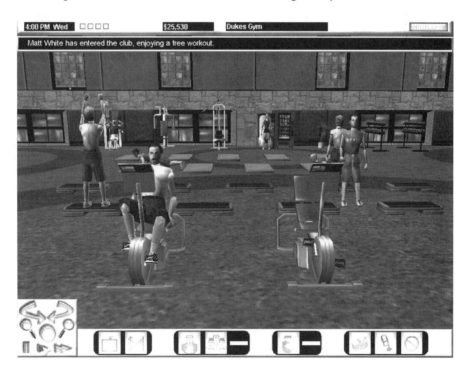

FIGURE 10.5 *Health & Fitness Tycoon* in action.

The output of the game's save function was a legal Lua script file that could be opened and examined in any editor. We even put in vital comments to assist in reviewing and debugging the file. Modifying the save/load functionality, as we added more complexity to the game, was simply a matter of editing one Lua function, because game-data loading was taken care of by Lua itself.

Probably the best benefit of this system was something we didn't anticipate at the outset. With the save-game data file being easy to understand Lua, we could edit the file to create specific game situations that allowed us to test the game more effectively. If we needed to see how the payday functions were handled, we could edit an existing save-game file so that it was the day before payday and then load in the data.

SUMMARY

In this chapter, we took a detailed look at using Lua as our primary data storage and retrieval tool for all of our runtime game data. Saving and loading of game data can be one of the most frustrating and time-consuming aspects of game development. Often, game data requires change during development, and frequently a development team has simply ignored updating their save and load code until they were forced to update it, because it pulled programmer resources away from more important tasks. By pulling the system into Lua, the script programmers and designers can manage the saving and loading and can easily modify the scripts to keep them current. Designers don't have to worry about input-parsing save-game data because Lua handles it already—and editing save-game files allows designers to create game situations to test easily.

Lua can be used to hold very simple game data, or we can expand the implementation to enable us to handle massive amounts of data, from either an external spreadsheet file or by creating the data in Lua itself.

We then explored how we can use Lua to write Lua files that capture the state of the game data at any given moment—and then, using Lua's own built-in functions, we can load that data and let Lua parse it for us.

With this information in hand, we've got the data structures handled for our *Take Away* game. In the next chapter, we'll turn our attention to the GUI system and learn how to implement a user interface from both the code side and the Lua side of the coin.

11 Lua-powered GUI

In This Chapter

■ Overview of the GUI System
■ C++ Classes for GUI
■ GUI LuaGlue
■ Next Steps
■ Lua Game Interfaces

One of the most natural uses of Lua in games is to create and control GUIs. This chapter will detail a full-featured environment in which to create and control a variety of GUI items, giving us the building blocks to make simple and complex interfaces. Beyond this, we'll look at our *Take Away* example game and explore the interfaces that make up the game and how they function and interact.

OVERVIEW OF THE GUI SYSTEM

As touched on in Chapter 8, the GUI system is built on the idea of an interface. An interface is defined as a collection of graphic elements and Lua code that allows interaction with the user. In our example GUI system, we will have three types of graphic elements available and will use the event-driven system for controlling the interface.

Three GUI Items

ON THE CD

The items that are implemented in the GUI system are sprites, four state buttons, and text objects. Sprites are static 2D graphic objects, buttons are a collection of sprites that react to the position and button status of the mouse, and text objects are text strings displayed in a selected font. To support these three items, the game shell has to support sprites and drawing text in a selected font. The sprite object is CSprite; the font object is called CFont. The code required to support these objects can be found in the DX9 project on the CD-ROM. The three items implemented in the GUI system just scratch the surface of GUI items that can be implemented.

C++ CLASSES FOR GUI

The majority of the code for the GUI is in the C++ portion of the program. The Lua code controls and formats the GUI objects, but the brute-force processing is done in C++. The code for every GUI item is based on the CGUIObject base class. The class definition is shown in Listing 11.1

LISTING 11.1 CGUIObject Class

```
class CGUIObject
{
public:
                        CGUIObject();
    virtual             ~CGUIObject();
    virtual const char   *GetObjectTypeName();
    virtual bool         Update(float fSecsElapsed,
                             CUserInterface *pParent);
    virtual bool         Render(void);
    virtual int          ItemCommand(const char *pCommand);
    virtual void         SetPosition(float fx, float fy,
                                 float fw, float fh,
                                 float z);
    virtual bool         SetFont(char *pFontName,
                                 float normalSize);
    virtual bool         KeyHit(int ascii);
    void                 SetID(unsigned int id);
    unsigned int         GetID(void);
    RECT                 GetScreenRect();
    virtual bool         StealsMouse(int x, int y);
    void                 Enable(bool bDisable,
                                 bool bKeepDrawing);
    bool                 isDisabled();
    bool                 isDrawing();
};
```

Method: Update

This method is called to inform the object that some amount of time has passed. If any processing outside the render loop is necessary, this is the place to do it.

Method: Render

This method is called in the render loop to have the object draw itself. The base behavior is to check if there is a sprite loaded and, if so, draw it to the screen. This implementation uses the DX9 Framework to accomplish this task.

Method: ItemCommand

The `ItemCommand` method is called from a LuaGlue function to do some item-specific operations. The base behavior is to do nothing, but items that are build on this base will use this for a number of applications.

Method: SetPosition

This method sets the screen position of the item. Any drawing should be limited to this area of the screen.

Method: SetFont

This method associates a font with the item. The main application for this method is to set the font used in the TextField item.

Method: KeyHit

This method is called to allow the item to consume a keypress. If the item uses the passed key, it should return `true`, which will stop key processing. If the key is unused (the default condition), the method will return `false`.

Method: SetID and GetID

Each GUI item in an interface must have a unique ID. This ID is set by the Lua code at the creation time of the item. These methods allow access to this value from the C++ code.

Method: GetScreenRect

This method returns the currently set screen area that is assigned to the item.

Method: StealsMouse

This method is called to ask the item if the item reacts to the mouse at the passed location.

Method: Enable

This method sets the enable state of the item. An item that is disabled can still be drawn or can disappear completely from the screen. The C++ code (and LuaGlue code) can determine the enabled state and the drawing state by using the `isDisabled` and `isDrawing` methods.

Because all GUI items are derived from this class, they all have some common functionality. For example, they all have a sprite as a background and a font with which to draw text. Most of the functionality that we have in the implemented items comes directly from this base class. Only the button item builds further on the base class.

GUI Item: Sprite

All the functionality for the sprite GUI item is already part of the base class (CGUIObject). A class is still derived for it so that the GetObjectTypeName method returns the proper value, and that future expansion (maybe rotation, scaling, or tiling) is made easier. The class definition is shown in the following example:

```
class CGUISprite : public CGUIObject
{
public:
                    CGUISprite();
    virtual         ~CGUISprite();
    virtual    const char    *GetObjectTypeName();
};
```

GUI Item: TextField

The TextField builds on the base class by storing a text string and drawing it at the object's position during render time. The class definition is shown in the next example:

```
class CTextField : public CGUIObject
{
public:
                    CTextField();
    virtual         ~CTextField();
    virtual const char    *GetObjectTypeName();
    virtual int         ItemCommand(const char *pCommand);
    virtual bool        Render(void);
};
```

The TextField class introduces the ItemCommand method. This method sets the string, clears the string, or returns the string's contents. This method is called from a LuaGlue function described later in this chapter. The Render method is also over-ridden so that the object can draw the string after calling the base class Render method.

GUI Item: Button

The button class is a specialized version of a sprite. The biggest difference between a button and a sprite is that the button reacts to the mouse position and has three images from which to choose as its display. The states of this button class are normal, hover, and pressed. This item will also create events for the Lua code to handle for the state changes of the button state. The class definition is shown in the following example:

```
class CButton : public CGUIObject
{
public:
                    CButton ();
    virtual         ~CButton ();
    virtual const char    *GetObjectTypeName();
    virtual int           ItemCommand(const char *pCommand);
    virtual bool          Update(float fSecsElapsed,
                            CUserInterface *pParent);
    virtual bool          Render(void);
};
```

Notice that the button class overrides the Update method. The button class uses this method to update the state of the button based on the position and button status of the mouse. The button also must have three sprites, one for each state, that are set at creation time (shown next) or using an ItemCommand. The events that the button can generate are GUI_EVENT_BUTTON_UP and GUI_EVENT_BUTTON_DOWN. The "down" event is when the user presses the button, and the "up" event is when the pressed button is released. The "up" event means the button has been clicked.

Interfaces

As we stated before, all GUI items are assigned to an interface. One interface is the "active" interface, which means it is drawn, updated, and gets input events sent to its event handler. The class definition is shown in Listing 11.2.

LISTING 11.2 CUserInterface class

```
class CUserInterface
{
public:
                CUserInterface();
    virtual     ~CUserInterface();
    bool        Init(const char *fname);
```

```
bool            Update(float fSecsElapsed);
bool            Render(void);
void            AddGUIObject(unsigned int id, CGUIObject *pObject);
void            DeleteGUIObject(unsigned int id);
void            SetGUIObjectPosition(unsigned int id,
                            float fx, float fy,
                            float fw, float fh);
void            SetGUIObjectFont(unsigned int id,
                            char *fontName, int fontSize);
int             ItemCommand(unsigned int id, const char *pCommand);
void            EnableObject(unsigned int id,
                            bool bDisable, bool bKeepDrawing);
void            SetEventHandler(const char *pHandlerName);
const char      *GetEventHandler(void) {return m_pEventHandlerName;}
bool            KeyHit(int ascii);
void            StartTimer(float fTime);
};
```

The main function of this class is to maintain a list of CGUIObjects and provide a central access point for the member GUI items.

The various methods associated with the GUI system used in *Take Away* are shown in Table 11.1.

TABLE 11.1 Methods associated with the GUI system used in *Take Away*

Method	Description
Init	When a new interface is created, this method is called to initialize the interface and to run the passed Lua file. This Lua file should create all the required GUI items and define an event handler for the interface. Examples of how to do this from Lua are described the next section.
Update	This method is called to inform the interface that some amount of time has passed. The interface will call the Update method of all GUI items in its list, allowing for each one to be updated.
Render	The interface does no rendering on its own but calls the Render method of all the GUI items in its list.
AddGUIObject	
DeleteGUIObject	These two methods add a new GUI item to the interface or remove an existing item from the list. →

Method	Description
SetGUIObjectPosition	This method finds the referenced GUI item and then sets the screen position of the item to the passed rectangle.
ItemCommand	This method finds the passed item and calls its `ItemCommand` method.
EnableObject	This method sets the enabled state of the passed item ID.
SetEventHandler	
GetEventHandler	These methods manipulate the name of the Lua event handler assigned to this interface.
KeyHit	This method is called to inform the interface that the user has pressed a key on the keyboard. The interface will offer the input key to all objects in the list and, if no item claims it, will cause the event `GUI_KEY_PRESS` to be sent to the interface's event handler.
StartTimer	Each interface has a timer for use by the Lua code. When the timer is started using this method, it counts down until the specified time has passed. An event (`GUI_TIMER_EXPIRED`) will be sent to the interface's event handler. After the event is sent, the timer becomes inactive.

The GUI Manager

The GUI Manager is the entry point for the C++ code to access the entire GUI system. This point is where all the interfaces are maintained and where the LuaGlue functions are stored. The CGUIManager object is a singleton, meaning there can be only one of these objects at a time. This characteristic allows us to access the entire system from this object. The class definition is shown in Listing 11.3.

LISTING 11.3 CGUIManager class

```
class CGUIManager
{
private:
    static CGUIManager    *m_pInstance;
public:
    static CGUIManager    *GetInstance();
public:
                CGUIManager();
    virtual     ~CGUIManager();
    bool        Init(cLua *pContext);
```

```
    bool              StartGUI(const char *pFilename);
    bool              Update(float fSecsElapsed);
    bool              Render();
    void              SendEvent(int iEventCode, int id,
                          float arg1 = 0.0f, float arg2 = 0.0f,
                          float arg3 = 0.0f, float arg4 = 0.0f);
    bool              KeyHit(int ascii);
};
```

Static Method: GetInstance

This method gives us the ability to get a pointer to the GUI Manager object from anywhere in the C++ code. The private pointer is updated in the object's constructor and destructor and is simply returned to any call to `CGUIManager::GetInstance()`. This feature makes it easy for GUI items to reference the system as a whole and for the main program to call methods in the instantiated object once created.

Method: Init

The `Init` method starts up the system and gives access to the Lua Environment of the main application. Once the system is ready for action, the Lua file `StartGUI.lua` will be run to start up the Lua side of the system.

Methods: Update and Render

The `Update` and `Render` methods are similar to the previous classes. These call their counterparts for the current interface (which calls them for all items).

Method: SendEvent

This method sends the passed event to the current interface's event handler.

Method: KeyHit

This method sends the passed keyboard input to the current interface.

GUI LUAGLUE

The LuaGlue functions for controlling the GUI system are closely tied to the earlier C++ implementation. The GUI's Lua component is initialized during system startup by running the file `StartGUI.lua`. At a minimum this script should start up an interface for the original interface screen. A catalog of the GUI LuaGlue functions that make up the Lua side of the GUI system follows.

RunGUI(filename)

This function creates a new interface or reruns an interface that was previously created. The file passed is a Lua file that creates the interface items and defines the event handler.

SetEventHandler(name)

This function tells the interface the name of the Lua event handler. Once set, this function will be called to handle all events generated by the system for this interface. Make sure that each interface has a unique event handler name, or you may run into problems when an interface that is restarted calls the wrong handler. The GUI event handler function takes parameters like the sample function shown in the following example:

```
function SampleEventHandler(itemID, eventCode, param1, param2, param3,
param4)
    -- event handler code here
end
```

CreateItem(id, type, item specifics)

Call this function to create interface items. The Lua coder assigned unique IDs to each item in an interface. The type of item (sprite, text field, or button) is passed, and additional parameters for each type of item are given. The additional parameters follows:

■ Sprite—A filename of the image to use as the sprite
■ TextField—None
■ Button—Names of the images to use for the three button states: normal, hover, pressed

DeleteItem(id)

This function removes an item from the interface completely.

SetItemPosition(id, x, y, w, h)

This function sets the screen position of the GUI item.

ItemCommand(id, command, ...)

This function passes a command to an item. Its parameters depend on the type of item and the command given. The item commands defined for our items follow:

- Sprite—None
- TextField

    1. SetString sets the display string to the next value passed.
    2. AddString appends the passed string to the current display string.
    3. GetString returns the current display string.
    4. SetColor sets the color of the display string text.

- Button—None

SetFont(id, fontname, fontsize)

This function sets the item's font. It is currently used only for TextField type items, but it could be used for a number of expanded items such as lists or edit boxes.

EnableObject(id, enable, draw)

This function sets the enable and draw states of an item. An item that is disabled can be set to draw but not interact with the user at all or to not draw at all.

StartTimer(time)

This function starts a GUI countdown timer. When the time expires, an event (GUI_TIMER_EXPIRED) will be sent to the interface's event handler, and the timer will be disabled (you can restart it in the event handler, if desired).

GUI Events

All the events that the GUI system can send to an interface's event handler are shown in the next example:

```
GUI_EVENT_BUTTON_UP
GUI_EVENT_BUTTON_DOWN
GUI_KEY_PRESS
GUI_ENTER_INTERFACE
GUI_REENTER_INTERFACE
GUI_TIMER_EXPIRED
```

GUI_EVENT_BUTTON_UP

This event is sent when the user clicks a GUI button. The id parameter is the ID of the button sending the event.

GUI_EVENT_BUTTON_DOWN

This event is sent when the user presses a GUI button but has not yet released it. The `id` parameter is the ID of the button sending the event.

GUI_KEY_PRESS

This event is sent when the user hits a key on the keyboard. The `id` parameter is the ASCII value of the key pressed.

GUI_ENTER_INTERFACE

This event is sent as the first event to a new interface. It lets the Lua code know that this is the first time this interface has been run and allows it to do some initialization.

GUI_REENTER_INTERFACE

This event is sent to an interface to signal that the interface is now being reentered after leaving the active state.

GUI_TIMER_EXPIRED

This event is sent in response to a `StartTimer` function call after the passed time has elapsed.

NEXT STEPS

The GUI items provided in our test game are only the beginning. The items you can create using this approach are limited only by your imagination (and your low-level coding skills). You can combine current items into compound items or create completely new items. Some of the possibilities are shown in Table 11.2.

TABLE 11.2   Possible GUI Items

GUI Item	Description
Scrolling List	A list of TextField objects that are drawn one below another in the item's rectangle. Buttons can be supplied to scroll the list up and down.
Text Edit/Entry	Takes keyboard input to edit the string of a TextField.
Text Banner	A TextField that scrolls a message across the item's rectangle.
Pie Chart	An item that displays a pie chart from given data. $\rightarrow$

GUI Item	Description
Progress Meter	A bar graph that shows the progress of an operation.
Radio Buttons	Linked buttons that allow only one to be in the "selected" state.
Check Boxes	Buttons that have "on" and "off" states. The mouse toggles the state.
Rotated Sprites	Modifies the current sprite item to use DX9 rotation.
Animated Sprites	A list of sprites. The `draw` function draws one from this list and advances the selected sprite at a specified time interval.
3D	Creates a new item that uses DX9 to display 3D scenes or simple objects.

To make new GUI items, make a new class that inherits from `CGUIObject` and add support for `ItemCommand` messages. Use the TextField item as an example. Once you have a new class, add code to create objects to the `CreateItem` LuaGlue (`GUI_Manager.cpp`). Once that is done, you are ready to use it in your Lua programs.

LUA GAME INTERFACES

Now that we've worked through the integration of a Lua interface system into our C++ game project, it's time to look at how we assemble an interface in Lua. The first step, of course, is the design, and we've already done that. If we look through our design, we can see that we've planned for a Lua implementation, and we've already laid out the skeleton files that will allow us to move forward in our game.

Beyond our example game, *Take Away*, it's a good idea to take this approach: design the Lua implementation and then create skeleton versions of the script files you'll be using in your project. This method will keep your scripting focused and operating within the constraints of your design.

When you complete your game, you obviously want it to look as polished as possible, but in the development process, it's often a great idea to get the components of your game up and running before you turn them over to an artist for a full implementation. Some developers call this *prototyping*—we prefer the term *rapid implementation*, because we're not really building a prototype but rather building the structure and flow of our game and enhancing it later, once we've validated our approach.

Interface Design 101

An interface is the visual (and often aural) vehicle that we use to communicate information about our game to the player. The interface is what the player sees, hears, clicks, and taps in a game. Many excellent books on interface design and how people respond and react to different interface approaches are available, and it's far beyond the scope of this book to travel down that path. Some good books to look at include *User Interface Design for Programmers* by Joel Spolsky and *Designing Web Usability* by Jacob Neilson (focused on Web design but great for game interfaces as well). We will provide a few simple guideposts for interface design:

Keep the interface simple: Don't create a complex, button-heavy interface if you don't need to. Make the display simple so that the player's eyes focus naturally on what's important.

Make the interface visually pleasing: Take care to create an interface that looks good and professional. Also remember that the interface is the primary manner in which you communicate the tone and feel of your game to the player. And don't go crazy with too much color or too much art!

Provide only vital information: If you give your player unlimited shots from a gun, don't have an ammo display. Show only the data that changes during play and that will mean something to the player.

Provide meaningful feedback on player progress: Make sure that the data you show the player tells him in an instant how he is doing in the game. This information could be the score, a health meter, an ammo counter (that means something!)—just be sure that the interface reflects the player's progress through the game in a meaningful way.

Get Your Interface Up Quickly

When it's time to roll up your sleeves and start scripting, don't let yourself get bogged down in the details of the art or the look and feel of your graphics. Use some sort of tool to quickly create your interface screens (if you've heard of the term *programmer art*, you know what we're talking about). We use Microsoft Visio® (see Figure 11.1) for our interface mockups, but almost any program will work (even a word processor). Find something that allows you to quickly create a layout for a full-screen interface, save it out as an image file, and then snip out the components for buttons and sprites.

By creating an interface rapidly, you can lay out the flow of all of your interface screens. This process will allow you to test the flow of your screens, see how the information is presented, and determine if you've forgotten anything vital—it'll only take a few hours.

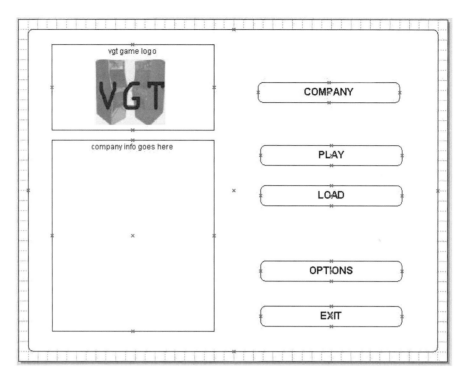

FIGURE 11.1 A quickly-created interface screen done in Visio.

Loading Screen

Most games begin with some sort of splash, or loading, screen, and we'll do the same in our *Take Away* game. Usually, a loading screen is displayed to the player while game data and assets are loaded into memory. *Take Away* is such a lean game data-wise, that there is no real loading time, but the screen gives the game a nice look and feel.

For this interface, we aren't doing anything too complicated at all. We'll show a background image, a copyright piece of text, and a progress bar (that's actually just a text string made up of periods).

In our GUI scripts, we have sections for initializing objects and performing `dofile()` calls for any sub-GUI objects (more about those next), but we don't need those for this interface, so those sections are blank. Earlier, we fleshed out this file with the `SetEventHandler("LoadingMenuEvent")` function to set up the event handler, and the control structure for reacting to an event. Soon, we'll look at capturing and reacting to events, but for now, let's set up the GUI objects.

Our first checkpoint in the process is the `StartGUI.lua` file. This file initializes our game constants. In this file we set up all of the ID constants for the GUI interfaces we'll be using in the game. As described earlier, a GUI is a stand-alone unit in the world of Lua scripting—a sprite in one GUI file can have the same ID in another GUI file and everything works fine. To keep things better organized, however, we've chosen to create a "master" GUI ID for each interface, as a constant. Doing so guarantees that each GUI element in our game will have a unique ID, and that every GUI element for a given interface will fall within a 1000 ID range (useful for sub-GUIs as you see later). For *Take Away*, our GUI constants follow:

```
-- Sub-interface constants
GUI_INGAME = 0
GUI_RUNTIME_SPRITES = 1000
GUI_MAIN_MENU = 2000
GUI_ESCAPE = 3000
GUI_KEY_SELECT = 4000
GUI_LOADING = 5000
GUI_END_GAME = 6000
```

The last item in `StartGUI.lua` calls the loading interface and gets the game underway with the following function call:

```
--Start with the loading screen
RunGUI("GUI_Loading.lua")
```

We now turn our attention to the `GUI_Loading.lua` file. First, we'll set up background sprite image with the next script chunk:

```
CreateItem(GUI_LOADING + 100, "Sprite", "ui_bg_loading.bmp")
SetItemPosition(GUI_LOADING + 100, 0, 0, 800, 600)
```

With these function calls, we create a GUI object, using the master GUI ID constant set in `StartGUI.lua`, that is a sprite and assign the bitmap image `ui_bg_loading.bmp` to the object. We then issue the `SetItemPossition()` command to set the object's position to 0,0 (the top-left portion of the screen) and the size of 800×600 (so it will fill up our entire screen).

The GUI objects, in the system we've implemented here, will draw from the lowest ID number to the highest ID number within a GUI. That's why we lay out our GUI files with the sprites as the 100s range, because often they are used as background images and other interface elements. To draw a sprite in front of a full-screen image, make sure the ID number is higher.

The Text Table

The next GUI objects in our loading screen are text objects, so let's take some time to explore how to handle text object. A text object can be defined very simply, such as with the following script:

```
CreateItem(myID,"TextField")
SetItemPosition(myID, 335, 20, 0, 0)
SetFont(myID, "Arial", 16)
ItemCommand(myID, "SetColor", 169,20,231,255)
ItemCommand(myID, "SetString", "Hello World!")
```

In this example, we create a TextField object with the ID specified by the variable myID. We then set the position (the size of a TextField is determined by the size of the font, so the size arguments to SetItemPosition() don't mean anything at all). We next set the font (this is a system font, so it must be installed on the system running the game and referred to exactly as it is in the Fonts Control Panel browser).

Our next step is to set the color—this is simply an RGBA value. The first three values are the RGB color values (from 0 to 255) of the color you want, and the fourth value is the alpha (transparency) of the text, with 255 being opaque.

Finally, we set the actual string to display by passing in a string as an argument. In this case, we can set the string by passing in the value directly, but if you are creating a game that needs any kind of localization, or if you'll want to "mass edit" strings later, it's a good idea to break the strings into their own Lua file (we already set this up in our design of the Lua implementation).

For our game, we use a file called Text.lua. It loads a table with data that will be displayed by text objects.

First, though, we'll create a simple function, shown in the following example, that allows us to get a text string easily:

```
function GetText(localID)
    return textTable[localID]
end
```

This simple function simply pulls the value from the table. If we ever need to change the table or manipulate the string data in any way, we can do it in this function rather than by searching for textTable references all through our scripts.

We initialize the textTable at the start of the file and then simply add entries, using the same GUI ID as the interface object for the table key (and we've already loaded this file from StartGUI.lua so the data is already in memory). The following elements are needed for the loading interface:

```
--define empty table
textTable = {}
--Loading text
textTable[GUI_LOADING + 200] = "Version 1.0"
textTable[GUI_LOADING + 201] = "Copyright 2005, Charles River Media"
```

You'll notice the table keys are based on the GUI interface objects, which will create lots of unused keys in our table. However, remember that Lua doesn't create the table based on a range of values, but rather it creates a table value when one is defined, so we don't have to sacrifice any wasted table space for this approach.

Now we can define our first two text elements for this interface as follows:

```
--200s Text items
CreateItem(GUI_LOADING + 200,"TextField")
SetItemPosition(GUI_LOADING + 200, 335, 20, 0, 0)
SetFont(GUI_LOADING + 200, "Arial", 16)
ItemCommand(GUI_LOADING + 200, "SetColor", 169,20,231,255)
ItemCommand(GUI_LOADING + 200, "SetString", GetText(GUI_LOADING + 200))

CreateItem(GUI_LOADING + 201,"TextField")
SetItemPosition(GUI_LOADING + 201, 220, 555, 0, 0)
SetFont(GUI_LOADING + 201, "Arial", 16)
ItemCommand(GUI_LOADING + 201, "SetColor", 169,20,231,255)
ItemCommand(GUI_LOADING + 201, "SetString", GetText(GUI_LOADING + 201))
```

Our final text object will become our progress bar, defined as follows:

```
loadString = "."
CreateItem(GUI_LOADING + 202,"TextField")
SetItemPosition(GUI_LOADING + 202, 212, 500, 0, 0)
SetFont(GUI_LOADING + 202, "Arial", 48)
ItemCommand(GUI_LOADING + 202, "SetColor", 177,174,255,255)
ItemCommand(GUI_LOADING + 202, "SetString", loadString)
```

We set this up as a regular string, but we use the variable loadString to hold the initial period (we'll check against the length of this string to determine how far the progress bar is moving). To actually make this run, we'll need to explore the event handling within this interface file.

Loading Screen Event Handling

The only event that we're working with in the loading screen is the timer event, and we start the timer ticking with the `StartTimer(0.25)` LuaGlue function call right before we set the event handler. This function starts the GUI timer for this interface ticking. It will also stop and fire off the `GUI_TIMER_EXPIRED` event when it is finished (after a quarter of a second, in this case). The core event-handling code for the event looks like the following example:

```
function LoadingMenuEvent(id, eventCode)
    if eventCode == GUI_TIMER_EXPIRED then
        if string.len(loadString) < 21 then
            loadString = string.format("%s%s", loadString, ".")
            ItemCommand(GUI_LOADING + 202, "SetString", loadString)
            StartTimer(.15)
        else
            RunGUI("GUI_MainMenu.lua")
        end
    end
end  -- event handler
```

For this handler, the code checks to see if the length of `loadString` value is less than 21 (that is, displaying 20 or fewer periods). If it is, the code adds another period to the `loadString` and sets the TextField to display the new value of `loadString`. Finally, the handler will start another timer counting down, which will call this handler again.

Once the progress bar is long enough, the `string.len()` function will bounce out of the `if` control structure, and the script will run the main menu GUI screen.

Loading Objects

In this example, we are simply walking through a timed progress bar with no actual progress tied to the bar. We can, however, use this approach to load any data we may have once we create a more data-intensive game project. Look at the following example, which was taken from another game:

```
if periodCount < 21 then
        if periodCount == 1 then
            LoadSounds()
    end
        if periodCount == 5 then
        AddImageToCache("female_thin.bmp")
        AddImageToCache("female_normal.bmp")
        AddImageToCache("female_heavy.bmp")
```

```
            AddImageToCache("male_thin.bmp")
            AddImageToCache("male_normal.bmp")
            AddImageToCache("male_heavy.bmp")
        end
        if periodCount == 10 then
            AddModelToCache("female_heavy.mlm")
        end
        if periodCount == 15 then
            AddModelToCache("female_normal.mlm")
        end
        loadString = string.format("%s%s", loadString, ".")
        ItemCommand(GUI_LOADING + 202, "SetString", loadString)
        StartTimer(.15)
    else
        RunGUI("GUI_MainMenu.lua")
    end
end
```

In this example, we capture discrete moments as the progress meter fills up and use that time to actually perform some important business—in this case, loading the sounds, some textures, and some models in memory.

If you create your own LuaGlue functions to pre-cache or load game data (the low-level type of data) or call Lua files via the dofile() function during this event loop, you can control the game loading right within Lua.

Main Menu Screen

The main menu in our *Take Away* game, shown in Figure 11.2, is the primary "staging area" for the player before he enters the game proper. Here, he can view the high scores, start a new game, load a saved game, re-map the control keys, or exit the game and return to the Windows desktop.

The interface features a background sprite image, several text fields (to hold the high scores and the date of the saved game), and four buttons. Setting up the background sprite and the text fields is handled the same way as in the loading menu, so we don't need to cover that territory again. We should note that because the text objects on this interface are derived from game data, they don't pull their values from the text table but from the data itself during an update function (see the following sections).

FIGURE 11.2.   The main menu in *Take Away*.

Buttons

The new GUI element here is the button. In *Take Away*, the New Game button is defined by the following script:

```
--300s Buttons
-- to start a new game
CreateItem(GUI_MAIN_MENU + 300, "Button", "uib_newgame_up.bmp",
"uib_newgame_hv.bmp", "uib_newgame_dn.bmp")
SetItemPosition(GUI_MAIN_MENU + 300, 452, 123, 293, 67)
```

Here, we create a GUI button object and assign it three bitmaps: for the up, down, and hover states of the button. See Figure 11.3. We then set the position and size of the button graphic.

For our example game, we try to keep the size of on screen graphical objects the same as the size of the source graphic; otherwise, you'll find some image degradation in the automatic scaling provided by DirectX.

FIGURE 11.3 The up, down, and hover states of the New Game button.

To use the button in the script, we capture the GUI_EVENT_BUTTON_UP event code. This event will also pass in the ID of the GUI object via the variable ID. We can check against this variable to capture a specific button press and then act on that button. The script to react to just the New Game button follows:

```
if eventCode == GUI_EVENT_BUTTON_UP then
      if id == GUI_MAIN_MENU + 300 then
          PlaySound(1, "button.wav")
          gFromEscape = "no"
          RunGUI("GUI_InGame.lua")
      end
end
```

You can see that we are testing for the ID value of the object, and if it matches, then we execute three lines of Lua script. Here, we play a simple sound effect of a button click, set a global variable (that will be used by the InGame GUI), and run GUI_InGame.lua, which will actually start the game.

Entering the Interface

If you look at the first two events listed in the Main Menu event handler, you'll see:

```
GUI_ENTER_INTERFACE
GUI_REENTER_INTERFACE
```

These events are fired when you first load an interface. The first event is fired the first time that an interface is run during a program sessions. The Reenter event is fired all of the subsequent times you enter the interface. Breaking this event into two events allows us to separate the "initialize only once" operations from the "initialize each time" operations.

In our *Take Away* game, all of the function calls refer to functions defined in the LuaSupport.lua file that we loaded at the start of the program execution (so they are already compiled and in memory).

If we look at what gets called during the first run of the interface (GUI_ENTER_INTERFACE), we see the following function calls:

```
LoadSettings()
SortScoreLists()
UpdateMainMenu()
```

Let's take a look at the first function, shown in the next example:

```
function LoadSettings()
--Loads the current setting and high scores
    --Creates the pathway for the file
    local fileName = io.open(("SaveGames\\Take_Away_Saved_Settings.lua"),
    "r")
    --Checks for the file's existence
    if fileName ~= nil then
        --Reads the file, closes it, and begins the action
        dofile("SaveGames\\Take_Away_Saved_Settings.lua")
        fileName:close()
    else
        gSavedGameDate = ""
        gThrustKey = 32
        gShootKey = 112
        gTurnLeftKey = 91
        gTurnRightKey = 93
        gHighScoreNum = 0
        myHighScoresDate = {}
        myHighScoresAmount = {}
        EnableObject(GUI_MAIN_MENU + 301, 0, 0)
    end
end
```

This function loads the file that holds the settings for the game. Notice that it first checks for the existence of the file, because it won't exist if no one has played the game yet. If the file is there, it will simply load and run the file using the dofile() function. If the file doesn't exist, it will load the appropriate variables with valid starting values.

The next function takes care of displaying the high scores list:

```
function SortScoreLists()
    if gHighScoreNum > 0 then
        for indx = 1, gHighScoreNum do
            for i = gHighScoreNum, indx+1, -1 do
                if myHighScoresAmount[i] > myHighScoresAmount[i-1] then
                    --swap numbers
                    t =  myHighScoresAmount[i]
                    myHighScoresAmount[i] = myHighScoresAmount[i-1]
                    myHighScoresAmount[i-1] = t
                    --swap dates
                    t =  myHighScoresDate[i]
                    myHighScoresDate[i] = myHighScoresDate[i-1]
                    myHighScoresDate[i-1] = t
                end
            end
        end
    end
end
```

This function walks through the myHighScoresAmount and sorts both that table and the corresponding values in myHighScoresDate. If we were dealing with a single table, we could use the table.sort() function, but because we wish to keep the dates linked with the scores, we need to manage this process manually.

Finally, we update the Main Menu's GUI displays with the following function:

```
function UpdateMainMenu()
--This updates the Date and Score portions of the Main Menu
    for indx = 1,10 do
        if myHighScoresDate[indx] == nil then
            ItemCommand(GUI_MAIN_MENU + 200 + indx, "SetString", "")
            ItemCommand(GUI_MAIN_MENU + 210 + indx, "SetString", "")
        else
            ItemCommand(GUI_MAIN_MENU + 200 + indx, "SetString",
            myHighScoresDate[indx])
            ItemCommand(GUI_MAIN_MENU + 210 + indx, "SetString",
            CommaFormatBigInteger(myHighScoresAmount[indx]))
        end
        ItemCommand(GUI_MAIN_MENU + 200, "SetString", gSavedGameDate)
        if gSavedGameDate == "" then
            EnableObject(GUI_MAIN_MENU + 301, 0, 0)
        else
            EnableObject(GUI_MAIN_MENU + 301, 1, 1)
```

```
            end
        end
    end
```

This function simply walks through the myHighScoresDate table (all 10 entries, whether they have values or not). If there are values in the table, it will populate TextFields with the date of the score and the score value. Finally, it will display the date of the last save game, just below the Load Game button.

If you look at the event scripts for the New Game and the Saved Game buttons, you'll notice only a single difference: the Saved Game buttons called the LoadGame() script after it calls the InGame GUI. The call to load the InGame GUI is done first, because the sprites that are the ships, enemies, crates, and projectiles are actually "owned" by the InGame GUI. The call to run the GUI actually changes the InGame GUI to the active interface, even though we are still in the Main Game interface.

The LoadGame() function is shown in the next example:

```
function LoadGame()
--Loads a saved game
    --Creates the pathway for the file
    local fileName = io.open(("SaveGames\\Take_Away_Saved_Game.lua"),
    "r")
    --Checks for the file's existence
    if fileName ~= nil then
        --Clears all projectiles
        for indx = 1,pCount do
            if myProjectiles[indx].PROJ_ID ~= nil then
                DeleteItem(myProjectiles[indx].PROJ_ID)
            end
        end
        --Clears all targets
        for indx = 1,targetCount do
            if myTargets[indx].T_ID ~= nil then
                DeleteItem(myTargets[indx].T_ID)
            end
        end
        --Reads the file, closes it, and begins the action
        dofile("SaveGames\\Take_Away_Saved_Game.lua")
        fileName:close()
        StartTimer(refreshRate)
    end
end
```

The function is actually quite simple. It first checks to see if the save-game file exists; if it does, all projectile and target data is cleared (this is done in case the game is being loaded during a session in which the game was already run—in that case, there will still be lingering target and projectile data that will corrupt the new game). Once the housecleaning is done, the new game data is loaded via the `dofile()` on the save-game file (the InGame interface already initializes all of the other data and the save-game file merely modifies the values). Finally, it starts the InGame timer, which is the primary control mechanism for the game's movement through time.

The Controls button simply loads the `GUI_KeySelect.lua` file, and we'll explore that interface below.

The Exit button calls the `SaveSettings()` function (found in `LuaSupport.lua`) which saves all of the master game settings. In function, it's very similar to the `SaveGame()` function we explored in the previous chapter, so we won't spend any time on it here. Simply look over the function in the script file and you'll be able to tell how it walks through and saves the meta game data (such as the scores and the key mappings).

Finally, the Exit buttons calls the LuaGlue function `QuitProgram()`, which signals the program to shut down the shell and the Lua environment and then exits the program.

Controls

The Controls interface allows the player to map his chosen keys to the four game controls (turn left, turn right, thrust, and fire). The player simply clicks a button that indicates the control he'd like to remap and then taps a key on the keyboard to select the key. This interface is defined in `GUI_KeySelect.lua`. See Figure 11.4.

We begin in standard fashion but create a sprite for the background image and set up the Buttons and TextFields. You'll notice that when we set the strings for the TextFields, we run the command variables through the following function:

```
ItemCommand(GUI_KEY_SELECT + 200, "SetString",
ASCIIToString(gThrustKey))
```

This function, found in `LuaSupport.lua`, processes the value (which is an ASCII code) into something we can understand more easily, as shown in the following example:

```
function ASCIIToString(id)
    if id == 8 then
        myString = "Backspace"
```

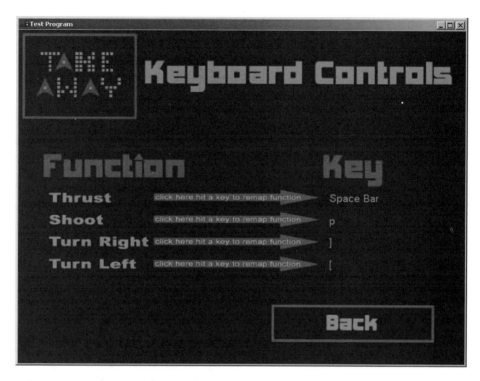

FIGURE 11.4 The Control screen in action.

```
    elseif id == 9 then
        myString = "Tab"
    elseif id == 13 then
        myString = "Enter"
    elseif id == 32 then --Space Bar
        myString = "Space Bar"
    else
        myString = string.char(id)
    end
    return myString
end
```

This function uses the `string.char()` function to return a readable character for our TextField. We've also added in some checks that capture keys that don't translate directly with the `string.char()` function, so we can understand them as well.

If we move down and look at the event handling, we use the Back button to rerun the Main Menu GUI. All of the other buttons are used to tell the program which key we'd like to remap. We handle this by creating a mode, defined by the `keySelect` variable, and using the following event-handling script:

```
    if id == GUI_KEY_SELECT + 301 then
        PlaySound(1, "button.wav")
        keySelect = 1
        HighlightText(GUI_KEY_SELECT + 200)
    end
```

This script sets the mode by setting the value of keySelect for each button clicked, plus it runs the HighlightText() function on the ID of the TextField that's associated with that command. That function is shown in the next example:

```
function HighlightText(id)
    for indx = GUI_KEY_SELECT + 200, GUI_KEY_SELECT + 200 + 3 do
        ItemCommand(indx, "SetColor", 176,173,254,255)
    end
    if (id > GUI_KEY_SELECT + 199) and (id < GUI_KEY_SELECT + 204) then
        ItemCommand(id, "SetColor", 255,0,0,255)
    end
end
```

This function first walks through all of the TextFields on this interface and sets them to the default color. It then sets the color of the TextField whose ID is passed in to red. You'll notice that it checks for the ID range of the four text fields, and if it's not in the range, it will simply set all fields to the original color. We use this function when we enter and reenter the interface to reset all text fields to the default value by calling HighlightText(0).

Finally, the event handler grabs keystrokes and runs a chunk of script depending on the current keySelect mode, by using the following structure:

```
elseif keySelect == 1 then
        --Thrust
        if (gShootKey ~= id) and (gTurnLeftKey ~= id) and
         (gTurnRightKey ~= id) and (27 ~= id) then
          gThrustKey = id
            ItemCommand(GUI_KEY_SELECT + 200, "SetString",
            ASCIIToString(id))
        end
        keySelect = 0
        HighlightText(0)
```

This code checks to make sure that you aren't assigning the same value to multiple keys, and if you're not, it will set the proper game variable, update the TextField, set the keySelect mode to 0 (no selection in progress), and finally set the colors of the text field to the default look.

InGame

We'll cover the majority of what goes on in the InGame interface in the next chapters, as we explore game flow and artificial intelligence, but we'll take a look at the interface elements here.

The core interface elements in InGame are a series of TextFields that indicate the labels (pulled from the textTable) and the values that display the players score, the shots fired, and how many crates they've lost.

Other than the core game flow elements, the most interesting aspect of this interface is the use of a sub-GUI to bring up an InGame menu. When you design your game interfaces, some interfaces are clearly full-screen interfaces, such as the main menu in our sample game. These interfaces stand on their own and are easily self-contained.

Often, when you are in real-time gameplay mode, you'll want to show different interface elements to a player at different times but to still keep the control flexible (remember than an interface "owns" all of a game's input). If I want to put up a small screen showing the inventory on my Barbarian fighter, I might want to still be able to click other buttons in the interface and perform operations that have nothing to do with my inventory display. In that case, we use the concept of sub-GUIs, to allow multiple interfaces to operate from within one master "parent" interface. See Figure 11.5 for an example of a sub-GUI.

Sub-GUIs are based on the concept of limited ID ranges for a GUI and nested event handlers. Earlier in the chapter, we looked at the ID anchors set as constants in StartGUI.lua. These values are the baseline and all of the IDs in a GUI build from that number, never taking more than 1000 IDs. Because of that, we can use the following functions to control the display of a GUI (found in LuaSupport.lua):

```lua
function ClearGUI(id)
    for indx = 1,1000 do
        EnableObject(id + indx, 0, 0);
    end
end
function RestoreGUI(id)
    for indx = 1,1000 do
        EnableObject(id + indx, 1, 1);
    end
end
```

These simple functions simply walk through all of the possible ID values and call the EnableObject() LuaGlue function to enable or disable the entire GUI (all non-used ID values are simply ignored). We simply pass in the anchor constant for the GUI we'd like to manipulate. Objects that have the Enable values set to 0 are not drawn and do not accept input.

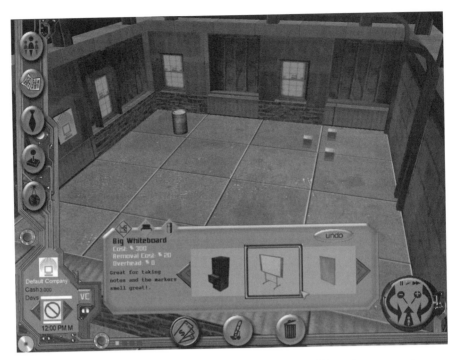

FIGURE 11.5 An example of a sub-GUI in action: the small interface to purchase objects exists within a larger InGame interface that is still active at the time.

If you look at the top of GUI_InGame.lua, you'll see the following statement:

```
dofile("Scripts\\GUI_Escape.lua")
```

This statement will load the Escape GUI (which pauses the game and allows you to save a game, resume the game, or quit). Almost immediately, the GUI_ENTER_INTERFACE event in InGame will call the InitialSetUp() function, and near the end, you'll find:

```
ClearGUI(GUI_ESCAPE)
gEscapeOn = 0
```

This function will clear out the Escape GUI at the outset. You'll also notice that we set the global variable gEscapeOn to 0. This value tells the program whether the Escape menu is on.

Take a look at the start of the InGame event handler; you'll see the following initial structure:

```
if EscapeEvent(id, eventCode) ~= 1 then
end -- escape event
```

This structure surrounds the entire "meat" of the InGame event handler; it tells the function to first run the function `EscapeEvent()` and evaluate the result before deciding if it should run the InGame event-handling script.

In `GUI_Escape.lua`, we have a function that looks like an event handler (but notice that we don't set it as an event handler with the `SetEventHandler()` function). At the start of the Escape event handler, we set the variable result equal to 0, and then if the Escape event handler captures and handles the input, it sets result to 1. This value is then passed back to the InGame event handler as the trigger to tell the script if the input has been handled.

By using this system of nested event handlers (and we've used this approach with as many as 12 sub-GUI interfaces), you can be sure that the input is captured by the right interface, while the other interfaces are still active.

You'll see that the InGame event handler captures the Esc key being pressed, as shown in the following example:

```
if id == 27 then --Esc
            if gEscapeOn == 0 then
                RestoreGUI(GUI_ESCAPE)
                gEscapeOn = 1
            end
    end
```

If the Escape menu isn't already displayed, it will restore the GUI and set the `gEscapeOn` global variable. Conversely, in the Escape event handler, if the Escape key is pressed there, it will run the next script:

```
if id == 27 then --Esc
            if gEscapeOn == 1 then
                ClearGUI(GUI_ESCAPE)
                gEscapeOn = 0
                StartTimer(refreshRate)
                result = 1
            end
    end
```

This script clears the GUI, sets the mode variable, and returns a `result` of 1, which tells the InGame handle to ignore the rest of its script. You'll also notice the `StartTimer()` function call—this restarts the game after it paused in the Escape menu.

SUMMARY

In this chapter, we learned how to construct the objects that would serve as the foundation for a GUI system within a Lua-enabled game. By linking object commands to LuaGlue functions, we can create and control GUI objects within our Lua scripts and react to interface events.

We then walked through the primary interfaces in our *Take Away* game to see how all of this comes together in the crucible of game development.

Our next step will be to explore the game logic and game-event system that will enable us to create a gameplay experience within our Lua environment.

12 Game Programming with Lua

In This Chapter

- The Game Loop
- Tic-Tac-Toe
- *Take Away*

In the previous chapters, we laid the groundwork to build a GUI system using LuaGlue functions and learned how to capture interface events. This was a major task, indeed, but it still doesn't get us to developing a game—we have just set up the foundation from which we can build a game.

In this chapter, we'll explore using Lua as the tool to write the game logic that will take us through an entire game, in both a turn-based model and in our real-time *Take Away* game. We'll learn about the master control system, or the Game Loop, that allows us to control the flow of an entire game from start to finish. We'll learn how to capture the events and the timing triggers that will move our game forward in time, and we'll take a detailed look under the hood at the growing complexity of our *Take Away* project.

THE GAME LOOP

So far, our *Take Away* game has been defined by a fairly static implementation—we've explored interface and initialization components, but we haven't yet had the concept of a game. Without going into the semantics of what defines a game once again, we do need to boil down things to the most bare level to give us the structure on which to build a game.

Think for a moment about one of the most basic of games: tic-tac-toe. Although the design of the game limits its challenge to about 30 seconds (and that's pushing it!), it is useful for our example. In tic-tac-toe, we see two core concepts in a game: each player takes a turn making an O or an X mark, and the game ends when a player gets three marks in a row or the board is filled up (a cat's game).

This game gives us the concepts of turns and victory conditions. Victory conditions are the parameters that must be met within the game world to signal the end of the game. In *Take Away*, we follow the old arcade-style design of an endless game with the end-game defined by player failure (and the player's success is the score value at the moment of failure). We simply play *Take Away* until all of our supply crates are dragged off screen.

The real challenge is to define the flow of the game within the context of our Lua script. Every game needs some level of master control game loop or function that walked the game through what must be done in each turn or each slice of time (for a real-time game such as *Take Away*). To get us started, we'll explore a simple tic-tac-toe game.

TIC-TAC-TOE

Tic-tac-toe is a turn-based game: one player makes a move and then the next and so on, until the end of the game is reached. If we break down this game even further, we can describe the events of a turn as follows:

- The player places a symbol (X or O) on an empty spot on the 3×3 board.
- If the player's symbol makes a row (horizontally, vertically, or diagonally) of three like symbols, that player wins.
- The winning player indicates his victory by drawing a slash through his three connected symbols.
- If the player places his symbol on the board in the last available square, and it does not make three in a row, the game is a draw.

Of course, this assumes that we begin with a blank board. To do this, we'll create a representation of our board that will allow us to track the state of the board at any given time (see Figure 12.1). From that data, we can draw the current state of the game world.

If we want to create a Lua data structure to match our image of the board shown in Figure 12.1, we can simply use a table such as the following:

```
myBoard = {0,0,0,0,0,0,0,0,0}
```

This code represents a blank board at the beginning of the game. At the start of every game, we need to set the game world to its neutral state, so that it can change during play as each turn moves the game closer to the fulfillment of the victory condition.

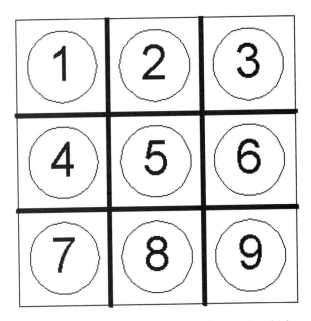

FIGURE 12.1 This diagram shows the way in which we will number the nine game cells for our tic-tac-toe game.

Initializing the Game

For our tic-tac-toe example, we are going to pre-populate the world with all of the possible graphical elements (because they are finite), and then simply turn those elements on or off to suit the current representation of the world. If you look at the GUI_InGame.lua file for the tic-tac-toe game on the CD-ROM, you'll see how we do this in the following code:

```
--board
CreateItem(100, "Sprite", "board.bmp")
SetItemPosition(100, 250, 150, 300, 300)

--X pieces
EX = 110
CreateItem(EX + 1, "Sprite", "piece_x.bmp")
SetItemPosition(EX + 1, 270, 170, 60, 60)
EnableObject(EX + 1, 0, 0)

CreateItem(EX + 2, "Sprite", "piece_x.bmp")
SetItemPosition(EX + 2, 370, 170, 60, 60)
EnableObject(EX + 2, 0, 0)
```

We explicitly create elements for every position of the X pieces, every position of the O pieces, and the lines that indicate the wins. Normally, doing all this is overkill, but this approach works just fine in a small game like this. We then use the `EnableObject()` function to control the rendering of the object. In `EnableObject()`, we first pass in the ID of the GUI object and then flag values to control rendering and input, as follows:

```
EnableObject(EX + 2, 0, 0)
```

A value of 1 as the second argument means the object is rendered to the screen. A value of 1 for the third argument means the object will react to user input.

We can then write a simple function that will initialize the game world and all the GUI elements, as shown in Listing 12.1.

LISTING 12.1   Function to initialize game world and GUI elements

```lua
function InitGame()
    --turn off graphics
    --first, the pieces
    for indx = 1,9 do
        EnableObject(EX + indx, 0, 0)
        EnableObject(OH + indx, 0, 0)
    end
    --the bars
    for indx = 1,3 do
        EnableObject(H_BAR + indx, 0, 0)
        EnableObject(V_BAR + indx, 0, 0)
    end
    EnableObject(D_BAR + 1, 0, 0)
    EnableObject(D_BAR + 2, 0, 0)
    --the text
    for indx = 1,5 do
        EnableObject(GUI_INGAME + 200 + (indx * 10), 0, 0)
    end
    --set up the game data
    myBoard = {0,0,0,0,0,0,0,0,0}
    theWinner = -1
    --set up for the first turn
    if math.random(1,100) > 49 then
        curTurn = EX
        ItemCommand(GUI_INGAME + 250, "SetString", "X's turn: left click
        to place")
    else
        ItemCommand(GUI_INGAME + 250, "SetString", "O's turn: left click
        to place")
```

```
        curTurn = OH
    end
    EnableObject(GUI_INGAME + 250, 1, 1)
end
```

This function walks through all of the GUI elements that define the game and sets them to the starting values. It then initializes the world table theWinner variable (which indicates whether the game is in progress, a cat's game, or a game in which one player has won). Finally, the function basically flips a coin to determine who goes first. After this function is run (initially run from the GUI_ENTER_INTERFACE even in GUI_InGame.lua), the game is ready to play. If the game is over, we simply have to rerun this function to reset the game world.

Handling the Game Turn

Now that we've set up things, it's time to take a look at how we handle a game turn. When a turn begins, only one player will make a move. Once he places his symbol on the board, the game will evaluate the world state and either end the game or switch the turn to the next player. The phrase "place his symbol on the board" is key here, because this gives us the clue for how to capture the end of a turn. In our example game, the player will use the mouse to click the board—it's this event, GUI_MOUSE_BUTTON_UP, that is our trigger in the game. We can now capture the event as follows:

```
if eventCode == GUI_MOUSE_BUTTON_UP then

    if theWinner == -1 then
            MakeMove()
    end
end
```

We use the if statement to check the value of theWinner variable—if its value is –1, then the game is ongoing, so we want to process the player's mouse click. By using this simple event, we now have the control to capture a turn and process the results. We do this in the MakeMove() function as shown in Listing 12.2.

LISTING 12.2 The MakeMove() function

```
function MakeMove()
    thePos = GetBoardLocation(GetMousePosition())
    if thePos ~= -1 then
        --turn on the space
        EnableObject(curTurn + thePos, 1, 1)
        --change text
```

```
            if curTurn == EX then
                ItemCommand(GUI_INGAME + 250, "SetString", "O's turn: left
                click to place")
            else
                ItemCommand(GUI_INGAME + 250, "SetString", "X's turn: left
                click to place")
            end
            --now update the table
            myBoard[thePos] = curTurn
            --check for win
            theWinner = -1
            theWinner, slashID = WinCheck()
            if theWinner == -1 then
                --no winner
                --now swap turns
                if curTurn == OH then
                    curTurn = EX
                else
                    curTurn = OH
                end
            elseif theWinner == 0 then
                --cat's game
                EnableObject(GUI_INGAME + 210, 1, 1)
                EnableObject(GUI_INGAME + 240, 1, 1)
                EnableObject(GUI_INGAME + 250, 0, 0)
            else
                --we have a winner
                EnableObject(GUI_INGAME + 250, 0, 0)
                EnableObject(GUI_INGAME + 240, 1, 1)
                EnableObject(slashID, 1, 1)
                if theWinner == EX then
                    EnableObject(GUI_INGAME + 220, 1, 1)
                else
                    EnableObject(GUI_INGAME + 230, 1, 1)
                end
            end
        end
    end
end
```

Let's spend some time walking through this function, because it contains the heart and soul of our tic-tac-toe game and sets us up for our more lengthy exploration of the game logic in our *Take Away* game. First, we need to see where on the board the player clicked, shown in the next line:

```
thePos = GetBoardLocation(GetMousePosition())
```

The function `GetMousePosition()` is a LuaGlue function written in C++ (covered in more detail in Chapter 13), which returns the x- and y-coordinates of the current mouse position. We send this result directly to the `GetBoardLocation()` function, which will return the board position (see earlier example) on which the player clicked (if the player clicks out of bounds, it will return a value of –1). The function is shown in Listing 12.3.

LISTING 12.3 The `GetBoardLocation()` function

```
function GetBoardLocation(myX, myY)
    --set default response (not valid)
    myPos = -1
    --modify values to make it easier to comprehend
    myX = myX - 250
    myY = myY - 150
    --now check for the click area
    if (myX > 0) and (myX < 100) and (myY > 0) and (myY < 100) then
        myPos = 1
    end
    if (myX > 100) and (myX < 200) and (myY > 0) and (myY < 100) then
        myPos = 2
    end
    if (myX > 200) and (myX < 300) and (myY > 0) and (myY < 100) then
        myPos = 3
    end
    if (myX > 0) and (myX < 100) and (myY > 100) and (myY < 200) then
        myPos = 4
    end
    if (myX > 100) and (myX < 200) and (myY > 100) and (myY < 200) then
        myPos = 5
    end
    if (myX > 200) and (myX < 300) and (myY > 100) and (myY < 200) then
        myPos = 6
    end
    if (myX > 0) and (myX < 100) and (myY > 200) and (myY < 300) then
        myPos = 7
    end
    if (myX > 100) and (myX < 200) and (myY > 200) and (myY < 300) then
        myPos = 8
    end
    if (myX > 200) and (myX < 300) and (myY > 200) and (myY < 300) then
        myPos = 9
    end
    if myPos ~= -1 then
        --if the click is legal, see if the space is occupied
        if myBoard[myPos] ~= 0 then
```

```
            myPos = -1
        end
    end
    return myPos
end
```

This function uses the literal screen coordinates of each of the nine cells to assign a position value to myPos, which is returned at the end of the function. If no valid board position is indicated, it will return the default value of −1.

Once the function is finished checking all locations, it then checks the table (myBoard) that contains the current world state to see if the selected position is already occupied. If it is, then the function will return a value of −1.

Once we have the current board position (if it is legal), we then turn on the player's symbol for that position with the following line:

```
EnableObject(curTurn + thePos, 1, 1)
```

We use the same value in curTurn as we do to define the two sets of GUI elements (EX and OH), and we set up the GUI elements to correspond to the table index, so we can simply use those values in the call to enable the GUI object for the current player at the indicated position.

The next major aspect of the function (aside from changing some on-screen text) is to actually update the game board. We do this with the following single line:

```
myBoard[thePos] = curTurn
```

All we do here is simply place the value (EX and OH) for the current turn into the indicated position in the game board table.

Our next task is to evaluate the newly modified game board to see if we have any change in the results. We do that with the next statement:

```
theWinner, slashID = WinCheck()
```

The WinCheck() function will return the state of the board (in theWinner variable) as well as the ID of the proper "slash" graphic. The function is shown in Listing 12.4.

LISTING 12.4 The WinCheck() function

```
function WinCheck()
    --set default for on-going
    theGame = -1
    theID = -1
```

```lua
--first, check for cat's game
openSpace = false
for indx = 1,9 do
    if myBoard[indx] == 0 then
        openSpace = true
    end
end
if openSpace == false then
    --no open spaces, so cat's game
    theGame = 0
end
    --now check for a win
    --row1
    if myBoard[1] == curTurn then
        if myBoard[2] == curTurn then
            if myBoard [3] == curTurn then
                theGame = curTurn
                theID = H_BAR + 1
            end
        end
    end
    --row2
    if myBoard[4] == curTurn then
    if myBoard[5] == curTurn then
            if myBoard [6] == curTurn then
                theGame = curTurn
                theID = H_BAR + 2
            end
        end
    end
    --row3
    if myBoard[7] == curTurn then
        if myBoard[8] == curTurn then
            if myBoard [9] == curTurn then
                theGame = curTurn
                theID = H_BAR + 3
            end
        end
    end
    --col1
    if myBoard[1] == curTurn then
```

```lua
        if myBoard[4] == curTurn then
            if myBoard [7] == curTurn then
                theGame = curTurn
                theID = V_BAR + 1
            end
        end
    end
    --col2
    if myBoard[2] == curTurn then
        if myBoard[5] == curTurn then
            if myBoard [8] == curTurn then
                theGame = curTurn
                theID = V_BAR + 2
            end
        end
    end
    --col3
    if myBoard[3] == curTurn then
        if myBoard[6] == curTurn then
            if myBoard [9] == curTurn then
                theGame = curTurn
                theID = V_BAR + 3
            end
        end
    end
    --diag1
    if myBoard[1] == curTurn then
        if myBoard[5] == curTurn then
            if myBoard [9] == curTurn then
                theGame = curTurn
                theID = D_BAR + 1
            end
        end
    end
    --diag2
    if myBoard[3] == curTurn then
        if myBoard[5] == curTurn then
            if myBoard [7] == curTurn then
                theGame = curTurn
                theID = D_BAR + 2
            end
```

```
                end
            end
        return theGame, theID
    end
```

The first thing this function does is walk through the entire board to see if all of the spaces are occupied. If so, there is a potential that it's a cat's game, so the value of theWinner is set to 0.

The script then walks through the board positions for all possible winning situations (there are eight in total), seeing if the current player has three symbols in a row, as shown in Figure 12.2. If three like symbols in a row are discovered, then theGame variable is set to the curPlayer and theID variable is set to the ID of the proper "slash" graphic. These values are then returned to the parent function.

FIGURE 12.2: We see that the O player has won with a diagonal three-in-a-row, and we display the slash graphic on top of the player's winning symbols.

Handling the WinCheck in C

For our tic-tac-toe example, writing some functions as LuaGlue functions is a good way to illustrate the way that custom functions can be implemented in specific cases. The LuaGlue code was placed in a new source file with a function to initialize the LuaGlue functions. This function, called during program initialization, is a good model for future expansion.

The `WinCheck()` LuaGlue functions for tic-tac-toe will use a simple nine-integer array to represent the game board, just as we did in Lua. The indexes 0, 1, and 2 are the top row; 3, 4, and 5 are the middle row; and 6,7, and 8 are the bottom row. Any spot having the value of 0 (zero) is considered "open" or free; any other value is considered to be the ID of the owning player. Having defined this structure, we can define all the winning combinations in the game. The winning combination list follows:

```
const int winningPositions[8][3] =
{
    {0, 1, 2},
    {3, 4, 5},
    {6, 7, 8},
    {0, 3, 6},
    {1, 4, 7},
    {2, 5, 8},
    {0, 4, 8},
    {2, 4, 6}
};
```

Now that the board format is set and the combinations for winning are defined, we can write the the LuaGlue function `WinCheck`. This function returns –1 if there is no winner and the board still has open slots. A return value of 0 (zero) denotes a draw, no winner, and no more open spots. If a win is found, the return value is the winner's board value. The code follows with commentary:

```
extern "C" int TTT_WinCheck(lua_State *L)
{
    cLua *lua = g_pBase->GetLua();
    int winner = -1;
    int argNum = 1;
    int board[9];
    for(int i=0; i<9; i++)
    {
        board[i] = (int) lua->GetNumberArgument(argNum++, 0);
    }
```

The first task is to get the `cLua` object and retrieve the board status from the caller. The code does this by getting the first nine passed arguments and placing them into our internal board format.

```
for(i=0; i<8; i++)
{
  if(board[winningPositions[i][0]]==board[winningPositions[i][1]] &&
     board[winningPositions[i][0]] == board[winningPositions
     [i][2]])
  {
    winner = board[winningPositions[i][0]];
  }
}
if(winner == -1)
{
    //didn't find a winner, check for draw
    bool bDraw = true;
    for(i=0; i<9; i++)
    {
        if(board[i])
            bDraw = false;
    }
    if(bDraw)
        winner = 0;
}
```

All the winning combinations are checked to see if the same player occupies all three members of the winning combination. If all three spaces belong to a player, the return value is that player's ID. If a win was not found, we have to check if the board is completely full. If there is even one open slot (a value of 0 denotes an open slot), then the game is ongoing. Now that the return value is determined, all there is left to do is return and exit, shown in the next lines:

```
lua->PushNumber(winner);
return 1;
}
```

As you work through your own games, experiment to see which situations are best handled in Lua exclusively and which are best handled in C++ with a LuaGlue function. In the case of the WinCheck() function, the answer is that neither approach is really better than the other. Using C++ will generally speed up the code, but for a turn-based game like tic-tac-toe, that isn't an issue at all. When thinking through this specific angle, how would you modify either the LuaGlue function (in C), or the Lua script that follows the function call to process the slash image that shows the winning move visually?

Wrapping Up the Game Turn

Once we return from the WinCheck() function, we simply swap turns if there is no winner (theWinner has a value of −1). If the game is a draw, we activate the proper text messages; if it's a winning game, we indicate that as well.

With theWinner equaling −1 (the game is still progressing), the next mouse input will process the move for the next player. If the game is over, then the check we placed in the GUI_MOUSE_BUTTON_UP event will block any further input. We can then reset the game by capturing a space bar tap and begin the process again, with the following script:

```
if eventCode == GUI_KEY_PRESS then
    if id == 32 then --space bar
        if theWinner ~= -1 then
            InitGame()
        end
    end
end
```

In this example, we covered the game loop logic for a turn-based game, and captured the change in turn by an input event from the player. We'll now turn our attention to the *Take Away* game and see how we handle game logic in real time using Lua.

TAKE AWAY

In *Take Away*, we have a real-time game that plays forward, whether or not the player is actually doing anything. To keep the game flowing, we use the concepts of a timer and the function StartTimer(), which is called from GUI_InGame.lua and generates the event GUI_TIMER_EXPIRED. This is the method we use to create and control the master game loop. In the pages that follow, we'll walk you through the logic of our example game.

InGame

Although compact in appearance, the GUI_InGame.lua file boasts a level of complexity not reached by any other script in the game. GUI_InGame.lua relies heavily on functions defined in LuaSupport.lua. To better understand the mechanics of *Take Away*, we will walk through each step of the game's logic in the order that it occurs during a typical session. With this thought in mind, it is best to skim the script down to the event handler, where the program first seeks direction.

When `GUI_InGame.lua` is first executed, we initialize the game world by creating a table, using the following script:

```
world = {}
```

This 40×30 table, which is populated directly below its creation, simply divides the standard 800×600 pixel screen into square blocks of 20×20 meta pixels. This table will be used in a moment to display the game's virtual boundaries. In the meantime, take note of the scripting found below the event handler.

After the Escape sub-GUI check, which we discussed in Chapter 11, the first function called in the `GUI_REENTER_INTERFACE`/`GUI_ENTER_INTERFACE` is `InitialSetUp()`, which can be found at the top of the script shown in Listing 12.5.

LISTING 12.5 The `GUI_REENTER_INTERFACE`/`GUI_ENTER_INTERFACE` function

```
function InitialSetUp()
    --Initial player constants
    myRotation = 1 --Player's rotation (#)
    myX = 390       --Player's x-coordinate (#)
    myY = 290       --Player's y-coordinate (#)
    myXThrust = 0 --Player's thrust along the x-axis (#)
    myYThrust = 0 --Player's thrust along the y-axis (#)
    alive = "yes"  --Player's life status ("yes" or "no")
    --Initial limits
    respawnInterval = 20   --Number respawnCounter must reach to respawn
    player (#)
    --Initial setting of counters
    respawnCounter = 0     --Player's death period (#)
    score = 0              --Player's score (#)
    timeCounter = 0        --Passage of time (#)
    targetDoneCounter = 0 --Targets stolen by enemies (#)
    --Preferred game speed
    refreshRate = .1 --Seconds between timer expirations (#)
    --Initial GUI setup
    ItemCommand(GUI_INGAME + 201, "SetString", GetText(GUI_INGAME + 201))
    ItemCommand(GUI_INGAME + 202, "SetString", GetText(GUI_INGAME + 202))
    ItemCommand(GUI_INGAME + 203, "SetString", GetText(GUI_INGAME + 203))
    ItemCommand(GUI_INGAME + 204, "SetString", "0")
    ItemCommand(GUI_INGAME + 205, "SetString", "0")
    ItemCommand(GUI_INGAME + 206, "SetString", "0")
    ClearGUI(GUI_ESCAPE)
    gEscapeOn = 0
    masterCellID = 100000 --Constant used for the IDs of the world's
    boundaries
end
```

Each of the items set in this function must be reset to their original values at the start of each session for the game to function properly. The values labeled as "initial player constants" refer to those variables that pertain to the player's ship. The "limit" serves as the number that a separate counter must reach for an event to occur (in this case, the event is the respawning of the player).

The "counters" are values that increment throughout the game based on different events that occur throughout the game. Some, such as timeCounter and respawnCounter, are time-based whereas others, like score and targetDoneCounter are increased by specific occurrences within gameplay. The "preferred game speed" is the time, in seconds, that the game timer is set to count down. Because much of the game's functionality is linked to the GUI_TIMER_EXPIRED event, the refreshRate value is essentially the key to the smoothness and pace of *Take Away*. Finally, those items listed under the "Initial GUI setup" section work to restore the TextFields to primary data.

Returning to the order of operations in the event handler, we see that MakeWorld() is called directly after InitialSetUp(). The MakeWorld() function uses the world table and the DrawCell() function to render the pink boundaries of the *Take Away* environment, as shown in the following script:

```
function MakeWorld()
    for x = 1,40 do
        for y = 1,30 do
            if world[y][x] == 1 then
                DrawCell(x,y)
            end
        end
    end
end
function DrawCell(x,y)
--x is the x-coordinate
--y is the y-coordinate
    CreateItem(masterCellID, "Sprite", "box1.bmp")
    SetItemPosition(masterCellID, (x-1) * 20, (y-1) * 20, 20, 20)
    masterCellID = masterCellID + 1
end
```

After the borders are in place, the InGame interface calls the EnemyInit() function to direct the creation of a set number of enemy ships. The various ship-specific data for each enemy is stored within a myEnemies table. This massive table allows for the easy recall of such information as well as the simple scanning of all enemy statistics as a whole. This function is just the first of many in this interface to utilize what can be found in the LuaSupport.lua, as shown in the next example:

```
function EnemyInit()
    enemyCount = 5 --Number of enemies in the game
    myEnemies = {} --Creates myEnemies table
    --Creates table, one entry per potential enemy
    for indx = 1,enemyCount do
        --Creates a table to hold the data for each enemy
        myEnemies[indx] = {}
        --Now initialize the enemy
        EnemyRespawn(indx)
    end
end
```

Similar to `MakeWorld()`, the `EnemyInit()` function calls a function nested in a `for` loop. In this instance, the `EnemyRespawn(indx)` function is used to populate the `myEnemies` table with the essential data. Once fully established, the `myEnemies` table is one of the most important bodies in the entire scripting of the game. To continue filling the table, it is necessary to examine the `EnemyRespawn(indx)` function, which also appears in the `LuaSupport.lua` file. For the sake of ease, let's break it down into segments, beginning with the "Initial values," shown in the next example:

```
function EnemyRespawn(indx)
--Fills/refills myEnemies table according to indx
--indx is the myEnemies table index assigned to the enemy
    --Initial values
    myEnemies[indx].XTHRUST = 0 --Thrust along the x-axis (#)
    myEnemies[indx].YTHRUST = 0 --Thrust along the y-axis (#)
    myEnemies[indx].ROT = math.random(1,8) --Rotation of enemy ship (#)
    myEnemies[indx].ID = GUI_RUNTIME_SPRITES + indx + 100 --Starts GUI
    identification at 101 (#)
    myEnemies[indx].E_TOW = "no" --Towing flag (target ID # or "no")
    myEnemies[indx].FIRE = 0 --Projectile firing time interval (#)
```

Each of the indexed values listed serves to define the enemy's various parameters. XTHRUST, YTHRUST, and ROT deal with the ship's acceleration and orientation whereas ID pertains to the ship's GUI identification. E_TOW is a flag that reveals the enemy's current towing state. For example, when the enemy has no target in tow, it displays no; otherwise, it is set to the GUI ID of the target that it is towing. Finally, the FIRE section refers to the number of times that the enemy's AI has proceeded through the `EnemyFacing(indx)` function without firing a projectile. This value is compared to the `enemyFireInterval` to determine the proper intermission between shots.

Continuing on, we come across the section of the script that determines the edge of the game environment from which the enemy will appear. Using Lua's simple `math.random` function, we simply generate an integer between one and four and attribute it to the `entrySide` variable. Then, by interpreting the `entrySide` value as one of the four sides of the computer monitor, we set the enemy's initial x- and y-coordinates so that the enemy will be created off of the appropriate side of the screen. In this way, the ship will appear to fly in from outside of the visible area at varied locations. For the sake of avoiding redundancy, we've included only about one-fourth of this segment of the function here, in the next example:

```
entrySide = math.random(1,4)
--if entrySide == 1 then        --Left
--     myEnemies[indx].EX = math.random(-40,-20) --X-coordinate (#)
--     myEnemies[indx].EY = math.random(-40,620) —Y-coordinate (#)
```

In the second half of the `EnemyRespawn(indx)` function, we define the parameters that affect the enemy's speed, agility, and projectile-firing capabilities. These aspects are set according to the passage of time in the game session, as marked by the incrementing of the `timeCounter` at the expiration of the game timer. Because the default `refreshRate` is .1 seconds, it must be understood that the `timeCounter` marks the amount of timer expirations at this rate. For example, a `timeCounter` value of 100 would equal 10 seconds of real time with the default setting in place, as shown in the following script:

```
if (timeCounter >= 0) and (timeCounter < 100) then
    myEnemies[indx].REACT = 5 --Reaction time interval (#)
    myEnemies[indx].MAX = 5 --Maximum thrust (#)
    enemyFireInterval = 9
elseif (timeCounter >= 100) and (timeCounter < 200) then
    myEnemies[indx].REACT = 4 --Reaction time interval (#)
    myEnemies[indx].MAX = 6 --Maximum thrust (#)
    enemyFireInterval = 8
```

When the `EnemyRespawn(indx)` is called on to recreate an enemy that has been "killed," the function checks the duration of the current session and decides the proper way to set the REACT and MAX parameters for the enemy's ship. The `enemyFireInterval`, on the other hand, acts to affect all of the enemies in the game. Because the REACT value is the number of timer expirations that must pass between cycles of the AI thought process, a *decrease* in this number over time acts to *increase* the enemy's responsiveness. Conversely, the MAX value (the maximum thrust allowed for the enemy) is positively correlated with time so that an *increase* in time will equal an *increase* in maximum speed.

In the final stage of this function, the enemy's TYPE is determined (see the next example script). This parameter establishes the AI process to be used with this particular ship. In our simple game, there are four AI types, and each features a unique ship design. The randomly determined TYPE creates the appropriate sprite object and sets its position in a process similar to the one used to set the EX and EY. Here we also note that the enemies with a TYPE of 3 will have a speed advantage. Each will be discussed in further detail when we focus on the EnemyFacing(indx) function.

```
myEnemies[indx].TYPE = math.random(1,4) --AI type (1,2,3, or 4)
if myEnemies[indx].TYPE == 1 then
    CreateItem(myEnemies[indx].ID, "Sprite", "e1_ship1.bmp")
elseif myEnemies[indx].TYPE == 2 then
    CreateItem(myEnemies[indx].ID, "Sprite", "e2_ship1.bmp")
elseif myEnemies[indx].TYPE == 3 then
    myEnemies[indx].MAX = 10
    CreateItem(myEnemies[indx].ID, "Sprite", "e3_ship1.bmp")
elseif myEnemies[indx].TYPE == 4 then
    CreateItem(myEnemies[indx].ID, "Sprite", "e4_ship1.bmp")
end
SetItemPosition(myEnemies[indx].ID, myEnemies[indx].EX,
myEnemies[indx].EY, 20, 20)
end
```

Traveling back to the event handler, we find the call to TargetInit(). The role of this function is similar to EnemyInit() in that it creates a table that stores data specific to objects within the game. However, the TargetInit() function pertains to data that concerns the crates in *Take Away*. These crates are simple sprites around which the whole game revolves, and although they are generally stationary, they can be towed by enemies. The parameters required for such attributes are accounted for in the myTargets table, and each crate is set in its proper place (found in LuaSupport.lua), as shown in Listing 12.6.

LISTING 12.6 The TargetInit() function

```
function TargetInit()
    targetCount = 8 --Number of targets in the game
    myTargets = {} --Creates myTargets table
    startID = GUI_RUNTIME_SPRITES + 200 --Starts GUI identification at
    200 (#)
    startX = 360
    startY = 260
    --Creates/fills table with initial values
    for indx = 1, targetCount + 1 do
        myTargets[indx] = {}
        myTargets[indx].T_ID = startID
        startID = startID + 1
```

```
        myTargets[indx].T_TOW = "no" --Towing flag (enemy ID #, "no", or
        "done")
        myTargets[indx].T_X = startX --x-coordinate (#)
        startX = startX + 30
        if startX > 420 then
            startX = 360
        end
        myTargets[indx].T_Y = startY --y-coordinate (#)
        if indx > 2 then
            if indx < 6 then
                startY = 290
            else
                startY = 320
            end
        end
    end
    --now delete the middle target, so the player can spawn in
    table.remove(myTargets, 5)
    --Creates targets (as sprites) and places them
    for indx = 1,targetCount do
        CreateItem(myTargets[indx].T_ID, "Sprite", "box2.jpg")
        SetItemPosition(myTargets[indx].T_ID, myTargets[indx].T_X,
        myTargets[indx].T_Y, 20, 20)
    end
end
```

In this structure, nine crates (known in script as *targets*) are created with T_ID, T_TOW, T_X, and T_Y parameters. The only variance between these parameters and those of the enemies is the T_TOW value. In the crates, the T_TOW harbors either the GUI ID of the enemy towing or the towing state of the crate (either no or done). The crates are grouped into a three-crate-by-three-crate box that is positioned in the center of the screen. However, only eight crates are desired, as noted by the targetCount value; therefore, the table.remove manipulator is used to delete the centermost crate, leaving eight crates arranged perfectly for the beginning of the game.

The last function called by the InGame event handler is ProjectileInit(). Only a few differences exist between this function and the other initiation functions that we've discussed. The pCount value refers to the total number of projectiles allowed to be drawn simultaneously within the game. By setting a limit, we spare the processor the hassle of storing data for infinite amounts of projectiles. The pIndx is the index key used to store the parameters of each projectile. When the pIndx reaches the pCount limit, it resets to 0; in effect, the pIndx is cyclical. It is necessary to have both the pCount and pIndx values, then, because the number of projectiles in the game will remain constant, but the index key will be cyclical. Also, the playerProjectiles counter keeps track of how many projectiles the player's ship has fired throughout the session. In addition to these different values, the `PROJ_SHIP` parameter in the `myProjectiles` table is new. This value stores either `player` or the index key of the enemy, who fired the projectile. All of these parts will be incorporated in the `Fire-Projectile(ship, xThrust, yThrust)` that we will discuss a little later.

Using the Timer

After initialization, the InGame event handler calls `StartTimer()` to start the movement of the game. Essentially, the timer is the core component of the *Take Away* game, because it manages our master game loop. With each expiration, this timer will act to refresh the screen display and set off several important functions (in C++, this is often done with a system timer or linked to the screen refresh rate).

With the default `refreshRate` setting of .1 seconds, the timer's expiration will seem instantaneous, resulting in a smooth gameplay experience for the player. With this in mind, let us walk through the first half of `GUI_TIMER_EXPIRED` portion of the `GUI_InGame.lua` script, as shown in the next example:

```
if eventCode == GUI_TIMER_EXPIRED then
    if gEscapeOn == 0 then
        if alive == "yes" then
            --Refreshes the player's ship image
            DrawShip(myRotation, myXThrust, myYThrust)
        else
            --Respawns the player after a certain period
            respawnCounter = respawnCounter + 1
            if respawnCounter == respawnInterval then
                myRotation = 1
                myXThrust = 0
                myYThrust = 0
                myX = 390
                myY = 290
                respawnCounter = 0
                alive = "yes"
            end
        end
    end
```

Every time the `GUI_TIMER_EXPIRED` event occurs, we check to see if the player's ship is "alive." If the `alive` variable is set to yes, the `DrawShip(myRot, x, y)` function is called. Essentially, this function refreshes the image of the player's ship in accordance with the player's rotation and thrust factors. A detailed explanation of this function is given later in this chapter, so we will continue to dissect the `GUI_TIMER_EXPIRED` event. If the `alive` value is no, the `respawnCounter` is incremented by one count. When this circumstance has occurred enough times to render the `respawnCounter` equal to the `respawnInterval` value (the default is 20 expirations), the player's ship parameters are reset. The player is then respawned at the center of the screen, and `alive` is set to yes.

The second portion of this event increments the `timeCounter` variable, shown in the next example. As mentioned previously, this value is associated with time-specific events such as the increase of the maximum speed allowances for enemies created later in the session.

```
--Directs each enemy based on its own REACT setting
timeCounter = timeCounter + 1
for indx = 1,enemyCount do
    if (timeCounter/myEnemies[indx].REACT) ==
    (math.floor(timeCounter/myEnemies[indx].REACT)) then
        EnemyFacing(indx)
    end
end
```

Within this event, the `timeCounter` is divided by the REACT value to determine the proper reaction time for an enemy. If the `timeCounter` happens to be perfectly divisible by the REACT setting, that enemy is allowed to orient itself toward its goal using `EnemyFacing(indx)`. The rest of this event is composed of function calls and a resetting of the timer, as shown in the following script:

```
--Updates entities
DrawProjectile()
DrawEnemyShip()
DrawTargets()
--Checks for various collisions
EnemyHitCheck()
EnemyTowCheck()
end
--Resets the timer
StartTimer(refreshRate)
end
end --Escape Sub-GUI
end
```

All of these functions will be clarified in later sections of this chapter, but to avoid confusion, a brief summary of their general operations is given here. The `DrawProjectile()`, `DrawEnemyShip()`, and `DrawTargets()` functions all serve to refresh their respective subjects' sprites according to their positions and check for collisions with the world boundaries. `EnemyHitCheck()` searches for collisions between the player's projectiles and the enemy ships, deleting the entities if necessary. `EnemyTowCheck()`, however, searches for collisions between the enemies and the supply crates, initiating a towing relationship if needed. Finally, the GUI timer is reset.

We have now walked through one cycle of the *Take Away* game logic. There are still more details to explore, but we now have a distinct concept of way the game functions through time.

Player Control

Returning to the GUI_InGame.lua script, we are going to observe player controls used throughout the game. Below the GUI_REENTER_INTERFACE/GUI_ENTER_INTERFACE event, we find the scripting for the GUI_KEY_PRESS event. Interpreting the ID as the ASCII representation of the keyboard key, we find that the first segment of this event is the Escape key functionality discussed in Chapter 11. Further down, we see the following lines of script:

```
if id == gTurnLeftKey then --Default [
    --Turns player's ship counterclockwise
    myRotation = myRotation - 1
    if myRotation < 1 then
        myRotation = 8
    end
end
```

The gTurnLeftKey (set in the Controls interface) reduces the myRotation value, effectively turning the player's ship counterclockwise. When it reaches 0, the myRotation value is set to 8 so that it remains headed in a cardinal or primary intercardinal direction (North, Northeast, East, Southeast, and so on). These directions form the range of the eight bitmaps that represent the player's ship. Altering the myRotation value affects the way the ship is drawn using the DrawShip(myRot, x, y) function. This functionality is tailored to the gTurnRightKey to turn the ship clockwise, giving the player full rotational control. The gThrustKey adjusts the myXThrust and myYThrust values, according to the player's ship orientation, within a range from –5 to 5. Such a limit ensures the game's challenge and pace. To finish the controls, the gShootKey functionality is defined in the following script:

```
if id == gShootKey then --Default p
    --Fires a projectile from the player
    if alive == "yes" then
        FireProjectile("player", myXThrust, myYThrust)
    end
end
```

When the key mapped to the gShootKey value is pressed, this scripting checks to see if the player's ship is onscreen and calls the FireProjectile(ship, xThrust, yThrust) function. Finished with the control section of the scripting, we will now turn our attention to this function (found in LuaSupport.lua), as shown in Listing 12.7.

LISTING 12.7 The FireProjectile(ship, xThrust, yThrust) function

```
function FireProjectile(ship, xThrust, yThrust)
--ship can either be "player" or the myEnemies index of the enemy
--xThrust is the projectile's thrust along the x-axis
--yThrust is the projectile's thrust along the y-axis
    pIndx = pIndx + 1
    myProjectiles[pIndx].PROJ_ID = GUI_RUNTIME_SPRITES + pIndx + 299 —
    Starts IDs at 300 (not including offset)
    if ship == "player" then
        --Player's projectile
        playerProjectiles = playerProjectiles + 1
        myProjectiles[pIndx].PROJ_SHIP = "player"
        myProjectiles[pIndx].PROJ_X = myX
        myProjectiles[pIndx].PROJ_Y = myY
        Rot = myRotation
        CreateItem(myProjectiles[pIndx].PROJ_ID, "Sprite", "box2.jpg")
    else
        --Enemy's projectile
        myProjectiles[pIndx].PROJ_SHIP = ship
        myProjectiles[pIndx].PROJ_X = myEnemies[ship].EX +
        myEnemies[ship].XTHRUST
        myProjectiles[pIndx].PROJ_Y = myEnemies[ship].EY +
        myEnemies[ship].YTHRUST
        Rot = myEnemies[ship].ROT
        CreateItem(myProjectiles[pIndx].PROJ_ID, "Sprite", "box3.jpg")
    End
```

The FireProjectile(ship, xThrust, yThrust) function creates a projectile's sprite image, sets it in the game environment, and uses the ship's parameters to calculate its speed and direction. Later functions in the game are concerned with the collisions of these projectiles, but for now we examine only their creation. At the beginning of this function, pIndx is incremented to create a new index key for the myProjectiles table. The script then determines, based on the ship value, which ship issued the command to fire a projectile. After this analysis, the parameters of the myProjectiles table are filled with the ship's current data. Rotation-specific values follow in the following format:

```
--Set the projectile's position and thrust
if Rot == 1 then --Up
    myProjectiles[pIndx].PROJ_X = myProjectiles[pIndx].PROJ_X + 8
```

```
        myProjectiles[pIndx].PROJ_Y = myProjectiles[pIndx].PROJ_Y
        myProjectiles[pIndx].PROJ_XTH = xThrust
        myProjectiles[pIndx].PROJ_YTH = yThrust - 10
    end
```

Last, the respective sprites are positioned in the environment in relative position to the ships. As long as the session is still underway, the game interface is updated to reflect the number of projectiles fired by the player. When the pIndx reaches the pCount, it is reset to 0, as shown in the next example:

```
    --Update the display
    SetItemPosition(myProjectiles[pIndx].PROJ_ID,
    myProjectiles[pIndx].PROJ_XTH, myProjectiles[pIndx].PROJ_YTH, 4, 4)
    if targetDoneCounter ~= targetCount then
        ItemCommand(GUI_INGAME + 204, "SetString",
        CommaFormatBigInteger(playerProjectiles))
    end
    if pIndx == pCount then
        pIndx = 0
    end
end
```

Although this process occurs every time a projectile is fired, the cyclical nature of the pIndx allows the processor to focus on more pertinent issues of gameplay. By "overwriting" values in the myProjectiles table when the pIndx reaches 50, we have developed a seemingly endless supply of projectiles without sacrificing the convenience of a closed projectile system.

Projectile Motion

Now that we've established a projectile, we must dictate its motion on a frame-by-frame basis. Revisiting the GUI_TIMER_EXPIRED portion of the GUI_InGame.lua file, we notice that the function DrawProjectile() is called at every incidence of this event. This function (found in LuaSupport.lua) refreshes the sprite images of all of the projectiles displayed at any given moment. The foundation for its operation is the standard for loop, shown in Listing 12.8.

LISTING 12.8 The DrawProjectile() function

```
function DrawProjectile()
    for indx = 1, pCount do
        if myProjectiles[indx].PROJ_ID ~= nil then
            DeleteItem(myProjectiles[indx].PROJ_ID)
            if myProjectiles[indx].PROJ_SHIP == "player" then
```

```
        --Player's projectile
        CreateItem(myProjectiles[indx].PROJ_ID, "Sprite",
        "box2.jpg")
    else
        --Enemy's projectile
        CreateItem(myProjectiles[indx].PROJ_ID, "Sprite",
        "box3.jpg")
    end
    myProjectiles[indx].PROJ_X = myProjectiles[indx].PROJ_X +
    myProjectiles[indx].PROJ_XTH
    myProjectiles[indx].PROJ_Y = myProjectiles[indx].PROJ_Y +
    myProjectiles[indx].PROJ_YTH
    SetItemPosition(myProjectiles[indx].PROJ_ID,
    myProjectiles[indx].PROJ_X, myProjectiles[indx].PROJ_Y, 4, 4)
```

Basically, `DrawProjectile()` scans the `myProjectiles` table and takes note of the projectiles present in the game. It deletes the sprites of these projectiles and replaces them with a fresh, repositioned sprite to indicate the movement of the projectile. See Figure 12.3. This process is mirrored in all of the "drawing" functions. So, why should we continuously create and delete these entities instead of simply resetting their positions every frame? The answer lies in the loading of the game.

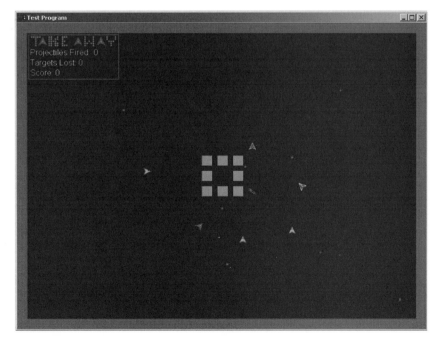

FIGURE 12.3 We can see enemy ships, projectiles, and storage crates all being handled in real time during the play of *Take Away*.

The constant creating and deleting of these sprites allows a loaded game to simply "turn on" an entity through the value of its table-based ID parameter. For instance, if the loaded game data reports that a projectile's PROJ_ID value is nil, it will not draw this projectile. However, if the loaded data reports that the PROJ_ID is a valid number, the DrawProjectile() function will automatically create and place that projectile's sprite.

Continuing with the last part of this function, we see that it detects collisions between the world boundaries and projectiles. When any part of a projectile intersects with a wall, its sprite is deleted and all of its data is cleared, as shown in the next script sample:

```
--Deletes projectiles when they pass the world's boundaries
if (myProjectiles[indx].PROJ_X > 780) or
 (myProjectiles[indx].PROJ_X < 20) or
 (myProjectiles[indx].PROJ_Y > 580) or
 (myProjectiles[indx].PROJ_Y < 20) then
     DeleteItem(myProjectiles[indx].PROJ_ID)
     myProjectiles[indx].PROJ_X = nil
     myProjectiles[indx].PROJ_Y = nil
     myProjectiles[indx].PROJ_XTH = nil
     myProjectiles[indx].PROJ_YTH = nil
     myProjectiles[indx].PROJ_ID = nil
     myProjectiles[indx].PROJ_SHIP = nil
 end
    end
  end
end
```

All that is necessary for this simple type of collision is a simple mathematical calculation by which we can determine if any part of a projectile has crossed a boundary line. According to the verdict rendered by this equation, we can delete the proper projectile. This kind of collision check is effective for projectiles because it does not require anything but the deletion of the colliding entity.

Ship Movement

The ships in *Take Away*, however, will collide with barriers in a different manner; they will bounce off of the walls as if they were ricocheting. Before we can explore the CollisionCheck(ship, x, y) function that will determine the correct deflection path, we must look at one of its components—the GetTravelDirection(xThrust, yThrust) function (found in LuaSupport.lua), shown in Listing 12.9.

LISTING 12.9 The `GetTravelDirection(xThrust, yThrust)` function

```lua
function GetTravelDirection(xThrust, yThrust)
--xThrust is a ship's thrust along the x-axis
--yThrust is a ship's thrust along the y-axis
    direction = 1
    if math.abs(xThrust) >= math.abs(yThrust) then
        --Left/right
        lrPercent = (math.abs(yThrust)/math.abs(xThrust)) * 100
        if lrPercent < 30 then
            if xThrust < 0 then
                direction = 7 --Left
            else
                direction = 3 --Right
            end
        else
            if xThrust < 0 then
                if yThrust < 0 then
                    direction = 8 --Up/left
                else
                    direction = 6 --Down/left
                end
            else
                if yThrust < 0 then
                    direction = 2 --Up/right
                else
                    direction = 4 --Down/right
                end
            end
        end
    else
```

The `GetTravelDirection(xThrust, yThrust)` function uses a series of `if-then` statements to determine the current direction of the ship, based on its x- and y-Thrust values. Essentially, it finds the ratio between the `xThrust` and `yThrust`—`lrPercent` or `udPercent` (not shown)—and utilizes this percentage to track down the ship's most prominent vector. The `direction` value relates to the eight directions illustrated in its eight bitmap textures, and it is the `direction` value that is returned at the end of the function.

Armed with the ability to ascertain a ship's current travel direction, we can now deal with the collisions between ships and world barriers. Calculating the ship's travel direction at the moment of impact will allow us to determine the proper trajectory for a deflection. This entire process is outlined in the `LuaSupport.lua` function `CollisionCheck(ship, x, y)`. We shall examine it in pieces. See Listing 12.10.

LISTING 12.10   The `CollisionCheck(ship, x, y)` function

```
function CollisionCheck(ship, x, y)
--ship can either be "player" or the myEnemies index of the enemy
--x is the ship's x-coordinate
--y is the ship's y-coordinate
    collision = NO
    if ship == "player" then
        --Player
        if (y <= 20) then
            myY = 25
            collision = HORIZONTAL
        elseif (y >= 560) then
            myY = 555
            collision = HORIZONTAL
        elseif (x <= 20) then
            myX = 25
            collision = VERTICAL
        elseif (x >= 760) then
            myX = 755
            collision = VERTICAL
        end
        travelDir = GetTravelDirection (myXThrust, myYThrust)
        --Set local variables to global values
        XThrust = myXThrust
        YThrust = myYThrust
    else
```

Initially, the function decides if the ship in question is the player or an enemy based on the ship value (which can either be player or the myEnemies index key of the enemy). After making this decision, the function compares the ship's position to the boundaries of the world and settles on what kind of collision it is; HORIZONTAL represents a collision with a left-and-right wall (such as the top or bottom of the screen) whereas VERTICAL represents a collision with an up-and-down wall (such as the left or right side of the screen).

It should be noted here that the enemies are not bound by the same boundaries that cage the player's ship. Looking in the script, you will find that the enemies' boundaries provide 60 more pixels of space (40 of which are off screen). This increased boundary allows the enemies to disappear off of the screen as the game demands, but it keeps them corralled so that they return quickly to gameplay. This approach provides logical order to the game environment and also keeps the game flow at an optimal level.

The function also corrects the ship's affected coordinate so that it is clear of the wall before ricocheting. In the event that the gThrustKey is continuously depressed, this small jump keeps the ship from being gradually working its way into the wall. Finally, this section sets the travelDir, Xthrust, and Ythrust variables consistently with the ship's data.

The second piece of the function serves to change the Xthrust or Ythrust values based on the collision and travelDir values, as shown in the next script:

```
if collision > NO then
--Set thrusts based on travel direction and collision
    if collision == HORIZONTAL then
        if travelDir == 1 then
            YThrust = YThrust * -1
        end
```

This structure is repeated for each of the eight travelDir possibilities and also for the VERTICAL collisions. This approach comprehensively accounts for every possible collision in *Take Away* while simultaneously maintaining its simplicity, as shown in the next sample:

```
        --Set global variables equal to local values
    if ship == "player" then
        myXThrust = XThrust
        myYThrust = YThrust
    else
```

Finally, the CollisionCheck(ship, x, y) function sets the global x- and y-Thrust values to the values of the newly altered intermediate variables. In the case of the player, myXThrust and myYThrust are set equal to their respective intermediates. Of course this process occurs with the enemies in the same manner (not shown), but their values are stored in the myEnemies table.

Now that the concept of border collision has been presented, we can successfully venture on to the three drawing functions that remain: DrawShip(myRot, x, y), DrawEnemyShip(), and DrawTargets(). Because all three of these functions employ the same basic structure as DrawProjectile(), we will cover only those areas that are specifically exclusive to each.

Drawing the Dynamic Entities

The aspects of DrawShip(myRot, x, y) that set it apart from the DrawProjectile() are its calls to CollisionCheck(ship, x, y) and CasualtyCheck() (another collision function that we will discuss later). By placing these calls within the refresh function, we have guaranteed that all important collisions will be isolated and dealt with in one-tenth of a second.

Because the DrawEnemyShip() function (found in LuaSupport.lua) must scan and manipulate the myEnemies table, it may seem much more complex than DrawShip(myRot, x, y). Even so, it still follows the same basic outline as DrawShip(myRot, x, y). As is customary, the function is contained entirely within a for loop and creates new x- and y-Thrust values by manipulating the XTHRUST and YTHRUST parameters according to the ROT value in the following manner:

```
--Determine enemy's new thrust
newThrust = math.random(0,2)
if myEnemies[indx].ROT == 1 then --Up
    myEnemies[indx].YTHRUST = myEnemies[indx].YTHRUST —
    newThrust
end
if myEnemies[indx].ROT == 2 then --Up/right
    myEnemies[indx].YTHRUST = myEnemies[indx].YTHRUST —
    newThrust
    myEnemies[indx].XTHRUST = myEnemies[indx].XTHRUST +
    newThrust
end
```

Later in the function, we make sure that the enemy's thrusts do not exceed the MAX value. In this way, we have a constant harness on the difficulty and pace of the gameplay experience. Following that portion of the function, we find the following lines of script:

```
--Checks for collisions and displays the new enemy ship
shipName = string.format("%s%d%s%d%s", "e",
myEnemies[indx].TYPE, "_ship", myEnemies[indx].ROT, ".bmp")
myEnemies[indx].EX = myEnemies[indx].EX +
myEnemies[indx].XTHRUST
myEnemies[indx].EY = myEnemies[indx].EY +
myEnemies[indx].YTHRUST
CollisionCheck(indx, myEnemies[indx].EX, myEnemies[indx].EY)
CreateItem(myEnemies[indx].ID, "Sprite", shipName)
SetItemPosition(myEnemies[indx].ID, myEnemies[indx].EX,
myEnemies[indx].EY, 20, 20)
        end
    end
end
```

The most important element to notice is how versatile the table system is in this function. By storing all of the data for the enemies in a comprehensive table we are able to construct entire bitmap file names, check for collisions, create and delete the ships, and set their positions. Tailoring this type of function to different entities is made so much easier by the various tables that we've assembled.

Such is the case with the DrawTargets() function (found in LuaSupport.lua). Once again with the same basic construction as the other drawing functions, DrawTargets() organizes its content into two massive for loops. After assessing the towing status of the crate, using the T_TOW parameter, the function focuses on those crates that are being towed by enemy ships (crates not being towed are simply redrawn using the last few lines of script housed in this function). Taking into account the rotation of the enemy that is towing the crate, we notice the crate placement in the following manner:

```
--Postition target behind enemy
if myEnemies[i].ROT == 1 then --Up
    myTargets[indx].T_X = myEnemies[i].EX
    myTargets[indx].T_Y = myEnemies[i].EY + 20
end
if myEnemies[i].ROT == 2 then --Up/right
    myTargets[indx].T_X = myEnemies[i].EX - 20
    myTargets[indx].T_Y = myEnemies[i].EY + 20
end
```

After adjusting the appropriate myTargets values so that the crate always appears behind the enemy's ship, we make sure to create the crate's sprite and set its position. At this point, we utilize the same functionality that we employed in the DrawProjectile() function, shown in the next script:

```
if (myTargets[indx].T_X > 800) or (myTargets[indx].T_X < -20) or
(myTargets[indx].T_Y > 600) or (myTargets[indx].T_Y < -20) then
    DeleteItem(myTargets[indx].T_ID)
    myTargets[indx].T_X = nil
    myTargets[indx].T_Y = nil
    myTargets[indx].T_ID = nil
    myTargets[indx].T_TOW = "done"
    myEnemies[i].E_TOW = "no"
```

Notice that the T_TOW and E_TOW parameters must be set to done and no, respectively. These settings indicate that the enemy has successfully stolen the crate and that the enemy is now capable of towing a different crate. More attention will be paid to these settings in the EnemyHitCheck(), EnemyTowCheck(), and CasualtyCheck() explanations. The last section of this function with which we will concern ourselves handles the stealing of the last crate; in effect, it manages the ending of the game, as shown in the following script:

```
--Update stolen target display and/or display game over string
targetDoneCounter = targetDoneCounter + 1
ItemCommand(GUI_INGAME + 205, "SetString",
CommaFormatBigInteger(targetDoneCounter))
    if targetDoneCounter == targetCount then
        for indx = 1,pCount do
            if myProjectiles[indx].PROJ_ID ~= nil then
                DeleteItem(myProjectiles[indx].PROJ_ID)
            end
            end
            DeleteItem(GUI_RUNTIME_SPRITES + 100)
            RunGUI("GUI_EndGame.lua")
        end
    end
```

This segment increments the targetDoneCounter and compares it to the total amount of crates in the game (targetCount). When they are equal—that is, when all of the crates have been stolen—we make sure to clear all of the projectiles and the player's ship so that they do not linger in the environment until the next session. Lastly, it directs the action to the GUI_EndGame.lua file.

SUMMARY

We now have a solid handle on the flow of the game in *Take Away*, which is a real-time game controlled by a GUI timer. We also explored using an event-driven system to handle the flow of a turn-based tic-tac-toe game. Using these approaches, you can see how you can control the flow of the game in something like a real-time strategy (RTS) game or a more advanced turn-based game.

Armed with this knowledge, our next step is to look into creating computer-controlled opponents within Lua, or, in other words, artificial intelligence. In the next chapter, we'll return to both our tic-tac-toe game and *Take Away*, plus explore other examples to give ourselves a solid grounding in using Lua to control computer opponents.

13 Using Lua to Define and Control AI

In This Chapter

- The Appearance of Intelligence
- Blackjack
- Tic-Tac-Toe
- Take Away
- Other AI Examples
- Finite State Machines
- Pathfinding

In previous chapters, we worked to build a simple arcade-style game. We wrote the scripts to allow us to control the movements of our small spaceship through a hostile world. But what makes the world hostile? In our game, computer-controlled enemies try to ram you, take away your crates, and shoot your ship. What controls those enemies is intelligence—artificial intelligence defined by the program code.

Artificial intelligence (AI) is the term that was coined to mean those instances when a computer appears to be thinking. We all know that computers can't actually think—not yet, at least—but computers are very good at processing data and behaving in a certain way based on that data. If done correctly, it can feel like the computer is thinking.

In this chapter, we will explore using Lua to define AI, not only in our *Take Away* game but in a larger context as well, covering such subjects as pathfinding and finite state machines.

THE APPEARANCE OF INTELLIGENCE

Artificial intelligence in games can exist in many ways, because many types of games can be created. AI can be used to determine the next best move in a board game, to place a bet in a poker game, to determine if a dealer will "hit" in blackjack, and to determine the best path through a debris-strewn battlefield.

We will touch on some basic elements of AI in this chapter and how they relate to the examples we've been exploring throughout this book. We'll also explore some other examples as well, such as pathfinding and some decision making in a card game. By looking through the examples, you should come away with a good grasp on how Lua can be used to control the computer opponents in your game—and from that knowledge, you should be well on your way toward building an AI system for your own game.

The key concept to get a handle on, in the context of game development, is that AI doesn't necessarily mean intelligence at all. Rather, it means the appearance of intelligence. For the player, AI is usually seen as the mechanisms that provide some challenge in a game (as well as some automation to complex entities under the player's control).

When you are constructing a system to control an enemy that will provide a challenge for the player, the player's perception of that enemy is of the utmost importance. The computer-controlled enemy doesn't need to actually go through all the thinking motions of assessing all the risks in the environment before it determines the best tactics to move on the player—rather, it should feel to the player that these things are happening under the surface, and that the result is a visceral challenge that keeps the player on his toes.

For years, there have been debates on the pros and cons of AI "cheating"—that is, giving a computer opponent access to game-world information that is not available to the player (such as precise movement tracking or knowing where the doors and keys are in a maze level). Our position on that subject is that it's really a non-issue: it's the player's experience that is at the core. If some cheating can provide the sense of a more engaging and exciting opponent without penalizing the player, then just go for it. It's all about the appearance of intelligence, after all, and you want your enemies and the challenge in your game to feel intelligent and just hard enough so the player can struggle but will prevail by the skin of his teeth.

BLACKJACK

One area of AI that is particularly well suited for Lua scripting is in creating computer opponents for card games. Card games deal with a random, finite "stack" of elements (the cards), in both a deck and a player's hand. Card games are governed by clear rules of valuation (this hand is better than that hand), and Lua is a good tool to manage this type of thinking.

ON THE CD

Let's begin our chapter on AI with a simple example: blackjack against a dealer. If you look at the resources for this chapter on the CD-ROM, you'll see a small blackjack game that pits you against the dealer. Before we dive into the simple AI for this example, let's look at how we set up the cards. We begin by creating the following list of constants that will make our later code more easily readable:

```
--blackjack constants
SPADE = 1
DIAMOND = 2
CLUB = 3
HEART = 4
```

```
ACE = 1
JACK = 11
QUEEN = 12
KING = 13
```

From here, we can now create a virtual deck of cards within a Lua table, as follows:

```
function CreateDeck()
    curDeckLocation = 1
    myDeck = {}
    cardNum = 1
    for suit = SPADE, HEART do
        for card = ACE, KING do
            myDeck[cardNum] = {}
            myDeck[cardNum].suit = suit
            myDeck[cardNum].card = card
            cardNum = cardNum + 1
        end
    end
end
```

This function walks through all the possible cards and creates one instance of each card (you could do this several times to create a "shoe" with several decks). Our next step is to shuffle the deck of cards, as follows:

```
function ShuffleDeck()
    shuffleValue = 1000
    for indx = 1, shuffleValue do
        card1 = math.random(1,52)
        card2 = math.random(1,52)
        hold = {}
        hold = myDeck[card1]
        myDeck[card1] = myDeck[card2]
        myDeck[card2] = hold
    end
end
```

This function iterates through 1,000 times, each time, taking two random cards in the deck and swapping their position. The net result is a deck that is effectively randomized, so that if you "pull" cards off the top, one at a time, you'll have a random distribution. See Figure 13.1.

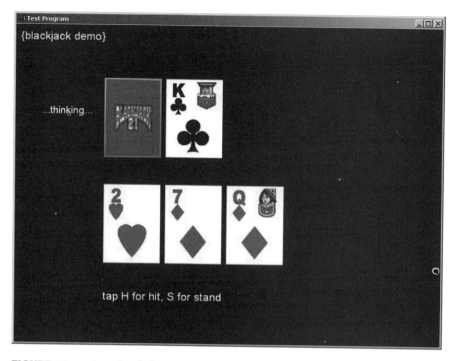

FIGURE 13.1   Our simple blackjack game controls the dealer against a single player.

Finally, we initialize the hands of the human player and the dealer with the following function:

```
function InitHands()
    theHand = {}
    theHand[DEALER] = {}
    theHand[HUMAN] = {}
end
```

This function sets up a nested table to hold the hand of each player. All a hand is, in this example, is the index number of the card in the myDeck table. We can then draw a card from the deck with the following simple function:

```
function GetCard(player)
    if curDeckLocation > 52 then
        print("Out of cards! Start new game!")
    else
        table.insert(theHand[player], curDeckLocation)
        DrawHand(player) -- draws the card on the screen
        curDeckLocation = curDeckLocation + 1
```

```
        end
    end
```

We use the variable curDeckLocation to track where we are on in the deck, and that value is simply added to the player's hand table. The DrawHand() function is the function that draws the cards on the screen, and we'll let you explore that rather straightforward function yourself.

With this mechanic, we can now look at the two functions in which we are most interested: valuing the hand and allowing the dealer to "think." In blackjack, the hand can be valued different ways, depending on how many aces you have in your hand. We use the function shown in Listing 13.1 to return the current value of the hand.

LISTING 13.1   The CheckHandValue function

```lua
function CheckHandValue(player)
    myValue = 0
    numAces = 0
    for indx = 1, table.getn(theHand[player]) do
        curCardValue = myDeck[theHand[player][indx]].card
        if curCardValue > 10 then
            curCardValue = 10
        end
        if curCardValue == ACE then
            --we have an ace
            numAces = numAces + 1
        else
            myValue = myValue + curCardValue
        end
    end
    if numAces > 0 then
        --deal with one ace
        if numAces == 1 then
            if myValue + 11 > 21 then
                myValue = myValue + 1
            else
                myValue = myValue + 11
            end
        end
        --deal with two aces
        if numAces == 2 then
            if myValue + 12 > 21 then
                myValue = myValue + 2
```

```
            else
                myValue = myValue + 12
            end
        end
        --deal with three aces
        if numAces == 3 then
            if myValue + 13 > 21 then
                myValue = myValue + 3
            else
                myValue = myValue + 13
            end
        end
        --deal with four aces
        if numAces == 4 then
            if myValue + 14 > 21 then
                myValue = myValue + 4
            else
                myValue = myValue + 14
            end
        end
    end
    return myValue
end
```

In this function, we walk through the cards in a player's hand, setting the value of the card to 10 if it's a face card. If the card is an ace, we don't add it to the total but rather keep a tally of how many aces we have in the hand. After we total the hand (without aces), we process the aces, if there are any. This function goes a little overboard in addressing every possibility, but it gives you a good idea of how it can determine automatically the value of the ace cards based on the current situation.

This function is used in the human player game loop (based on the GUI_KEY_PRESS events in GUI_InGame.lua) to determine if his hand is a bust after taking another card (by pressing the H key).

When the player is done with his hand, it is the dealer's turn. In true Vegas fashion, the dealer's first card is dealt down, but the card value exists in his hand. Once the player presses the S key, the dealer's thinking takes over and is completely encapsulated in the next function:

```
function Think(player)
    result = THINKING
    if CheckHandValue(player) < HOUSE_STAND then
        GetCard(player)
```

```
        else
            result = DONE_THINKING
        end
        if CheckHandValue(player) > 21 then
            result = BUST
        end
        return result
    end
```

This is a very simple example of computer-opponent AI—the value at which the dealer must stand is defined in the constant HOUSE_STAND (which is set to 17—in casinos, dealers are often required to stand on their hand when the value is 17 or higher). The dealer simply compares his value to this value and makes a decision that could lead to one of three results: still thinking, done thinking, or busted.

We use the timer function to handle the looping through the dealer's thinking with the following event code:

```
if eventCode == GUI_TIMER_EXPIRED then
    progress = Think(DEALER)
    if progress == BUST then
        EnableObject(GUI_INGAME + 205, 0, 0)
        gameState = DEALER_DONE
        DrawHand(DEALER)
        ItemCommand(MESSAGE, "SetString", "Dealer busts... YOU
        WIN!!")
    elseif progress == THINKING then
        StartTimer(1.5)
    else
        --dealer is done...process results
        EnableObject(GUI_INGAME + 205, 0, 0)
        gameState = DEALER_DONE
        DrawHand(DEALER)
        if CheckHandValue(HUMAN) > CheckHandValue(DEALER) then
            theScore = tostring(CheckHandValue(HUMAN))
            ItemCommand(MESSAGE, "SetString",
            string.format("%s%s%s","You win the hand with a ",
            theScore, "!"))
        else
            theScore = tostring(CheckHandValue(DEALER))
            ItemCommand(MESSAGE, "SetString",
            string.format("%s%s%s","Dealer takes the hand with a
            score of ", theScore, "."))
        end
        EnableObject(GUI_INGAME + 202, 1, 1)
```

```
        end
    end
```

This section of code simply calls the `Think()` function and then, based on the returned results, reports the results. If the result is "still thinking," the timer is started and this game loop is re-executed.

In the previous example, we can see a simple use of AI that provides the same level of challenge as a dealer on the Vegas strip who must also follow the house rules for standing and hitting.

TIC-TAC-TOE

Let's return for a moment to our tic-tac-toe game from the previous chapter to see how we can create a computer opponent for us, this time, using C++ to create a LuaGlue function that will allow us to determine the player's moves.

First, let's look at what we need to do to integrate a computer opponent into the two-player tic-tac-toe game. In the human-only game, we determined where on the board the player was placing his symbol by using the next function:

```
thePos = GetBoardLocation(GetMousePosition())
```

This function retuned a value from 1 to 9 to indicate where the move was to be placed, and a value of −1 if there is no valid move possible. After this, the `MakeMove()` function deals with drawing the symbol, checking for a win, and managing on-screen text. Ideally, our computer opponent would be powered by a single function that works very much like the preceding function and returns the same values. That way, we can integrate it into the same `MakeMove()` function to reuse as much existing script as possible.

The LuaGlue function looks like the following example:

```
thePos = GetMove(myBoard[1],myBoard[2],myBoard[3],myBoard[4],
myBoard[5],myBoard[6],myBoard[7],myBoard[8],myBoard[9],OH)
```

In this function, we pass in the board and the current player (we must pass in the table manually, because C can't deal with Lua tables directly as parameters to LuaGlue functions). See Figure 13.2.

FIGURE 13.2 We've taken our tic-tac-toe game from the last chapter and added a LuaGlue function that allows us to play against a computer-controlled opponent.

In our tic-tac-toe example, we are going to make the O player computer controlled, and the X player human. When the game initializes, it randomly assigns who moves first. We simply add the following script immediately after initialization:

```
if eventCode == GUI_ENTER_INTERFACE then
    InitGame()
    if curTurn == OH then
        StartTimer(1.5)
    end
end
```

This script checks to see if the current player is the OH player, and if so, we start a timer. Then, at the timer event, we handle it with the code shown in Listing 13.2.

LISTING 13.2 Script for handling a timer event

```
if eventCode == GUI_TIMER_EXPIRED then
    MakeMove()
end
```

This is really all we need to change in our GUI_InGame.lua logic. Now the revised MakeMove() function looks like this:

```lua
function MakeMove()

    if curTurn == EX then
        --X human player
        thePos = GetBoardLocation(GetMousePosition())
    else
        --O AI player
        thePos = GetMove(myBoard[1],myBoard[2],myBoard[3],myBoard[4],
        myBoard[5],myBoard[6],myBoard[7],myBoard[8],myBoard[9],OH)
    end
    if thePos ~= -1 then
        --turn on the space
        EnableObject(curTurn + thePos, 1, 1)
        --change text
        if curTurn == EX then
            ItemCommand(GUI_INGAME + 250, "SetString", "O's turn: AI
            thinking")
        else
            ItemCommand(GUI_INGAME + 250, "SetString", "X's turn: left
            click to place")
        end
        --now update the table
        myBoard[thePos] = curTurn
        --check for win
        theWinner = -1
        theWinner, slashID = WinCheck()
        if theWinner == -1 then
            --no winner
            --now swap turns
            if curTurn == OH then
                curTurn = EX
            else
                curTurn = OH
            end
        elseif theWinner == 0 then
            --cat's game
            EnableObject(GUI_INGAME + 210, 1, 1)
            EnableObject(GUI_INGAME + 240, 1, 1)
            EnableObject(GUI_INGAME + 250, 0, 0)
        else
            --we have a winner
            EnableObject(GUI_INGAME + 250, 0, 0)
```

```
                    EnableObject(GUI_INGAME + 240, 1, 1)
                    EnableObject(slashID, 1, 1)
                    if theWinner == EX then
                        EnableObject(GUI_INGAME + 220, 1, 1)
                    else
                        EnableObject(GUI_INGAME + 230, 1, 1)
                    end
                end
            end
            if (curTurn == OH) and (theWinner == -1) then
                StartTimer(1.5)
            end
        end
    end
```

The previous function is the same as that used in our two-player version of the game, with the exception of the check at the start of the function. If the player is human (EX), then we'll process the GetBoardLocation() function; if the player is computer-controlled, we then call the LuaGlue GetMove() function.

At the end of this function, we test to see if the current player (we've switched turns already) is the computer player and whether is the game is in progress. If so, we then call the timer function (we do this just to allow the human to feel like the computer player is taking some time to act—it feels more "natural"), which triggers the next MakeMove() call.

GetMove() LuaGlue

AI move searches have many approaches, from simple to complex. Tic-tac-toe is a simple game, so a brute-force, rules-based solution seems best. This implementation also allows for the reader to tinker with the process easily to improve the performance of the computer player. Next, we have the start of the function in C:

```
extern "C" int TTT_GetMove(lua_State *L)
{
    cLua *lua = g_pBase->GetLua();
    int move = -1;
    int argNum = 1;
    int board[9];
    for(int i=0; i<9; i++)
    {
        board[i] = (int) lua->GetNumberArgument(argNum++, 0);
    }
    int sidetomove = (int) lua->GetNumberArgument(argNum++, 0);
```

As with the previous function, we build the board to be evaluated by getting the nine values from the caller. This function requires us to know who is to move so that we can search for a move for that player. We then need to make a list of the legal moves, as shown in the following script:

```
std::list<int> legalMoves;
for(i=0; i<9; i++)
{
    if(board[i] == 0)
        legalMoves.push_back(i);
}
```

All the legal moves are placed into an STL list to process each one in the next step. Each slot of the board is examined, and if it is an open space, it is added to the legal move list. Once this is done, we can search through this list using the following code:

```
int bestVal = 0;
std::list<int>::iterator it = legalMoves.begin();
while(it != legalMoves.end())
{
    // look at each winning move and count the
    // spaces (with this move made) that are in it
    for(i=0; i<8; i++)
    {
        int val = 0;
        if(((*it) == winningPositions[i][0]) ||
            (board[winningPositions[i][0]] == sidetomove))
            ++val;
        if(((*it) == winningPositions[i][1]) ||
            (board[winningPositions[i][1]] == sidetomove))
            ++val;
        if(((*it) == winningPositions[i][2]) ||
            (board[winningPositions[i][2]] == sidetomove))
            ++val;
        if((board[winningPositions[i][0]] != sidetomove) &&
            (board[winningPositions[i][0]] != 0))
            val = -1;
            if((board[winningPositions[i][1]] != sidetomove) &&
                (board[winningPositions[i][1]] != 0))
            val = -1;
        if((board[winningPositions[i][2]] != sidetomove) &&
            (board[winningPositions[i][2]] != 0))
            val = -1;
```

```
            if(val > bestVal)
            {
                move = (*it);
                bestVal = val;
            }
        }

        ++it;
    }
```

Each legal move is evaluated and given a score based on how good a move it is and is used to choose the best move from all possible moves. This score is calculated by counting how many matching slots in a winning combination the move would make. The score is overridden if the winning combination cannot be made because the opponent owns one of the slots. After the score is generated, the score is compared to the best score found so far. If the new best score is better than the previous best, the new score is recorded as the best for future tests. This mechanism, called "king of the hill," is useful for many other applications. When all combinations have been checked, it is time to move on to the next step, which is checking for a "no move available" condition, as shown in the next example:

```
    if(move == -1)
    {
        move = (*legalMoves.begin());
    }

    lua->PushNumber(move+1); // adjust for 1 base in Lua code
    return 1;
}
```

If no move has been found that the evaluator likes, you return to the first legal move in the list. This function is only the beginning—there are lots of ways to improve the computer player's "brains." One suggestion to get you thinking is to put in some sort of defense check: check if the move would prevent a win by the other player and rate that move very highly.

TAKE AWAY

Now let's turn our attention to our *Take Away* game and walk through the various control mechanisms, shown in Figure 13.3, used to direct the various types of enemies the player will encounter in the game.

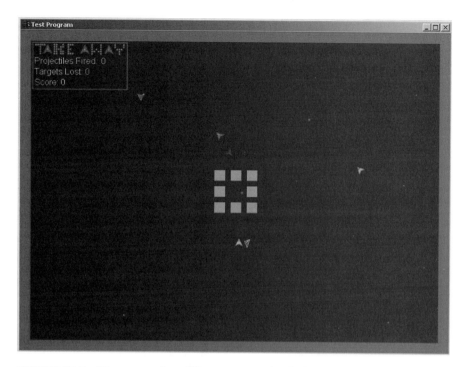

FIGURE 13.3 We process four different types of AI behavior in *Take Away*.

The hub of the enemy's intellect is contained in the EnemyFacing() function, called in the GUI_TIMER_EXPIRED event in an association with the REACT setting of an enemy. As a whole, it is one of the most complex functions in the game. However, EnemyFacing() can be easily separated into four distinct sections, each managing a different AI type. Each utilizes EnemyFacing() to locate a specific destination (we will call it a "goal") and then employs SetTravelDirection(indx, tX, tY) to orient the ship toward that goal. In *Take Away*, we've established four distinct classes of enemies: Box Grabbers, Shooters, Rammers, and Hybrids.

Box Grabbers

```
function EnemyFacing(indx)
--indx is the myEnemies table index assigned to the enemy
    if myEnemies[indx].ID ~= nil then
        if myEnemies[indx].TYPE == 1 then --Box grabbers
            for i = 1,targetCount do
                if myEnemies[indx].E_TOW == "no" then --Enemy not towing
                    if myTargets[i].T_TOW == "no" then --Target free
                        SetTravelDirection(indx, myTargets[i].T_X + 10,
```

```
                            myTargets[i].T_Y + 10)
                    end
            end
        end
```

As seen in the previous script, the Box Grabber's sole objective is to tow away supply crates. Without regard for its own safety, a Box Grabber will speed toward a motionless crate, attach to it, and tow it off of the screen (returning immediately to begin the cycle again). This action is accomplished by searching through the `myTargets` table in search of a free crate. Once one is located, we establish the center of the crate using the `T_X` value, `T_Y` value, and half the distance of the crate's dimensions. We then call `SetTravelDirection(indx, tX, tY)`, subbing in the coordinates of the crate's center for the coordinates of the goal (`tX` and `tY`).

Shooters

```
elseif myEnemies[indx].TYPE == 2 then --Shooters
    SetTravelDirection(indx, myX + 10, myY + 10)
    --Enemy shooting script (see EnemyRespawn(indx) function)
    myEnemies[indx].FIRE = myEnemies[indx].FIRE + 1
    if myEnemies[indx].FIRE == enemyFireInterval then
        FireProjectile(indx, myEnemies[indx].XTHRUST,
        myEnemies[indx].YTHRUST)
        myEnemies[indx].FIRE = 0
    end
```

The Shooter's only intention is to eliminate the player by firing an unlimited amount of projectiles at the player's ship. The call to `SetTravelDirection(indx, tX, tY)` considers the significant coordinates of the human ship to be its goal. The unique feature of the Shooter-related script is the portion that controls the firing of the enemy's projectiles. Every time `EnemyFacing()` is called by a Shooter, its `FIRE` parameter is incremented. When the `FIRE` parameter reaches the `enemyFireInterval`, `FireProjectile(ship, xThrust, yThrust)` is called and the `FIRE` parameter is reset. This system allows for a fixed period between shots that is adjustable based on the `enemyFireInterval` and the `REACT` parameter of the enemy. Such flexibility permits the AI to become increasingly difficult as the session progresses in line with the game's design.

Rammers

```
elseif myEnemies[indx].TYPE == 3 then --Rammers
    SetTravelDirection(indx, myX + 10, myY + 10)
```

The simplicity of the preceding AI might lead one to believe that the Rammer is the least formidable opponent in the game. After all, from this small section of scripting, it appears as if the Rammer is simply a Shooter deprived of projectile-firing capability. However, the advantage of the Rammer lies in its maximum speed (MAX value). With a top speed that is initially twice that of other enemies, the Rammer packs more of an arsenal than what might be deduced from the `EnemyFacing()` function.

Hybrids

A Hybrid combines the towing capabilities of a Box Grabber with the projectile-firing facilities of a Shooter. The factor that determines whether a Hybrid will pursue a crate or shoot at the player is simply the distance from each. The basic logic of the Hybrid compares the distance from the player with the distance from the nearest target and chooses the closest option. Once it has determined the nearest entity, it will call `SetTravelDirection(indx, tX, tY)`, substituting in the appropriate goal's coordinates, as shown next:

```
elseif myEnemies[indx].TYPE == 4 then --Hybrids
    if myEnemies[indx].E_TOW == "no" then --Enemy not towing
        --Determine distance from player
        playerDistance = math.sqrt(((myEnemies[indx].EX + 10) -
        (myX + 10))^2 + ((myEnemies[indx].EY + 10) - (myY +
        10))^2)
        targetDistance = 10000
```

Initially, we find the distance between the center of the Hybrid ship and the center of the player's ship (`playerDistance`) by using a simple variation of the Pythagorean Theorem. Then we set the variable `targetDistance` to an astronomical value. To understand the reasoning for this last step, we must look further into the Hybrid logic, shown in the following script:

```
for i = 1,targetCount do
    if myTargets[i].T_TOW == "no" then --Target free
        --Determine distance from closest target
        tempTargetDistance = math.sqrt((
        (myEnemies[indx].EX + 10) - (myTargets[i].T_X +
        10))^2 + ((myEnemies[indx].EY + 10) —
        (myTargets[i].T_Y + 10))^2)
        if tempTargetDistance < targetDistance then
            targetDistance = tempTargetDistance
```

Next, we begin a `for` loop that will cycle through all of the crates and find the Hybrid's relative distance from each (`tempTargetDistance`). If the distance from the current crate (`tempTargetDistance`) is smaller than the distance from the previously closest crate (`targetDistance`), the current crate's distance will become the new standard by which the following crates' distances will be judged. The huge value that we initially placed on the `targetDistance` ensures that a crate distance will be found at a closer distance and, thus, will allow for a legitimate comparison between the distances of the closest crate and the player's ship, as shown in the following script:

```
                        --Evaluate for the closest option
                        if playerDistance < targetDistance then
                            tX = myX + 10
                            tY = myY + 10
                            --Enemy shooting script
                            myEnemies[indx].FIRE =
                            myEnemies[indx].FIRE + 1
                            if myEnemies[indx].FIRE ==
                            enemyFireInterval then
                                FireProjectile(indx,
                                myEnemies[indx].XTHRUST,
                                myEnemies[indx].YTHRUST)
                                myEnemies[indx].FIRE = 0
                            end
                        else
                            tX = myTargets[i].T_X + 10
                            tY = myTargets[i].T_Y + 10
                        end
                    end
                else
                    tX = myX + 10
                    tY = myY + 10
                end
            end
        end
        SetTravelDirection(indx, tX, tY)
    end
end
end
end
```

If the player's ship is closest, the Hybrid will set it as its goal and step through the enemy shooting script. If the crate is closer, the Hybrid will choose to set it as its goal and disregard the player's ship. Although the script may appear complex at first glance, it truly is a simple system for making a factor-based decision.

Managing Travel Direction

After successfully exploring the `EnemyFacing(indx)` function, only one more function remains to investigate in the realm of the artificial intelligence in *Take Away*. Of course, the tool being discussed is `SetTravelDirection(indx, tX, tY)`. Although we've observed its frequent use, we have not examined its components and developed an understanding of its core structure. Specifically, `SetTravelDirection(indx, tX, tY)` alters the `ROT` value of an enemy based on the mathematical relationship between the enemy's coordinates and those of its goal. The `myEnemies` `ROT` value is then used in `DrawEnemyShip()` to appropriately alter the `XTHRUST` and `YTHRUST` values to cause the enemy ship to track and pursue its goal. This function can be divided into three distinct parts based on the comparison of the x-coordinates of the centers of the two entities. The first section manages the instances when the goal's x-coordinate is less than the enemy's, as shown in the following script:

```
function SetTravelDirection(indx, tX, tY)
--indx is the myEnemies table index assigned to the enemy
--tX is the X coordinate of the goal (target or player's ship)
--tY is the Y coordinate of the goal (target or player's ship)
    if tX < myEnemies[indx].EX then
        if tY < myEnemies[indx].EY then
            if (myEnemies[indx].EY - tY) > 150 then
                if (myEnemies[indx].EX - tX) > 150 then
                    myEnemies[indx].ROT = 8 --Up/left
                else
                    myEnemies[indx].ROT = 1 --Up
                end
            elseif (myEnemies[indx].EY - tY) > 30 then
                myEnemies[indx].ROT = 8 --Up/left
            else
                myEnemies[indx].ROT = 7 --Left
            end
        elseif tY == myEnemies[indx].EY then
            myEnemies[indx].ROT = 7 --Left
        elseif tY > myEnemies[indx].EY then
            if (tY - myEnemies[indx].EY) > 150 then
                if (myEnemies[indx].EX - tX) > 150 then
                    myEnemies[indx].ROT = 6 --Down/left
                else
                    myEnemies[indx].ROT = 5 --Down
                end
            elseif (tY - myEnemies[indx].EY) > 30 then
                myEnemies[indx].ROT = 6 --Down/left
            else
```

```
                myEnemies[indx].ROT = 7 --Left
        end
    end
```

A smaller segment is devoted to the occasions where the x-coordinates are completely equal, shown next:

```
elseif tX == myEnemies[indx].EX then
    if tY <= myEnemies[indx].EY then
        myEnemies[indx].ROT = 1 --Up
    else
        myEnemies[indx].ROT = 5 --Down
    end
```

The previous section manages the occurrences in which the goal's x-coordinate is greater than the enemy's. However, because this section is so similar in structure to the first section, we will not cover it here. After reading the brief synopsis of the first portion, a quick look at the scripts will reveal the third portion to be rather self-explanatory.

Collision Detection

We now move onward to the final major segment of the InGame processes: collision detection. The three functions that handle the collisions between the various entities are EnemyTowCheck(), EnemyHitCheck(), and CasualtyCheck(). These LuaSupport.lua functions are the most complex, and perhaps the most vital, components of the InGame construction. Although each has its own distinctive characteristics, they all have a similar configuration. We begin our exploration of collision detection with EnemyTowCheck() (found in LuaSupport.lua and shown in the next example). It determines if a Box Grabber or Hybrid comes in contact with a free crate, resulting in the towing of that crate by the enemy ship.

```
function EnemyTowCheck()
    for i = 1,enemyCount do
        if myEnemies[i].ID ~= nil then
            j = 1
            while ((myEnemies[i].E_TOW == "no") and (j < (targetCount +
            1))) do
                if (myTargets[j].T_TOW == "no") and ((myEnemies[i].TYPE
                == 1) or (myEnemies[i].TYPE == 4)) then --Enemies are
                box grabbers or hybrids & the target is free for towing
```

The entire body of the function is contained within the bounds of a `for` loop that walks through every enemy in the game. After making sure that the enemy is present in the game, we continue on to create a `while` statement that will progress through the crates present in the game. The `while` statement is also based on the E_TOW status of the current enemy. These two factors (the E_TOW status and the number of crates in the game) permit the loop to progress through all of the crates in the game while continually verifying that the current enemy is not in possession of a crate. The use of the `while` control structure is important because the operations of the loop, as we will see, have the ability to change the E_TOW status. In a `for` loop, the E_TOW status would be evaluated only once (at the beginning of the statement), which would result in the loop processing dated information. Viewing the next segment of the function will assist us in explaining this concept:

```
if ((myEnemies[i].EX + 20) < myTargets[j].T_X) or
(myEnemies[i].EX > (myTargets[j].T_X + 20)) or
((myEnemies[i].EY + 20) < myTargets[j].T_Y) or
(myEnemies[i].EY > (myTargets[j].T_Y + 20)) then
    --No collision
else
    --Collision
    --Indexes the ID of each entity into the
    appropriate portion of the other's table
    myTargets[j].T_TOW = myEnemies[i].ID
    myEnemies[i].E_TOW = myTargets[j].T_ID
end
end
j = j + 1
end
end
end
end
```

Using a calculation based on where the two entities are *not* positioned, we determine the occurrences of collisions. If a collision occurs, the table indexes of the entities are stored into the other's tow-based parameter. Finally, the index key for the incrementing of the crates is increased. In summary, the general construction of the function works as follows: for each enemy, every available crate is checked for a collision. In the event that a collision does occur, the E_TOW and T_TOW values of the respective entities are changed to declare their newfound connection, and the `while` statement terminates its loop, resulting in the next enemy in the `for` loop stepping up for collision inspection.

This simple construction is seen also in the EnemyHitCheck() function (found in LuaSupport.lua). Because the two functions are so similar, the portion that we will focus on will be the result of the collision between a player's projectile and an enemy ship, as shown next:

```
--Collision
if myEnemies[i].E_TOW ~= "no" then --Enemy
    was towing
        for k = 1,targetCount do
            if myTargets[k].T_TOW ==
            myEnemies[i].ID then
                --Makes the target available for
                towing again
                myTargets[k].T_TOW = "no"
            end
        end
end
```

When a collision occurs, we check for the presence of a crate that the enemy might have been towing. If one is found, it is "dropped"—it remains stationary in its last position. The important area here is to notice that the T_TOW parameter is set to no because the target is not off of the screen; it doesn't warrant done status. Finally, the two objects are dealt with, as shown in Listing 13.3.

LISTING 13.3   Deleting the enemy and clearing its table

```
--Deletes the enemy and clears its table

indexes
DeleteItem(myEnemies[i].ID)
    myEnemies[i].XTHRUST = nil
    myEnemies[i].YTHRUST = nil
    myEnemies[i].ROT = nil
    myEnemies[i].EX = nil
    myEnemies[i].EY = nil
    myEnemies[i].ID = nil
    myEnemies[i].E_TOW = "no"
    myEnemies[i].FIRE = nil
    --Respawns the enemy if the game is not over
    if targetDoneCounter ~= targetCount then
        UpdateScore(myEnemies[i].TYPE)
        EnemyRespawn(i)
    end
    --Deletes the projectile and clears its table
```

```
                                indexes
                                DeleteItem(myProjectiles[j].PROJ_ID)
                                myProjectiles[j].PROJ_X = nil
                                myProjectiles[j].PROJ_Y = nil
                                myProjectiles[j].PROJ_XTH = nil
                                myProjectiles[j].PROJ_YTH = nil
                                myProjectiles[j].PROJ_ID = nil
                                myProjectiles[j].PROJ_SHIP = nil
                            end
                        end
                    end
                    j = j + 1
                end
            end
        end
    end
```

The sprites of both the projectile and the enemy ship are deleted, and their individual table allocations are primarily set to nil. Like T_TOW, however, the E_TOW parameter must be reset to indicate its available status. Also occurring at this time is the updating of the scoreboard (see UpdateScore(enemyType) in GUI_InGame.lua). If the game is not finished, EnemyRespawn(indx) is also called using the specified index of the recently deceased enemy. This system guarantees a consistent flow of enemies in the game, as well as the conservation of the processor (because the data of only a few enemies must be stored simultaneously).

The final function to be considered in the realm of collision detection is CasualtyCheck(), which searches for the collisions between the player's ship and hazardous entities (enemies and enemy projectiles). Whereas EnemyHitCheck() and EnemyTowCheck() were called by the GUI_TIMER_EXPIRED event, this function is utilized by the DrawShip(myRot, x, y) function, which is called only when the player is "alive." The function is divided into halves—the first half deals with ship collisions and the second half manages projectile collisions. Because the last two-thirds of the ship-collision portion are nearly identical to the EnemyHitCheck() structure, and because the second half of this function is closely related to the first, we will discuss only the first few lines of the first half, as shown in the next example:

```
function CasualtyCheck()
    --Collisions with enemies
    i = 1
    while ((alive == "yes") and (i < (enemyCount + 1))) do
        if myEnemies[i].ID ~= nil then
            if ((myEnemies[i].EX + 20) < myX) or (myEnemies[i].EX > (myX
```

```
        + 20)) or ((myEnemies[i].EY + 20) < myY) or (myEnemies[i].EY
        > (myY + 20)) then
            --No collision
        else
            --Collision
            --Delete the player's ship
            DeleteItem(GUI_RUNTIME_SPRITES + 100)
            alive = "no"
```

The main parts to notice this time through the collision structure are the conditions embedded in the `while` statement. Particularly of note is the inclusion of the `alive` value. This value is necessary because, once again, the value may be altered within the loop itself. Thus, if the player's ship is deleted, this loop will break, and no enemies will be checked for collisions with the player's deleted ship. The second half of this function operates in a similar manner. A quick scanning of the second half of this function in the scripts will prove it easy to understand without extra documentation.

This concludes our illumination of multiple-entity collision-detection functions. Equipped with this last piece of the InGame logic, you may confidently regard your model of the *Take Away* gameplay experience as complete. We have traversed the functions required to power the game, and now it may be easier to understand how each portion of the game interacts with the others. Using a unique assortment of game events, GUI interfaces, functions, tables, global and local variables, and the tools provided by the Lua language, we have constructed an interactive environment that challenges, entertains, and enlightens. Our hope is that the skills and concepts learned in the design of this program will be the building blocks of your own Lua-based creations.

OTHER AI EXAMPLES

ON THE CD

We'll now spend some time looking at some variants to the behaviors that we built into *Take Away*. These variants can be found in the AI Sandbox folder in this chapter's materials on the CD-ROM. The executable for this is the same as for *Take Away*—only the scripts have changed. The demo will take you through eight examples of variant behavior, via changing scripts. You can see how the scripts are selected via the `GUI_MainMenu.lua` button events.

Stationary Track

This example shows how an enemy can hone in on a stationary target. Here, we are using a mechanism similar to what we did in *Take Away* for the enemies that were going after the storage crates. The important function in this example is `Stationary-TrackSetTravelDirection()`. In this function, the enemy will set its facing based on its target, as shown in Listing 13.4.

LISTING 13.4 The `StationaryTrackSetTravelDirection()` function

```
function StationaryTrackSetTravelDirection(indx, tX, tY)
--indx is the myEnemies table index assigned to the enemy
--tX is the X-coordinate of the goal (target or player's ship)
--tY is the Y-coordinate of the goal (target or player's ship)
    if tX < myEnemies[indx].EX then
        if tY < myEnemies[indx].EY then
            if (myEnemies[indx].EY - tY) > 150 then
                if (myEnemies[indx].EX - tX) > 150 then
                    myEnemies[indx].ROT = 8 --Up/left
                else
                    myEnemies[indx].ROT = 1 --Up
                end
            elseif (myEnemies[indx].EY - tY) > 30 then
                myEnemies[indx].ROT = 8 --Up/left
            else
                myEnemies[indx].ROT = 7 --Left
            end
        elseif tY == myEnemies[indx].EY then
            myEnemies[indx].ROT = 7 --Left
        elseif tY > myEnemies[indx].EY then
            if (tY - myEnemies[indx].EY) > 150 then
                if (myEnemies[indx].EX - tX) > 150 then
                    myEnemies[indx].ROT = 6 --Down/left
                else
                    myEnemies[indx].ROT = 5 --Down
                end
            elseif (tY - myEnemies[indx].EY) > 30 then
                myEnemies[indx].ROT = 6 --Down/left
            else
                myEnemies[indx].ROT = 7 --Left
            end
        end
    elseif tX == myEnemies[indx].EX then
        if tY <= myEnemies[indx].EY then
            myEnemies[indx].ROT = 1 --Up
        else
            myEnemies[indx].ROT = 5 --Down
        end
```

```
            elseif tX > myEnemies[indx].EX then
                if tY < myEnemies[indx].EY then
                    if (myEnemies[indx].EY - tY) > 150 then
                        if (tX - myEnemies[indx].EX) > 150 then
                            myEnemies[indx].ROT = 2 --Up/right
                        else
                            myEnemies[indx].ROT = 1 --Up
                        end
                    elseif (myEnemies[indx].EY - tY) > 30 then
                        myEnemies[indx].ROT = 2 --Up/right
                    else
                        myEnemies[indx].ROT = 3 --Right
                    end
                elseif tY == myEnemies[indx].EY then
                    myEnemies[indx].ROT = 3 --Right
                elseif tY > myEnemies[indx].EY then
                    if (tY - myEnemies[indx].EY) > 150 then
                        if (tX - myEnemies[indx].EX) > 150 then
                            myEnemies[indx].ROT = 4 --Down/right
                        else
                            myEnemies[indx].ROT = 5 --Down
                        end
                    elseif (tY - myEnemies[indx].EY) > 30 then
                        myEnemies[indx].ROT = 4 --Down/right
                    else
                        myEnemies[indx].ROT = 3 --Right
                    end
                end
            end
        end
```

This function uses a brute-force method to see in which of the 45-degree-angle slices the target exists, and then sets the enemy ship's rotation to that quadrant. In the next chapter, you'll see a much different approach to the same problem.

Proximity Track

In this demo, we place two supply crates randomly in a game world that is occupied by a single enemy (of the towing type found in *Take Away*). We can press the 1 key to tell the enemy to target the closest crate and the 2 key to tell it to target the furthest crate from its current position. The target differentiation is handled in the `ProximityTrackEnemyFacing()` function, shown in Listing 13.5.

LISTING 13.5   The `ProximityTrackEnemyFacing()` function

```lua
function ProximityTrackEnemyFacing(indx)
--indx is the myEnemies table index assigned to the enemy
    if (myEnemies[indx].E_TOW == "no") and (desiredTarget ~= "none") then
    --Enemy not towing and seeking target
        if desiredTarget ~= "set" then --Initial run
            --Determine distance from targets
            targetDistance = {}
            for i = 1,targetCount do
                if myTargets[i].T_TOW == "no" then --Target free
                    targetDistance[i] = math.sqrt(((myEnemies[indx].EX +
                        10) - (myTargets[i].T_X + 10))^2 +
                        ((myEnemies[indx].EY + 10) - (myTargets[i].T_Y +
                        10))^2)
                end
            end
            if (targetDistance[1] ~= nil) and (targetDistance[2] ~= nil)
            then
            --Evaluate for the distance options
                if targetDistance[1] < targetDistance[2] then
                    nearIndx = 1
                    farIndx = 2
                else
                    nearIndx = 2
                    farIndx = 1
                end
                if desiredTarget == "near" then
                    tX = myTargets[nearIndx].T_X + 10
                    tY = myTargets[nearIndx].T_Y + 10
                    desiredTarget = "set"
                elseif desiredTarget == "far" then
                    tX = myTargets[farIndx].T_X + 10
                    tY = myTargets[farIndx].T_Y + 10
                    desiredTarget = "set"
                end
                ProximityTrackSetTravelDirection(indx, tX, tY)
            end
        else
            ProximityTrackSetTravelDirection(indx, tX, tY)
        end
    end
end
```

This function relies on a three-state variable, desiredTarget, to determine the current target of the enemy. It begins being set to "none," indicating it is not tracing any target. The enemy ship will simply fly in a straight line out of the game world. The key-press event handlers set this variable to near or far.

We use some algebra to calculate the distance to both targets, and then perform a simple check of the distance values, targetDistance[index], to determine which of the two coordinates is closest. We then load the tX and tY values with the position of the nearest or furthest target, depending on the current state.

Moving Track

In this example, we introduce the player-controlled human ship. The player can turn, thrust, and move the ship—which is the target of the enemy. We use the same approach to determine facing as we did in the stationary example, but this time, the target is moving, so the enemy is always reacting to the player's movement. This action is handled in the function MovingTrackSetTravelDirection(), which sets the rotation quadrant of the enemy with the target, whose position has the potential to change every time cycle.

Anticipation Track

In the realm of aerial dogfighting, anticipating a plane's movement so that you can better hit it with your weapons is called deflection shooting. It is nothing more than the human pilot performing some on-the-fly geometric calculations (mostly by feel and experience) to estimate where the enemy plane will be in the time it takes his bullets to fly through the air.

In this example, we add this capability to the enemy, as shown in Figure 13.4. We begin with the capabilities of the last example, but we add the ability of the enemy to anticipate a point ahead of where the human-controlled ship is moving.

This behavior is handled in the AnticipationTrackSetTravelDirection() function. This function is the same as the function described in the previous section but with some extra calculations at the start, as shown in Listing 13.6.

LISTING 13.6   The AnticipationTrackSetTravelDirection() function

```
local enemyDistance = math.sqrt((((myX + 10) - (myEnemies[indx].EX +
10))^2 + ((myY + 10) - (myEnemies[indx].EY + 10))^2)
local enemyRate = math.sqrt(((myEnemies[indx].XTHRUST)^2) +
((myEnemies[indx].YTHRUST)^2))
local time = enemyDistance / enemyRate

local playerRate = math.sqrt(((myXThrust)^2) + ((myYThrust)^2))
local playerDistance = playerRate * time
```

FIGURE 13.4   In this demo, the computer-controlled enemy ship anticipates the movement vector of the human-controlled ship.

```lua
if playerDistance > 25 then
    playerDistance = 25
end
local playerXVector = math.sqrt(((playerDistance)^2) --
((myYThrust)^2))
local playerYVector = math.sqrt(((playerDistance)^2) --
((myXThrust)^2))
local dir = GetTravelDirection(myXThrust, myYThrust)
if dir == 1 then --Up
    tY = tY - (playerDistance)
elseif dir == 2 then --Up/right
    tX = tX + (playerXVector)
    tY = tY - (playerYVector)
elseif dir == 3 then --Right
    tX = tX + (playerDistance)
elseif dir == 4 then --Down/right
    tX = tX + (playerXVector)
    tY = tY + (playerYVector)
elseif dir == 5 then --Down
    tY = tY + (playerDistance)
```

```
    elseif dir == 6 then --Down/left
        tX = tX - (playerXVector)
        tY = tY + (playerYVector)
    elseif dir == 7 then --Left
        tX = tX - (playerDistance)
    elseif dir == 8 then --Up/left
        tX = tX - (playerXVector)
        tY = tY - (playerYVector)
    end
    SetItemPosition(GUI_RUNTIME_SPRITES + 150, tX, tY, 4, 4)
```

This extra script uses some basic geometric algebra to determine a point ahead of the human player's ship's movement vector, based on rotation, speed, and how far away the enemy is. The script modifies the tx and tY values to create a new, dynamically changing target value that becomes the position that the enemy is trying to reach.

In the previous example, it was fairly easy to fly your ship and evade the enemy, and this was all the logic that we put into the *Take Away* game. In this example, you'll find that it's much harder to escape colliding with the enemy, because the enemy now has knowledge of your ship's movement patterns, and the update speed of the program (controlled by the StartTimer() function calls) is a touch quicker than we can think. With this example, you can see how a simple adjustment to an existing process can give the appearance of even more intelligence.

Turret Fire

In this example, we create a turret that will rotate to face the closest enemy (either computer controlled or human controlled) and will fire at the enemy. The turret determines it's facing the same way the enemy ship did when it was considering a moving target (you could increase the intelligence of the turret by allowing it to anticipate enemy position by incorporating the approach described in the previous section).

The turret chooses the closest enemy within the TurretFireTurretFacing() function, shown in Listing 13.7.

LISTING 13.7   The TurretFireTurretFacing() function

```
function TurretFireTurretFacing()
    --Determine distance from player
    playerDistance = math.sqrt(((turX + 10) - (myX + 10))^2 + ((turY +
    10) - (myY + 10))^2)
    enemyDistance = 10000
    for i = 1,enemyCount do
```

```
            if myEnemies[i].ID ~= nil then --Enemy exists
                --Determine distance from closest enemy
                tempEnemyDistance = math.sqrt(((turX + 10) - (myEnemies[i].EX
                + 10))^2 + ((turY + 10) - (myEnemies[i].EY + 10))^2)
                if tempEnemyDistance < enemyDistance then
                    enemyDistance = tempEnemyDistance
                end
                --Evaluate for the closest option
                if playerDistance < enemyDistance then
                    tX = myX + 10
                    tY = myY + 10
                else
                    tX = myEnemies[i].EX + 10
                    tY = myEnemies[i].EY + 10
                end
            else
                tX = myX + 10
                tY = myY + 10
            end
            turFireCounter = turFireCounter + 1
            if turFireCounter == 5 then
                TurretFireFireProjectile(0, 0)
                turFireCounter = 0
            end
        end
        TurretFireSetTravelDirection("turret", tX, tY)
    end
```

This function uses simple right-triangle $a^2 + b^2 = c^2$ algebra to determine the distance values for the player (from the turret) and all enemies active in the game. It then sets the target position to whatever entity is closest and then calculates what direction to turn using the `TurretFireSetTravelDirection()` function. You'll notice that the rotation function is also the same as that used by the enemies, with a simple check at the beginning of the function.

Avoid Fire

In this example, the enemy ship will react to being fired on. If the enemy is not fired on, it will move and act as in the previous example. If a projectile comes close, however, it will turn tail and move away. This behavior is done first in the `AvoidFireEnemyFacing()` function, shown in Listing 13.8.

LISTING 13.8   The AvoidFireEnemyFacing() function

```
function AvoidFireEnemyFacing(indx)
--indx is the myEnemies table index assigned to the enemy
    --Determine distance from projectiles
    projectileDistance = 100
    tX = myX + 10
    tY = myY + 10
    state = "none"
    for i = 1, pCount do
        if myProjectiles[i].PROJ_ID ~= nil then --Projectile exists
            --Determine distance from closest target
            tempProjectileDistance = math.sqrt(((myEnemies[indx].EX + 10)
            - (myProjectiles[i].PROJ_X + 2))^2 + ((myEnemies[indx].EY +
            10) - (myProjectiles[i].PROJ_Y + 2))^2)
            if tempProjectileDistance < projectileDistance then
                projectileDistance = tempProjectileDistance
                tX = myProjectiles[i].PROJ_X + 2
                tY = myProjectiles[i].PROJ_Y + 2
                state = "avoid"
            end
        end
    end
    AvoidFireSetTravelDirection(indx, state, tX, tY)
end
```

The projectileDistance variable sets how close a projectile needs to travel to an enemy (in pixels) before the enemy notices it. We use the same distance calculation as was used previously. If the distance is less than the "notice" distance, then the state of the enemy is set to "avoid."

In the AvoidFireSetTravelDirection() function, we simply then add the following code at the end to handle this situation:

```
        if state == "none" then
            myEnemies[indx].ROT = Rot
        else
                myEnemies[indx].ROT = Rot + 4
            if myEnemies[indx].ROT > 8 then
                dif = myEnemies[indx].ROT - 8
                myEnemies[indx].ROT = 0 + dif
            end
        end
```

This code checks for the state; if the state is set as "avoid," the code will set the rotation to the opposite direction than it would normally be (which is the current target), so that the next movement cycle will begin the "run away" movement. Because it will take several turns for the projectile to move through the 100-pixel "warning box" around the enemy, the enemy will work to avoid the target for several cycles at least.

Protection Fire

This example is nearly identical to that shown in the previous section, with the exception that the enemy ship is trying to move to a position behind a protective wall (not using proper pathfinding—we'll cover that next). If the enemy is fired on, it will attempt to avoid the projectiles and then return to getting behind the wall. This is accomplished using the ProtectionFireEnemyFacing function, shown next:

```
function ProtectionFireEnemyFacing(indx)
--indx is the myEnemies table index assigned to the enemy
    --Determine distance from projectiles
    projectileDistance = 100
    tX = 100
    tY = 300
    state = "protection"
    for i = 1, pCount do
        if myProjectiles[i].PROJ_ID ~= nil then --Projectile exists
            --Determine distance from closest target
            tempProjectileDistance = math.sqrt(((myEnemies[indx].EX + 10)
            - (myProjectiles[i].PROJ_X + 2))^2 + ((myEnemies[indx].EY +
            10) - (myProjectiles[i].PROJ_Y + 2))^2)
            if tempProjectileDistance < projectileDistance then
                projectileDistance = tempProjectileDistance
                tX = myProjectiles[i].PROJ_X + 2
                tY = myProjectiles[i].PROJ_Y + 2
                state = "avoid"
            end
        end
    end
    ProtectionFireSetTravelDirection(indx, state, tX, tY)
end
```

The default tx and ty values are the position behind the wall. This example could be expanded by making that target value dynamic, such as a home base or something like that. The enemy works to avoid fire when it has to and works to "get home" otherwise.

Damage Fire

In this example, we introduce the concept of damage to the enemy, by adding the
`myEnemies[indx].DAMAGE` key to the enemy data table. When the enemy is hit, it will
take damage. In the `DamageFireEnemyFacing()` function, showing Listing 13.9, the
enemy ship assesses its state.

LISTING 13.9   The `DamageFireEnemyFacing()` function

```lua
function DamageFireEnemyFacing(indx)
--indx is the myEnemies table index assigned to the enemy
    --Determine distance from projectiles
    projectileDistance = 100
    tX = myX + 10
    tY = myY + 10
    state = "none"
    if (myEnemies[indx].DAMAGE >= 3) and (myEnemies[indx].DAMAGE < 6)
    then
        print("Now in Avoidance Mode")
        for i = 1, pCount do
            if myProjectiles[i].PROJ_ID ~= nil then --Projectile exists
                --Determine distance from closest target
                tempProjectileDistance = math.sqrt(((myEnemies[indx].EX +
                    10) - (myProjectiles[i].PROJ_X + 2))^2 +
                ((myEnemies[indx].EY + 10) - (myProjectiles[i].PROJ_Y +
                2))^2)
                if tempProjectileDistance < projectileDistance then
                    projectileDistance = tempProjectileDistance
                    tX = myProjectiles[i].PROJ_X + 2
                    tY = myProjectiles[i].PROJ_Y + 2
                    state = "avoid"
                end
            end
        end
    elseif (myEnemies[indx].DAMAGE >= 6) then
        tX = 100
        tY = 300
        state = "protection"
        print("Now in Protection Mode")
    end
    DamageFireSetTravelDirection(indx, state, tX, tY)
end
```

In this example, the enemy doesn't care at all about projectiles whizzing past until it is first hit—at that point, it will avoid the projectiles but will still hone in on the enemy. Once it's received a significant amount of damage, it will seek the protection of the wall, as shown in Figure 13.5.

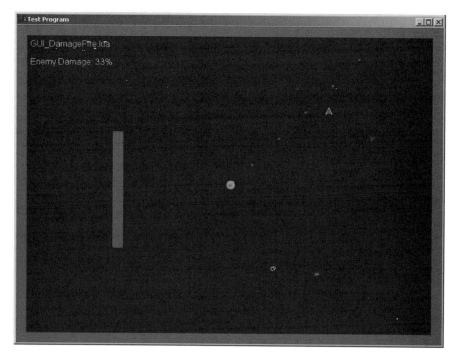

FIGURE 13.5 In this example, the enemy will attempt to flee behind the wall once it's taken some damage.

Next, you'll learn about an interesting way to control the internal states of computer-controlled entities. You might want to come back to this example and see how you could incorporate that system as a way to manage these behaviors.

FINITE STATE MACHINES

A powerful tool in the realm of artificial intelligence is the finite state machine (FSM). This is a "virtual machine" that allows program code to move from state to state. Consider yourself for a moment. Although you are a very complicated bio-mechanical object, in some ways you are like an FSM. You have moods that control how you act. At times you are happy, sad, angry, shy, amorous, and such. Each of these emotional states governs how you act; you behave much differently when you are angry than when you are shy. And certain triggers in the environment can change your state. Imagine being in a thoughtful, contemplative state, reading this book, and walking barefoot through your living room. Now imaging that you stub your toe on the leg of a table—instantly, your state has changed and you will act differently.

This is very similar to how an FSM functions in the computer realm. It is simply a mechanism that handles the logging of the current state, the processing of what happens in a state, and the determination of what causes a change from one state to the next. Think of some generic real-time strategy (RTS) game for a moment—an AI-controlled military unit might have several states: hold position, pursue target, patrol area, and flee. An FSM mechanism will allow you to control the state of that unit (and all other units independently) but still feel confident that you are processing the right actions during your game loop.

Although FSM programming could be a subject of an entire book itself, let's just take a look at how to build a simple FSM in Lua. Consider the following simple function:

```
function ProcessState(currentState, stateTable)
    if stateTable[currentState] ~= nil then
        return stateTable[currentState]()
    end
    return "Error"
end
```

These lines of code are all that's needed to build an FSM. Consider the next four functions:

```
function HoldFunction()
    --unit holds position
    if EnemeyNearby() then
            return "pursue"
      else
        return "hold"
      end
end
function PursueFunction()
    if DistanceToEnemy() > 10 then
        return "to_base"
    elseif DistanceToEnemy() > 5 then
        return "pursue"
```

```
        else
            return "attack"
        end
end
function AttackFunction()
    if EnemyHealth() > 0 then
        return "attack"
    else
        return "to_base"
    end
end

function ToBaseFunction()
    if DistanceToBase() > 0 then
        return "to_base"
    else
        return"hold"
    end
end
```

These functions indicate the actions that can be taken by our imaginary military unit: hold position, pursue enemy, attack enemy, or return to base. Inside these functions, we can write the scripts that define what happens in each of these states, but you can see that we built in, via some imaginary functions, the information we need to control how a state might change.

Now we set up a table (which represents a single unit) as follows:

```
Unit = {}
Unit.CurrentState = "hold"
Unit ["hold"] = HoldFunction
Unit ["pursue"] = PursueFunction
Unit ["attack"] = AttackFunction
Unit ["to_base"] = ToBaseFunction
```

In this table, the keys to the table are the string values that are our representation of the various states of this unit. The values are the actual name of the function, which allows our FSM to process them.

We can now issue the following command in our main game loop to process the actions (and potential state changes) for our unit:

```
Unit.CurrentState = ProcessState(Unit.CurrentState, Unit)
```

This single function will then cause the unit to execute the `CurrentState` function (which is currently "hold" and points to `HoldFunction()`) and then, when done, it will return the new state (which could either be "hold" or "pursue") and set the `CurrentState` key to that value. In this way, you can set up a game loop that walks through an arbitrary number of entities, each with its own state and agenda, and manages the execution of the actions and state changes in just a few lines of script.

PATHFINDING

One of the most important aspects in any game that simulates movement through space (such as an RTS, war game, or action game) is the ability to determine the best way in which a computer-controlled entity can get from point A to point B. This process is called pathfinding. Over the years, many approaches to this problem have been developed, but one of the most widely used and functional is the A* (pronounced "A Star") algorithm. There are many variations and optimizations of this approach, but we'll explore a basic implementation in Lua. From this, you can build a system to suit your needs in your own game.

ON THE CD For this example, refer to the PathFinding folder in this chapter's content on the CD-ROM. The executable is the same as in our *Take Away* game, but the scripts and graphics are unique to this example.

Algorithm Overview

For our discussion, let's think of a grid of meta pixels, like that shown in Figure 13.6, just like what we used for drawing the border in our *Take Away* game and our walls in the previous AI examples. We can call these meta pixels squares or nodes or anything we'd like (in other writing about this algorithm, the term is generally *node*).

This algorithm is made up of two lists: an open list and a closed list. The open list contains all nodes that we should explore as a possible point on the "best path" we are trying to create. The closed list is a more refined list of efficient nodes—within this list lies our path.

For our example, a node contains the following information:

The position in the world: The x- and y-value in our 2D world.

The parent of the node: Where we came from to reach this node.

The G value of the node: The movement cost from the starting node to this node, following the path thus far.

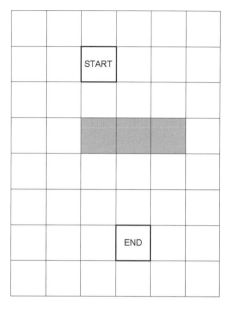

FIGURE 13.6   Here is a small example world with the start and target (end) nodes marked, plus an obstacle between them.

The H value of the node: An estimated movement cost to get from this node to the target node.

The basics of this algorithm follow:

1. Add the starting node to the open list (our "current" node).
2. Look at all the adjacent nodes surrounding the starting node that you can get to (you can't get to a wall square, for example). Add these to the open list, and mark the starting node as the parent of these nodes.
3. Remove the starting node from the open list, and add it to the closed list,
4. Now we start through a loop:
5. Search all nodes on the open list, and grab the node with the lowest F value (which is G + H).
6. Remove that node from the open list, add it to the closed list, and make it our current node.
7. Check all the adjacent nodes to the current node, ignoring the places you can't get to and any nodes already on the closed list.
8. If a node is already on the open list, check the current G value and see if it's lower that what exists already on the open list. If so, we change the parent of that node; if not, we do nothing.

9. We stop when the current node is our target node.
10. We now "walk through" the closed list, starting at the target node, follow the chain of parents, and build our path.
11. Now that we have the algorithm in place, let's look at the Lua implementation.

The Pathfinding Demo

Run the pathfinding demo—you'll see a maze composed of pink squares, as shown in Figure 13.7. The mode is set so that you can enter a starting location. Right-click to place the starting node.

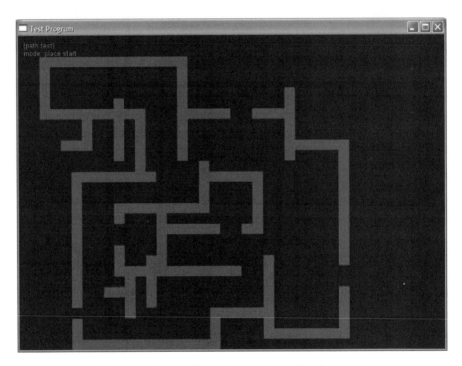

FIGURE 13.7 This maze is a good test for our A* Lua implementation.

Now press the space bar to change modes so that you can place the target node. Right-click again within the maze to place the target. The program will now calculate the best path and draw it using gray squares, as shown in Figure 13.8. You can reset the demo by pressing the Enter key.

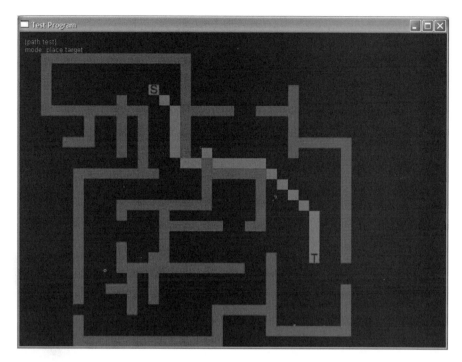

FIGURE 13.8   Once you place the target node, the program will generate the best path.

If you look at LuaSupport.lua, you can see how the world is defined in a large two-dimensional table. You can edit the 1 and 0 values to create your own maze or pathfinding test.

Lua Implementation

In our Lua implementation, we use three tables, all defined in the InitWorld() function:

```
open = {}
closed = {}
path = {}
```

The open and closed tables will hold our nodes, and the path table will hold the direct, usable results of our search: the x- and y-positions of the best path.

When the start position is selected by the player (via a right-click), we place it in the open table with the following function:

```
function DefineStart(myX, myY)
    startX = myX
    startY = myY
    --add start location to first item in open list
    open[1] = {}
    open[1].X = startX
    open[1].Y = startY
    open[1].Parent = 0
    open[1].G = 0
    open[1].H = 0
end
```

Because this is the first node, we don't need to calculate the G, H, or F values at all, and it has no parent.

When the player right-clicks to place the target, we execute a function that starts the pathfinding operation, as follows:

```
function PlaceTarget(myX, myY)
    RefreshWorld()
    DrawStart(startX,startY)
    DefineStart(startX, startY)
    myX = math.floor(myX/20)
    myY = math.floor(myY/20)
    if (myX < maxX-1) and (myX > 1) and (myY < maxY-1) and (myY > 1) then
        if world[myY][myX] ~= 1 then
            DefineTarget(myY, myX)
            DrawTarget(targetX,targetY)
            --is the line below needed?
            --open[1].H = 10*(math.abs(startX-targetX) + math.abs(startY-
            targetY))
            repeat
                targetFound = FindPath()
            until targetFound
            BuildPath()
            DrawPath(path)
        end
    end
end
```

The first part of this function is self-explanatory (and like placing the start); it normalizes the screen coordinates into our world coordinates, redraws the world, and gets us ready to find the path. The meat of this function is the repeat control structure that runs through the FindPath() function, until it sets targetFound to true. After that, we build the path from the closed table and then draw it on screen.

Let's now turn our attention to the FindPath() function, as shown in Listing 13.10.

LISTING 13.10 The FindPath() function

```
function FindPath()
    targetFound = false
    openIndx = FindLowestF(open)
    closedIndx = table.getn(closed) + 1
    table.setn(closed, closedIndx)
    closed[closedIndx] = {}
    closed[closedIndx].X = open[openIndx].X
    closed[closedIndx].Y = open[openIndx].Y
    closed[closedIndx].Parent = open[openIndx].Parent
    closed[closedIndx].G = open[openIndx].G
    closed[closedIndx].H = open[openIndx].H
    --Dump()
    --now check out the squares around it
    curX = closed[closedIndx].X
    curY = closed[closedIndx].Y
    --square1
    if not targetFound then
        myX = curX - 1
        myY = curY - 1
        if (myX > 0) and (myY > 0) and (world[myX][myY] ~= 1) then
            --in bounds and in play
            --does it exist?
            ProcessNode(myX, myY)
        end
    end
    --square2
    if not targetFound then
        myX = curX - 1
        myY = curY
        if (myX > 0) and (myY > 0) and (world[myX][myY] ~= 1) then
            --in bounds and in play
            --does it exist?
            ProcessNode(myX, myY)
        end
    end
    --square3
    if not targetFound then
        myX = curX - 1
        myY = curY + 1
```

```lua
        if (myX > 0) and (myY > 0) and (world[myX][myY] ~= 1) then
            --in bounds and in play
            --does it exist?
            ProcessNode(myX, myY)
        end
    end
    --square4
    if not targetFound then
        myX = curX
        myY = curY - 1
        if (myX > 0) and (myY > 0) and (world[myX][myY] ~= 1) then
            --in bounds and in play
            --does it exist?
            ProcessNode(myX, myY)
        end
    end
    --square5
    if not targetFound then
        myX = curX
        myY = curY + 1
        if (myX > 0) and (myY > 0) and (world[myX][myY] ~= 1) then
            --in bounds and in play
            --does it exist?
            ProcessNode(myX, myY)
        end
    end
    --square6
    if not targetFound then
        myX = curX + 1
        myY = curY - 1
        if (myX > 0) and (myY > 0) and (world[myX][myY] ~= 1) then
            --in bounds and in play
            --does it exist?
            ProcessNode(myX, myY)
        end
    end
    --square7
    if not targetFound then
        myX = curX + 1
        myY = curY
        if (myX > 0) and (myY > 0) and (world[myX][myY] ~= 1) then
            --in bounds and in play
            --does it exist?
            ProcessNode(myX, myY)
```

```
            end
        end
        --square8
        if not targetFound then
            myX = curX + 1
            myY = curY + 1
            if (myX > 0) and (myY > 0) and (world[myX][myY] ~= 1) then
                --in bounds and in play
                --does it exist?
                ProcessNode(myX, myY)
            end
        end
        --Dump()
        table.remove(open, openIndx)
        return targetFound
    end
```

This function begins by finding the node with the lowest F value in the open table. We do that by using the next function:

```
function FindLowestF(nodeTable)
    count = table.getn(nodeTable)
    minF = 1000000
    minFIndex = 0
    if count > 0 then
        for indx = 1,count do
            curF = nodeTable[indx].G + nodeTable[indx].H
            if curF <= minF then
                minF = curF
                minFIndex = indx
            end
        end
    end
    return minFIndex
end
```

This simple function simply walks through the nodes in the table, always comparing the F value (which is the G and H of the nodes added together) to the lowest value it has found so far. When the function has walked through the table, it will return the index value of the node with the lowest F.

With the index of the node with the lowest F known, the FindPath() function then increments the closed table and adds this node to it. This is now the "current node" that we check around.

You'll notice a commented out Dump() function call–this will print to a file the nodes as you discover them. It's very useful to see just how this algorithm works.

We now walk through each of the eight surrounding nodes of the current node. The script from the first node follows:

```
--square1
if not targetFound then
    myX = curX - 1
    myY = curY - 1
    if (myX > 0) and (myY > 0) and (world[myX][myY] ~= 1) then
        --in bounds and in play
        --does it exist?
        ProcessNode(myX, myY)
    end
end
```

We set the value of the node we are looking for by setting the myX and myY variables, and then we check to see if they are "in bounds" and if the location is open. If so, we then process the node with the function shown in Listing 13.11.

LISTING 13.11   The ProcessNode() function

```
function ProcessNode(newX, newY)
    targetFound = false
    exists = AlreadyExists(newX, newY)
    if exists == -1 then
        --it's a new open node
        --is it the target????
        if (newX == targetX) and (newY == targetY) then
            --target is found
            targetFound = true
            print("target found")
        else
            --it's a new open node
            NewOpenEntry(newX, newY)
            print("new entry")
        end
    else
        --the node is already in the open table
        print("exists!")
        existingG = open[exists].G
        curValue = 0
        parentG = closed[closedIndx].G
```

```
    if (open[exists].X == closed[closedIndx].X) or (open[exists].Y ==
    closed[closedIndx].Y) then
        --NOT diagonal
        curValue = 10
    else
        curValue = 14
    end
    newG = parentG + curValue
    if newG < existingG then
        --open[exists].Parent = openIndx
        open[exists].Parent = closedIndx
    end
end
return targetFound
end
```

We first check to see if the node already exists, using the `AlreadyExists()` function. If the function doesn't exist, we first check to see if it's the target (in which case we're done). If it's not the target, we add it to the open table with the following function:

```
function NewOpenEntry(newX, newY)
    myIndx = table.getn(open) + 1
    table.setn(open, myIndx)
    open[myIndx] = {}
    open[myIndx].X = newX
    open[myIndx].Y = newY
    open[myIndx].Parent = closedIndx
    open[myIndx].G = FindG(open, myIndx)
    open[myIndx].H = FindH(open[myIndx].X,open[myIndx].Y,targetX,targetY)
end
```

This function is straightforward, except at the end, where we have to calculate the G and H values for the node. To calculate the G value, we use the next function:

```
function FindG(nodeTable, node)
    parentG = closed[nodeTable[node].Parent].G
    if (nodeTable[node].X == closed[nodeTable[node].Parent].X) or
    (nodeTable[node].Y == closed[nodeTable[node].Parent].Y) then
        --NOT diagonal
        curValue = 10
    else
        curValue = 14
    end
```

```
        myG = parentG + curValue
        return myG
    end
```

The G value is calculated by adding to the G of the parent of the node in question the value of its distance from the current node. For this, we make it as simple as possible and use the value of 10 for a vertically or horizontally adjacent square and a value of 14 for a diagonal square.

It's in this function that you would add in any modifications to take into consideration the movement costs of different terrain types (such as road, field, or rubble).

To determine the H value of the node we're processing, we use the following function:

```
function FindH(curX,curY,tarX,tarY)
    --manhattan distance
    myH = 10*(math.abs(curX-tarX) + math.abs(curY-tarY))
    return myH
end
```

This simple function calculates the "Manhattan distance" from the current node to the target. The Manhattan distance is simple a way to calculate a stair-step distance between two points, as if you were walking the city streets of Manhattan (where you can't go diagonally). This is an estimate of how far the node under consideration is from the target (it doesn't take into account the terrain obstacles), but for our process, this is all we need right now.

Returning back to the ProcessNode() function, our other case is if the node already exists in the open table. If so, we check the G values to see if we are looking at a more efficient node at the moment. If so, we change parent references in the open table. If not, we do nothing.

Returning to the FindPath() function, we work through this process for all surrounding nodes, quitting immediately once we find that we are trying to add the target node to the open table. At the end of the function, we remove the current node from the table and return from the function. We'll loop through this process until we find our target.

When we are done, we have a closed table that is populated by nodes, some of which are on our desired path and some that aren't. To make sense out of this, we must process the closed table as follows:

```
function BuildPath()
    --once the path is found, this will build the path table
    --load the first node, the target
```

```
count = 1
path[count] = {}
path[count].X =  targetX
path[count].Y =  targetY
--load in the last node in the closed table
count = count + 1
path[count] = {}
pathIndx = table.getn(closed)
path[count].X =  closed[pathIndx].X
path[count].Y =  closed[pathIndx].Y
newPathIndx = closed[pathIndx].Parent
--now walk through closed table
while newPathIndx ~= 1 do
    count = count + 1
    path[count] = {}
    path[count].X =  closed[newPathIndx].X
    path[count].Y =  closed[newPathIndx].Y
    oldPathIndx = newPathIndx
    newPathIndx = closed[oldPathIndx].Parent
end
path = ReverseTable(path)
--FinalDump()
end
```

This function walks us through the nodes in the closed table, moving through the nodes based on the parents, and adding the x- and y-coordinates to the path table. When the `newPathIndex` equals 1, we would be adding the start node to the path table, so we are done. At this point, we have a series of coordinates, from back to front, describing the best path from our start to finish. The last step before we draw the path is to reverse our path table with the next function:

```
function ReverseTable(myTable)
    hold = {}
    endCount = table.getn(myTable)
    for indx = 1, table.getn(myTable) do
        hold[indx] = myTable[endCount]
        endCount = endCount -1
    end
    return hold
end
```

This function reverses all of the elements in a table (which could be useful in other situations as well, which is why it's generic). In this context, we end up with a path table that takes us from the start location to the target location, which we can now draw using the following function:

```
function DrawPath(myPath)
    --x is the down coordinate
    --y is the across coordinate
    if table.getn(myPath) > 0 then
        for indx = 1, table.getn(myPath) do
            CreateItem(masterCellID, "Sprite", "box_path.bmp")
            SetItemPosition(masterCellID, (myPath[indx].Y * 20) +
            worldOffset, (myPath[indx].X * 20) + worldOffset, 20, 20)
            masterCellID = masterCellID + 1
        end
    end
    --now draw the end as the target
    DrawTarget(myPath[table.getn(myPath)].X,myPath[table.getn
    (myPath)].Y)
end
```

Although this example is certainly limited, we have constructed it in a general enough way that it deals with a start and target value (imaging the current location of a tank and where on a game map you right-clicked). The result we get is a series of coordinates that indicates our "checkpoints" toward the target. We can feed this data into any movement function we have to move a vehicle across a map, for example. We can also dump the path data and recalculate at any time, when a player clicks a new movement location for something that is still moving. Imagine keeping a table of multiple targets—waypoints. You can change the current target to the start location and remove the top element of the table as the new target to create a queued list of waypoint movement orders.

You now have a solid foundation on how to use Lua to determine a best-fit path through an arbitrary environment.

SUMMARY

The demos in this chapter only scratch the surface of AI implementation in Lua. In games that we've developed in our studio, we've used Lua-powered AI to run a simulated presidential campaign, play Texas Hold 'Em poker, be a customer at a health club, and play shuffleboard and miniature golf. Lua, when used as the primary AI language, either alone or working with custom LuaGlue functions you write, allows you to rapidly prototype, test, and revise your AI algorithms with a speed that just isn't possible with a compiled language.

Hopefully, this chapter has you thinking of ways in which you could craft computer opponents for your own games. In the next chapter, we'll dive into more sophisticated work with the GUI system and the Sprite class, giving you more visual options and even more tools for your growing Lua toolbox.

14 Lua and Graphics

In This Chapter

- Running the Graphics Demos
- Linear Movement
- Collision Detection
- 2D Particle System

In the previous chapters, we worked through our example game, *Take Away*, and used some fairly primitive old-school sprite graphics to display our ships, crates, and such. Although Lua wasn't created as a tool to manage high-performance graphics, we can turn it into a fairly robust 2D graphical-control system with the addition of just a few additional LuaGlue functions.

In this chapter, which is aimed more at the hobbyist developer, we will expand our core *Take Away* code base to include more graphical options and give you the tools you need to create robust and sophisticated 2D games.

RUNNING THE GRAPHICS DEMOS

ON THE CD
In the folder for this chapter on the CD-ROM, you'll find the graphics_demos folder. This demo uses the same executable as our *Take Away* game. Simply run the executable, and you'll be able to run the individual example scripts, which we'll discuss later. The examples begin from the most basic and grow in complexity. As we work through the examples, think about ways in which you can expand the demo into a function or feature of your own Lua-powered game.

To run a demo, click the button to the right of the filename. When you are done with a demo, press the Esc key to return to the main menu.

Fingerprint Demo

This first example doesn't introduce any new LuaGlue functions; instead it uses what we already have to create an interesting animated graphic of a fingerprint scan. If you look in the textures directory, you'll see that there are 17 "frames" to this animation. We want the scan to rotate so that it looks like the scanning bar (more like a squiggle) moves up and down over the fingerprint in an endless loop. See Figure 14.1.

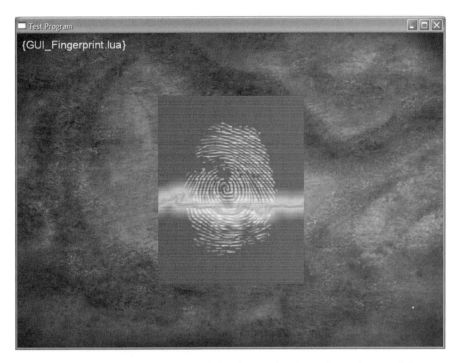

FIGURE 14.1 The animated sprite of the fingerprint demo "scans" up and down based on the timer event.

We control this sprite with the StartTimer() function, which is called when the interface is first loaded. We can then see the control loop in the GUI_TIMER_EXPIRED event, as shown in the next example:

```
if eventCode == GUI_TIMER_EXPIRED then
    if printDir == POSITIVE then
        printCounter = printCounter + 1
        if printCounter > 17 then   -- max number of 2d pics, so
        reverse direction
         printDir = NEGATIVE
         printCounter = 16
        end
    else
        printCounter = printCounter - 1
        if printCounter < 1 then   -- min number of  2d pics, so
        reverse direction
         printDir = POSITIVE
         printCounter = 2
        end
```

```
        end
        AnimatePrint()
    end
```

This loop controls two variables. First is `printDir`, which indicates if the scan should move up or down. The value of that variable indicates if we should increment or decrement the second variable, `printCounter`, which holds the value of the current animation frame we want to draw.

The image is then drawn with the next function, which is called at the end of our control loop shown in the previous example:

```
function AnimatePrint()
    local pic = "ui_tp_01.bmp"
    if printCounter < 10 then
        pic = string.format("%s%d%s","ui_tp_0",printCounter,".bmp")
    else
        pic = string.format("%s%d%s","ui_tp_",printCounter,".bmp")
    end
    CreateItem(GUI_INGAME + 101, "Sprite", pic)
    SetItemPosition(GUI_INGAME + 101, 264, 120, 272, 360)
    StartTimer(.09)
end
```

This function uses the `string.format()` function to build the string that is the filename for the current frame to draw. Then we create a sprite and set it to the current frame image. Because we are calling the `CreateItem()` function on an already-existing GUI item, we are replacing its data with the new data and not creating a new instance of a Sprite GUI object. The function wraps up with a call to `StartTimer()` to send it back to the control loop.

Explosion Demo

In this demo, you can click the screen to view an animated explosion at the location of your click. The explosion sequence is 13 frames long, and the images are Targa files (with a *.tga extension) with an alpha channel, to allow the explosion to "overlap" any graphics behind it.

If you are using explosions like this in your game, be sure that the ID number of the explosion sprite is higher than any of the other objects on screen, so you'll be able to see the explosion. The GUI system draws objects with the lowest ID first.

This demo uses the same control mechanism as the fingerprint demo described earlier, but it is all contained within the GUI_TIMER_EXPIRED event code. For this animation, it's not a looping animation but rather a single animation that will play through once. In the control loop, we are always firing the timer, even if no explosion is happening. However, we only show an explosion because we set the frame counter in the mouse event handler as follows:

```
if eventCode == GUI_MOUSE_BUTTON_UP then
    if id == LEFT then
        if explosionFrame == 0 then
            tarX, tarY = GetMousePosition()
            explosionFrame = 1
        end
    end
end
```

You'll also notice that this is a new event for us, and we make use of a new LuaGlue function: GetMousePosition().

Mouse Button Events

To trigger the explosion, we need to be able to capture a simple mouse-click event that was not linked to a button object. The events GUI_MOUSE_BUTTON_DOWN and GUI_MOUSE_BUTTON_UP were defined and sent when the mouse buttons changes its pressed state. Both the left and the right mouse buttons are supported, and the ID value returned with this event indicates which button was pressed.

GetMousePosition

The C++ code tracks the position of the mouse using the Windows message system. Windows sends a message to the program whenever the mouse is moved. The C++ code tracks these movements and saves the pointer position for internal use. To allow the Lua code access to this value was a simple matter of writing a new LuaGlue function GetMousePosition() and returning the x- and y-values to the caller. This process is easy due to Lua's ability to return multiple values from a function call. The GetMousePosition() function makes use of this feature and returns two values (x,y). The Windows message-handling code follows (from WinMain.CPP):

```
case WM_LBUTTONDOWN:
    g_mouseButtons |= MOUSE_LBUTTON_DOWN;
    CGUIManager::GetInstance()->NotifyMouseButtonDown(1);
    break;
case WM_LBUTTONUP:
    CGUIManager::GetInstance()->NotifyMouseButtonUp(1);
```

```
            g_mouseButtons &= ~MOUSE_LBUTTON_DOWN;
            break;
        case WM_RBUTTONDOWN:
            CGUIManager::GetInstance()->NotifyMouseButtonDown(2);
            g_mouseButtons |= MOUSE_RBUTTON_DOWN;
            break;
        case WM_RBUTTONUP:
            CGUIManager::GetInstance()->NotifyMouseButtonUp(2);
            g_mouseButtons &= ~MOUSE_RBUTTON_DOWN;
            break;
        case WM_MOUSEMOVE:
            g_mousePoint.x = LOWORD(lParam);
            g_mousePoint.y = HIWORD(lParam);
            break;
```

The message handler tracks all mouse-button-state changes as well as all mouse-movement messages. The variables g_mousButtons and g_mousePoint are updated constantly and used by the code in a number of places. This code also calls the GUI system to notify it of changes in the mouse state. The GUI system then sends the new events to the Lua event handler. A value of 1 indicates the message is for the left mouse button; a value of 2 indicates the right mouse button. To allow the Lua code access to this value was a simple matter of writing a new LuaGlue function GetMousePosition() and returning the x- and y-values to the caller. This is much easier due to Lua's ability to return multiple values from a function call. The GetMousePosition() function makes use of this feature and returns two values (x,y). The code from GUIManager.CPP follows:

```
extern int g_mouseButtons;
extern POINT g_mousePoint;
extern "C" int GUI_GetMousePosition(lua_State *L)
{
    cLua *lua = CGUIManager::GetInstance()->GetLuaContext();
    lua->PushNumber(g_mousePoint.x);
    lua->PushNumber(g_mousePoint.y);
    return 2;
}
```

Notice that the LuaGlue function returns "2". This tells Lua that there are two return values on the Lua stack.

Sprite Rotation

In our *Take Away* game, we used a tried-and-true method for handling the rotation of our ship and its enemies: we simply used a different graphic to indicate its rotation. This worked fine, but we were limited to only eight increments of rotation, in 45-degree changes. This was the approach used in many of the first RTS games that were developed. Now that we are working through DirectX, which thinks of everything in terms of 3D textures, we can take advantage of this capability and use some of the power built into the system. See Figure 14.2.

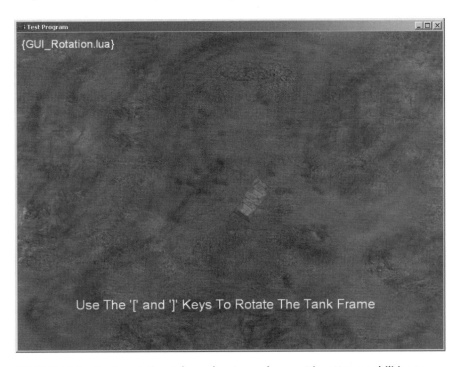

FIGURE 14.2 Sprite rotation takes advantage of some DirectX 9 capabilities to give us smooth rotation on screen.

In this example, you can rotate a spite by pressing the [and] keys. The meat of this demo is in the scripts attached to the key press event handlers, shown in the next example:

```
if id == 91 then --[
    tankRot = tankRot + .1
    if tankRot > 6.2 then
        tankRot = 0
```

```
                    end
                    ItemCommand(tankID, "SetRotation", tankRot)
                end
```

Here, we simply increment the rotation value, tankRot, by .1 every time the user presses the [key (as indicated by its ASCII value of 91). The SetRotation item command actually performs the rotation on the sprite. The rotation is in radians, so we reset the values at approximately 2$\prod$ and 0.

Sprite Rotation LuaGlue

The rotation command was implemented as an ItemCommand function for sprite items. The class CGUISprite (found in the file GUISprite.cpp) was expanded to include support for ItemCommands, and the DX9 class CSprite class (found in the file DXSprite.cpp) was modified to keep track of a rotation angle and to draw the sprite using a standard point-rotation formula.

The GUI sprite object gets the ItemCommand() through the normal GUI process. The command processor gets the rotation from the Lua Stack and sets the DXSprite object. The next time the sprite is drawn (the next frame), it will appear at the new rotated value. Code from GUISprite.CPP follows:

```
int     CGUISprite::ObjectCommand(const char *pCommand)
{
    cLua     *L = CGUIManager::GetInstance()->GetLuaContext();
    int retVal = 0;
    if(strcmp(pCommand, "SetRotation") == 0)
    {
        // rotate this arg rot (in radians)
        float rot =  (float) L->GetNumberArgument(3);
        m_pTexture->SetRotation(-1, -1, rot);
    }
    return retVal;
}
```

The DXSprite object sets a flag when the position or rotation values change so that the new position can be calculated at the next update. The DXSprite Update Position method (from DXSprite.CPP) is shown in Listing 14.1.

LISTING 14.1 The DXSprite UpdatePosition method

```
void Sprite::UpdatePosition(void)
{
    if(m_vb)
```

```
{
    SpriteVertex* pVertices;
    m_vb->Lock(0, 0, (void **)&pVertices, 0);
    pVertices[0].diffuse = pVertices[1].diffuse =
    pVertices[2].diffuse = pVertices[3].diffuse =
        D3DCOLOR_ARGB(255,255,255,255);
    pVertices[0].rhw = pVertices[1].rhw =
    pVertices[2].rhw = pVertices[3].rhw = 1.0f;
    pVertices[0].u0           = 0.0f;
    pVertices[0].v0           = 0.0f;
    pVertices[1].u0           = 1.0f;
    pVertices[1].v0           = 0.0f;
    pVertices[2].u0           = 0.0f;
    pVertices[2].v0           = 1.0f;
    pVertices[3].u0           = 1.0f;
    pVertices[3].v0           = 1.0f;
    pVertices[0].x            = m_x - 0.5f;
    pVertices[0].y            = m_y - 0.5f;
    pVertices[1].x            = m_x + m_width - 0.5f;
    pVertices[1].y            = m_y - 0.5f;
    pVertices[2].x            = m_x - 0.5f;
    pVertices[2].y            = m_y + m_height - 0.5f;
    pVertices[3].x            = m_x + m_width - 0.5f;
    pVertices[3].y            = m_y + m_height - 0.5f;
    if (m_rot != 0)
    { // apply rotation of m_rot radians
        m_centerX = m_x + m_width/2;
        m_centerY = m_y + m_height/2;
        float sn = sinf(m_rot);
        float cs = cosf(m_rot);
        float x = m_x - m_centerX;
        float y = m_y - m_centerY;
        pVertices[0].x = (x * cs) - (y * sn) + m_centerX;
        pVertices[0].y = (x * sn) + (y * cs) + m_centerY;
        x = m_x + m_width - m_centerX;
        y = m_y - m_centerY;
        pVertices[1].x = (x * cs) - (y * sn) + m_centerX;
        pVertices[1].y = (x * sn) + (y * cs) + m_centerY;
        x = m_x - m_centerX;
        y = m_y + m_height - m_centerY;
        pVertices[2].x = (x * cs) - (y * sn) + m_centerX;
        pVertices[2].y = (x * sn) + (y * cs) + m_centerY;
        x = m_x + m_width - m_centerX;
        y = m_y + m_height - m_centerY;
```

```
        pVertices[3].x = (x * cs) - (y * sn) + m_centerX;
        pVertices[3].y = (x * sn) + (y * cs) + m_centerY;
    }
    pVertices[0].z          = m_z - 0.5f;
    pVertices[1].z          = m_z - 0.5f;
    pVertices[2].z          = m_z - 0.5f;
    pVertices[3].z          = m_z - 0.5f;
    m_boundingRect.top = (long) ( __min (__min (pVertices[0].y,
        pVertices[1].y), __min (pVertices[2].y, pVertices[3].y)));
    m_boundingRect.left = (long) ( __min (__min (pVertices[0].x,
        pVertices[1].x), __min (pVertices[2].x, pVertices[3].x)));
    m_boundingRect.bottom = (long) ( __max (__max (pVertices[0].y,
        pVertices[1].y), __max (pVertices[2].y, pVertices[3].y)));
    m_boundingRect.right = (long) ( __max (__max (pVertices[0].x,
        pVertices[1].x), __max (pVertices[2].x, pVertices[3].x)));
    m_vb->Unlock();
    }
}
```

This code is run whenever the "dirty flag" is set. It checks to be sure that a DirectX vertex buffer exists for the sprite before doing anything; if the buffer does not exist, the process is aborted. The vertex buffer is locked, thereby giving access to the vertices that make up the sprite. First we set the sprite to the unrotated positions and then check if the rotation value is set to anything but 0. If there is a rotation value, each of the vertices is rotated around the center of the sprite m_rot radians. Last, we build a new bounding rectangle, which is affected by the rotation (if any) of the sprite.

LINEAR MOVEMENT

In the movement example, we take a different approach to moving a sprite object than we did for the enemies in *Take Away*. In *Take Away*, the enemies identified a target and then would work to rotate so that they were pointing toward the target, using their thrust to make their way there. The result, especially against a moving target (without anticipating anything), was that they would sort of loop toward the target, getting closer and closer, but not taking any direct path.

In this demo, we move a sprite in a linear fashion to a target that is set by clicking somewhere on the terrain. This approach forces us to brush off some simple trigonometry, but we'll come out of it with a function that is useful in a wide array of situations. The idea is that we need to determine the angle toward the target, and then, with an imaginary line drawn from our tank to the target, determine how many x- and y-values we must move given our current time and speed values, so that we move toward our goal. This process is handled in the `Movement ApproachTarget()` function, shown in the Listing 14.2.

LISTING 14.2 The `MovementApproachTarget()` function

```lua
function MovementApproachTarget(curX, curY, tarX, tarY, moveSpeed)
    --first, figure out the sides of the triangle:
    a = curY - tarY
    b = curX - tarX
    c = math.sqrt((a*a)+(b*b))
    --now, find the angle to the target:
    angle = math.acos(b/c)
    --now, determine the presence of negatives:
    if a > 0 then
        yNeg = -1
        if b > 0 then
            xNeg = -1
        elseif b == 0 then
            xNeg = 0
        else
            xNeg = -1
        end
    elseif a == 0 then
        yNeg = 1
        if b > 0 then
            xNeg = -1
        else
            xNeg = -1
        end
    else
        yNeg = 1
        if b > 0 then
            xNeg = -1
        elseif b == 0 then
            xNeg = 0
        else
            xNeg = -1
        end
    end
    --now, determine the x and y movement:
    movX = math.floor(moveSpeed * math.cos(angle) * xNeg)
    movY = math.floor(moveSpeed * math.sin(angle) * yNeg)
    --now, update your current position:
```

```
        curX = curX + movX
        curY = curY + movY
        tankX = curX
        tankY = curY
        SetItemPosition(tankID, tankX, tankY, 78, 34)
    end
```

We begin by first determining the distance to the target, not as a Manhattan-distance, which is a "stairstep" approach, but as a true straight line. This process is done by realizing that we have a right triangle on our hands and that the value we want is actually the hypotenuse of that triangle. See Figure 14.3.

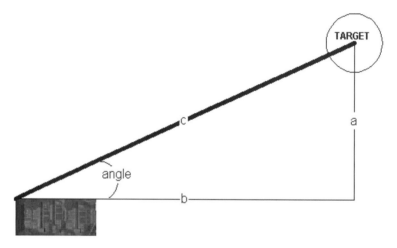

FIGURE 14.3 In this diagram, we can easily determine a and b, and then use a little math to get both c and the angle to the target.

Once we know the distance, we can now figure out the angle to the target with the next line:

```
angle = math.acos(b/c)
```

Our next step is to handle the strange values we might have, because our game coordinate system has 0,0 in the top-left corner of the screen and both x and y increase as we move diagonally down to the right (which is not how a traditional math Cartesian grid is laid out).

Once we have handled the odd coordinates, we determine the x- and y-values for our next position during the next update cycle with the following line:

```
movX = math.floor(moveSpeed * math.cos(angle) * xNeg)
```

This gives us our delta X for movement toward the target, based on `moveSpeed` (this is how far along c we want to travel in one update cycle) and the adjustment for the coordinate system (`xNeg`). We use `math.floor()` to drop the decimal value (we could also round by adding .5 to the value), because we care only about integer values here. Finally, we simply set the item position of the sprite to the new location with the next script:

```
SetItemPosition(tankID, tankX, tankY, 78, 34)
```

Like many of our other demos, this one is controlled via the `GUI_TIMER_EXPIRED` event, as follows:

```
if eventCode == GUI_TIMER_EXPIRED then
        if ((tarX ~= nil) and (tarY ~= nil)) then
            MovementApproachTarget(tankX, tankY, tarX, tarY, tankSpeed)
            hitTable = HitTest(tarX, tarY)
            for index,value in ipairs(hitTable) do
                if value == tankID then
                    tarX = nil
                    tarY = nil
                end
            end
        end
    end
    StartTimer(.1)
end
```

To see if we have reached our goal, we use another new LuaGlue function, `HitTest()`. This function is part of two new LuaGlue functions that introduce the idea of collision detection into our growing Lua-powered game system. `HitTest()` returns a table of all GUI objects the passed-in point "collides" with. We then walk through the table using the `ipairs()` iterator to see if our sprite has collided with our target point; if so, we set `tarX` and `tarY` to `nil`, which indicates that we are done processing movement.

GetCollisions

Because sprites were being used as more than just static images, a way to detect collisions between sprites was needed. The C++ code was the logical place to do this because it has all the information needed for the process. The rotation of sprites made this function a bit trickier because of the odd shapes that sprites could take on the screen. The passed sprite could collide with more than one sprite, so a table needed to be constructed to return all the sprites with which the passed sprite collides. Building a table and returning it is easy once you play around with the code a little. The following LuaGlue function calls the collision test function and builds the table from a Standard Template Library list (found in GUIManager.CPP):

```
extern "C" int GUI_GetCollisions(lua_State *L)
{
    cLua *lua = CGUIManager::GetInstance()->GetLuaContext();
    unsigned int id = (unsigned int) lua->GetNumberArgument(1);
    // create the return table on the stack
    lua_newtable (L);
    CUserInterface *pUI = CGUIManager::GetInstance()->GetCurrentUI();
    unsigned int i = 1;
    if(pUI)
    {
        std::list<unsigned int> list = pUI->SpriteCollision(id);
        std::list<unsigned int>::iterator it = list.begin();
        while(it != list.end())
        {
            lua_pushnumber(L, i);
            lua_pushnumber(L, (*it));
            lua_settable (L, -3);
            ++i;
            ++it;
        }
    }
    // now add the number of entries in the table as member "n" (t.n)
    lua_pushstring(L, "n");
    lua_pushnumber(L, i-1);
    lua_settable (L, -3);
    return 1;
}
```

The table has to be created on the Lua Stack, and then the index and the value have to be placed on the Lua Stack as well. After a call to the Lua API, the table is back on top of the stack and the table data is inserted. As a shortcut for the Lua programmer, the member n is also put into the table that contains the number of entries in the table (not including n). In this example, the table has members table[1] through table [table.n]. This makes it easy for the Lua programmer to write a loop to process all the returned ID values. The following example shows the basic loop to process the returned table:

```
T = GetCollisions(1)
for indx = 1,T.n do
    -- Process collision of sprite ID 1 and sprite ID T[indx]
end
```

The function that actually generates the collision list is in UserInterface.CPP. It relies on the next function to detect if a point is inside a rectangle (found in GUI Manager.CPP):

```
bool InRect(int x, int y, const RECT &r)
{
  if((x < r.left) || (x > r.right))
    return false;
  if((y < r.top) || (y > r.bottom))
    return false;
  return true;
}
```

If the x-coordinate is less than the left side of the rectangle or is greater than the right side of the rectangle, then the point cannot be inside the rectangle. If the y-coordinate is less than the top of the rectangle or is greater than the bottom of the rectangle, then the point cannot be inside the rectangle. If the function reached the end, the point must be in the rectangle. We now check against the sprites with the code shown in Listing 14.3 (found in UserInterface.CPP).

LISTING 14.3   Checking against the sprites

```
std::list<unsigned int> CUserInterface::SpriteCollision(unsigned int id)
{
    std::list<unsigned int> retVal;
    CGUISprite *pSprite = (CGUISprite *)FindObject(id);
    if(pSprite && (strcmp(pSprite->GetObjectTypeName(),
    kpSpriteName)==0))
    {
        // the passed GUI object is indeed a sprite
        RECT rOne = pSprite->GetBoundingRect();
        std::map<unsigned int,CGUIObject *>::iterator it =
            m_mapObjects.begin();
        while(it != m_mapObjects.end())
        {
            bool bBoom = false;
            if(( (*it).first != id) &&
                strcmp((*it).second->GetObjectTypeName(),
```

```
                kpSpriteName)==0)
        {
            CGUISprite *pTarget = (CGUISprite *) (*it).second;
            RECT rTwo = pTarget->GetBoundingRect();
            // see if the rects collide
            if(InRect(rTwo.right, rTwo.top, rOne))
            {
                bBoom = true;
            }
            else
            {
                if(InRect(rTwo.right, rTwo.bottom, rOne))
                {
                    bBoom = true;
                }
                else
                {
                    if(InRect(rTwo.left, rTwo.top, rOne))
                    {
                        bBoom = true;
                    }
                    else
                    {
                        if(InRect(rTwo.left, rTwo.bottom,
                                                    rOne))
                        {
                            bBoom = true;
                        }
                    }
                }
            }
        }
        if(bBoom)
        {
            retVal.push_back((*it).first);
        }
        it++;
        }
    }
    return retVal;
}
```

All the items that belong to the user interface are checked. All sprites are then subjected to a collision test. If any of the corners of the found sprite are inside the passed sprite, the ID of the found sprite is added to the collision list. When all the items have been checked, the list is returned to the caller.

HitTest

This test is very similar to the `GetCollisions()` LuaGlue function except it tests all GUI items against a single point (usually the mouse pointer location from `GetMousePosition()`). Any GUI item that is hit by the passed point will end up in the returned table. The returned table is just like the table returned from `GetCollisions()`.

The Next Step

To create a robust unit-movement system for something like an RTS game, you would couple this approach with the pathfinding demo we explored in the previous chapter. You would take the path table output and use the top value as the current target; when that is reached, remove it from the table and set the next target to the new top value in the path table.

COLLISION DETECTION

The next example showcases the collision between two sprites. In this example, we can move our tank around exactly as in the previous example, but the world is also populated by several randomly placed huts, which are defined in the following function:

```
function HutInit()
    hutCount = 3 --Number of huts in the game
    myHuts = {} --Creates myHuts table
    --Creates table, one entry per potential hut
    for indx = 1,hutCount do
        --Creates a table to hold the data for each hut
        myHuts[indx] = {}
        myHuts[indx].ID = GUI_INGAME + 100 + indx--GUI identification
        number (#)
        myHuts[indx].X = math.random(0,760) --X coordinate (#)
        myHuts[indx].Y = math.random(0,520) --Y coordinate (#)
        if (myHuts[indx].X > 325) and (myHuts[indx].X < 500) then
            myHuts[indx].X = 500
        end
        myHuts[indx].DAMAGE = 0
        CreateItem(myHuts[indx].ID, "Sprite", "hut1.bmp")
        SetItemPosition(myHuts[indx].ID, myHuts[indx].X, myHuts[indx].Y,
```

```
        40, 80)
     end
  end
```

This table creates a randomly placed hut and loops through the function as in-dicated by the value of hutCount. See Figure 14.4.

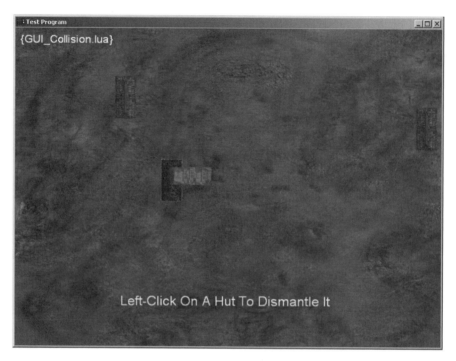

FIGURE 14.4 The tank has just collided with a hit, and the collision was detected by the CollisionCheck() LuaGlue function.

In the GUI_TIMER_EXPIRED event handler, we do the same thing as in the previ-ous example, but we make a call to CollisionCheck() at the end of our event pro-cessing. The next function takes care of checking for collisions between our tank and the huts:

```
function CollisonCheck()
    for indx = 1, hutCount do
        if myHuts[indx].DAMAGE ~= 1 then
            hitTable = GetCollisions(myHuts[indx].ID)
            for index,value in ipairs(hitTable) do
                if value == tankID then
                    myHuts[indx].DAMAGE = 1
```

```
                        SetTexture(myHuts[indx].ID, "hut3.bmp")
                    end
                end
            end
        end
    end
```

In this function, we walk through all of the huts and call `GetCollisions()` with the hut GUI ID. We then process the returned table (using the `ipairs()` iterator) to see if our tank is in the collision list. If so, we then change the damage state for the hut and use a new LuaGlue function, `SetTexture()`, to change the hut graphic to a damaged state.

The `SetTexture()` function could also be used. It is more efficient for things like our fingerprint and explosion examples.

SetTexture LuaGlue

To allow the Lua code to change the graphic that a sprite displays, the method `SetTexture` had to be exposed via a LuaGlue function. Previously, the following function was called when a sprite was created to load the graphic file for display (from `GUIManager.CPP`):

```cpp
extern "C" int GUI_SetTexture(lua_State *L)
{
    cLua *lua = CGUIManager::GetInstance()->GetLuaContext();
    unsigned int id   = (unsigned int) lua->GetNumberArgument(1);
    char *texName = (char *) lua->GetStringArgument(2);
    CUserInterface *pUI = CGUIManager::GetInstance()->GetCurrentUI();
    if(pUI)
    {
        CGUIObject *pObject = pUI->FindObject(id);
        if(pObject)
        {
            pObject->SetTexture(texName, false);
        }
    }
    return 0;
}
```

This LuaGlue function finds the passed item and calls the `SetTexture` method, as shown in Listing 14.4. Note that the `GUIObject` base class, not the `GUISprite` class, is used. This is because the actual graphic data to be displayed is part of the base class (found in GUIObject.CPP).

LISTING 14.4 The SetTexture method

```
bool CGUIObject::SetTexture(char *pTextureName, bool bSetPos)
{
    if(!pTextureName)
        return true;
    float rotx=0.0f, roty=0.0f, rot=0.0f;
    float oldx=0.0f, oldy=0.0f, oldz=0.0f, oldw=0.0f, oldh=0.0f;
    if(m_pTexture)
    {
        m_pTexture->GetRotation(rotx, roty, rot);
        m_pTexture->GetPosition(oldx, oldy, oldz);
        m_pTexture->GetDimensions(oldw, oldh);
        SAFE_DELETE(m_pTexture);
    }
    m_pTexture = new Sprite();
    m_pTexture->SetTexture(pTextureName);
    if(bSetPos)
    {
        m_pTexture->SetPosition(0, 0, 0);
        int w, h;
        DXContext::GetInstance()->GetScreenDimensions(w, h);
        m_pTexture->SetDimensions((float) w, (float) h);
    }
    else
    {
        // reset the location and dims
        float w, h;
        w = m_rScreen.right - m_rScreen.left;
        h = m_rScreen.bottom - m_rScreen.top;
        m_pTexture->SetPosition(oldx, oldy, oldz);
        m_pTexture->SetDimensions(oldw, oldh);
        m_pTexture->SetRotation(rotx, roty, rot);
    }
    return true;
}
```

If this object currently has image data, save the rotation and position information and remove the image. We delete the image because we are planning to replace it with new data. Next, create the new sprite and load the passed image file. If the user requests that the default screen position be set, set it to full screen. If not, set the position, dimensions, and rotation that were saved from the old sprite.

Tank Demo

This final demo in our `graphics_demo` example brings together all of the previous examples. You can click to move your tank, but this time we've added a turret that rotates with the tank. The turret can also be controlled with the bracket keys.

The first thing you'll notice is that the tank will turn to face the target. This action is done in the function shown in Listing 14.5 and found in `LuaSupport.lua`.

LISTING 14.5   Making the tank face the target

```lua
function FaceTarget(object, curX, curY, curRot, tarX, tarY)
    --first, figure out the sides of the triangle:
    a = curY - tarY
    b = curX - tarX
    c = math.sqrt((a*a)+(b*b))
    --now, find the angle to the target:
    angle = math.acos(b/c)
    --now, determine the presence of negatives:
    if a > 0 then
        if b > 0 then
            angle = math.pi + angle    -- Upper-Left
            print("Upper-Left")
        elseif b == 0 then
            angle = 1.5 * math.pi      -- Directly Up
            print("Directly Up")
        else
            angle = math.pi + angle    -- Upper-Right
            print("Upper-Right")
        end
    elseif a == 0 then
        if b > 0 then
            angle = math.pi            -- Directly Left
            print("Directly Left")
        else
            angle = 2 * math.pi        -- Directly Right
            print("Directly Right")
        end
    else
        if b > 0 then
            angle = math.pi - angle    -- Lower-Left
            print("Lower-Left")
```

```
        elseif b == 0 then
            angle = .5 * math.pi        -- Directly Down
            print("Directly Down")
        else
            angle = math.pi - angle    -- Lower-Right
            print("Lower-Right")
        end
    end
    if curRot > angle then
        angleDif = curRot - angle
        if angleDif < math.pi then
            angleDif = "ccwise"
        else
            angleDif = "cwise"
        end
    else
        angleDif = angle - curRot
        if angleDif < math.pi then
            angleDif = "cwise"
        else
            angleDif = "ccwise"
        end
    end
    if angleDif == "ccwise" then
        curRot = curRot - .1
        if curRot < .1 then
            curRot = 6.2
        end
    else
        curRot = curRot + .1
        if curRot > 6.2 then
            curRot = 0
        end
    end
    if object == "tank" then
        tankRot = curRot
        ItemCommand(tankID, "SetRotation", tankRot)
        if angleDif == "ccwise" then
            turRot = turRot - .1
            if turRot < 0 then
                turRot = 6.2
            end
        else
            turRot = turRot + .1
```

```
                if turRot > 6.2 then
                    turRot = 0
                end
            end
            ItemCommand(turID, "SetRotation", turRot)
        end
        if (curRot < (angle + .1)) and (curRot > (angle - .1)) then
            orientation = "done"
        else
            orientation = "processing"
        end
    end
```

You'll notice that this function is similar to our earlier example in which we determined how to move toward our target. Here, we need to get the angle to the target, and then determine what sort of angle it is relative to our current rotation. Then, using the SetRotation command to the ItemCommand() function, we set an incremental rotation. Because we rotate first and then move, we use the state variable orientation to let the control loop know on which part of tank movement we are working. The game loop in the GUI_TIMER_EXPIRED event is much more complex now that many things are happening during a single update cycle, as shown in Listing 14.6.

LISTING 14.6   The game loop in the GUI_TIMER_EXPIRED event

```
    if eventCode == GUI_TIMER_EXPIRED then
        if ((tarX ~= nil) and (tarY ~= nil)) then
            if orientation == "done" then
                ApproachTarget("tank", tankX, tankY, tarX, tarY,
                tankSpeed)
                hitTable = HitTest(tarX, tarY)
                for index,value in ipairs(hitTable) do
                    if value == tankID then
                        tarX = nil
                        tarY = nil
                    end
                end
            else
                FaceTarget("tank", tankX, tankY, tankRot, tarX, tarY)
            end
        end
        for indx = 1,pCount do
            if myProjectiles[indx].ID ~= nil then
                ApproachTarget(indx, myProjectiles[indx].X,
```

```
                    myProjectiles[indx].Y, myProjectiles[indx].TARX,
                    myProjectiles[indx].TARY, proSpeed)
            end
        end
        HutHit()
        if explosionFrame > 0 then
            if explosionFrame < 10 then
                pic = string.format("%s%d%s","kaboom_0",
                explosionFrame,".tga")
            else
                pic = string.format("%s%d%s","kaboom_",
                explosionFrame,".tga")
            end
            CreateItem(GUI_INGAME + 105, "Sprite", pic)
            SetItemPosition(GUI_INGAME + 105, myHuts[burningHut].X+1,
            myHuts[burningHut].Y+21, 38, 38)
            explosionFrame = explosionFrame + 1
            if explosionFrame > 13 then
                DeleteItem(GUI_INGAME + 105)
                explosionFrame = 0
            end
        end
        StartTimer(.1)
    end
```

In this larger game loop, we begin with a state check to see if our tank is in the act of rotating or moving, and we call the proper function (either ApproachTarget() or FaceTarget()). We then walk through our list of current projectiles and use the same ApproachTarget() function to handle the movement of the projectiles. We then check to see if any projectiles hit any hut with the HitHut() function, and finally, we manage the animation of any currently active explosion. See Figure 14.5 for a summary of the game.

This type of game-loop processing is fairly typical for a more robust real-time game. The actions of this loop could be made even cleaner if the concepts of a finite state machine, as discussed in the previous chapter, were put to use.

Another interesting experiment for this demo would be to code the rotation and the movement together, so that the tank rotated as it moved. To look realistic, you would have to modify its "move toward" target to be in relation to the current facing of the tank, so the vehicle didn't slew sideways.

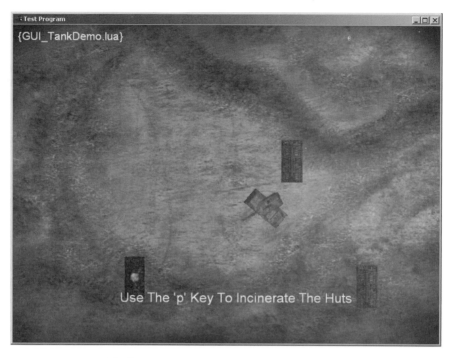

FIGURE 14.5 In this demo, we put together all the pieces and rotate our tank and our turret together, plus we fired projectiles to destroy the huts.

2D PARTICLE SYSTEM

Particle systems are used to simulate a wide variety of natural phenomena, from smoke to fire to the movement of clouds (see Figure 14.6). 3D particles systems have been used in 3D games for years, but they made their first appearance in 2D games well before that.

A particle system uses the concept of an "emitter"—basically a point in space that carries with it certain parameters of behavior. This emitter will spawn a particle, which is simply a graphical element with some behavior parameters. As time passes, the emitters create new particles and the already-existing particles move, change size, and follow a pattern of behavior until their life span instructs the particle-controlling function to delete them from the world.

ON THE CD
The demo for a simple 2D particle system is in the 2D_particle folder in this chapter's folder on the CD-ROM. This demo will create a small smoke system (using one of the graphical elements from the explosion) whenever the player clicks the screen.

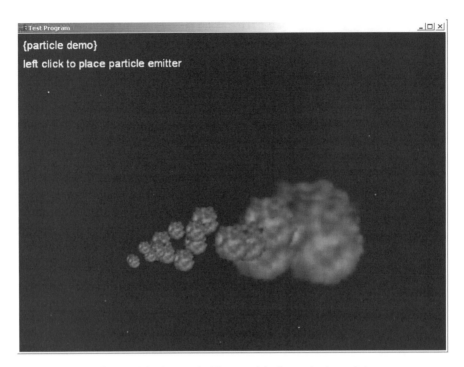

FIGURE 14.6 The particle demo choking out black smoke in real time.

The particle system is defined by the following table of value parameters:

```
partSystem = {}
partSystem.Texture = "kaboom_11.tga"
partSystem.BirthRate = .1
partSystem.AvgLife = 2
partSystem.LifeVariance = 1
partSystem.X = 200
partSystem.XVariance = 10
partSystem.Y = 200
partSystem.YVariance = 10
partSystem.XDrift = 10
partSystem.XDriftVariance = 6
partSystem.YDrift = -5
partSystem.YDriftVariance = 6
partSystem.Scale = 25
partSystem.ScaleVariance = 4
partSystem.ScaleChange = 1.08
partSystem.ScaleChangeVariance = .1
partSystem.BaseID = 1000
```

```
partSystem.Life = 20
```

The general idea with these parameters is that each particle is "born" with the default parameters, plus or minus some random value between 0 and the variance value. This idea creates some uniqueness to each particle.

When the player clicks on the screen, the x- and y-values of the mouse position are placed into the particle table, the particle system is initialized (the particles table is set to an empty table and the cumulative counter is set to 0), and the timer is started with the value of timeSlice. Once the timer expires, we call the master particle control function, which is shown in Listing 14.7.

LISTING 14.7   The master particle control function

```
function ProcessParticles()
    --increment cumulative counter
    curTime = curTime +  timeSlice
    if curTime < partSystem.Life then
        --new particle born
        if EvenDivide(curTime, partSystem.BirthRate) then
            CreateNewParticle()
        end
    end
    removeMe = nil
    --apply particle changes
    for index,value in ipairs(particles) do
        --increment age
        value.Age =  value.Age + timeSlice
        --process drift
        myValue = math.random(1, partSystem.XDriftVariance)
        if math.random(1,100) > 50 then
            value.X = value.X + partSystem.XDrift + myValue
        else
            value.X = value.X + partSystem.XDrift - myValue
        end
        myValue = math.random(1, partSystem.YDriftVariance)
        if math.random(1,100) > 50 then
            value.Y = value.Y + partSystem.YDrift + myValue
        else
            value.Y = value.Y + partSystem.YDrift - myValue
        end
        --process scale change
        myValue = math.random(0, partSystem.ScaleChangeVariance * 10)
        if math.random(1,100) > 50 then
```

```
            value.Scale = (value.Scale + (myValue/10)) *
            partSystem.ScaleChange
        else
            value.Scale = (value.Scale - (myValue/10)) *
            partSystem.ScaleChange
        end
        --render particle
        if value.Age < value.Life then
            CreateItem(value.ID, "Sprite", partSystem.Texture)
            SetItemPosition(value.ID, value.X, value.Y, value.Scale,
            value.Scale)
        else
            DeleteItem(value.ID)
            removeMe = index
        end
    end
    --now remove old particles
    if removeMe ~= nil then
        table.remove(particles, removeMe)
    end
    if table.getn(particles) > 0 then
        StartTimer(timeSlice)
    end
end
```

This function, which is called from the GUI_TIMER_EXPIRED event, first begins by updating the cumulative timer. We then check to see if the entire system's life span is over. If not, we process any new births through a "fuzzy" Boolean function (one that approximates the division of the ongoing time into the birth value, rather than treating it as absolute) that checks to see if the birth value is approximately an even division into the cumulative time value. If so, we create a new particle as follows:

```
function CreateNewParticle()
    tempPart = {}
    tempPart.Age = 0
    idCounter = idCounter + 1
    myValue = math.random(1, partSystem.LifeVariance * 10)
    if math.random(1,100) > 50 then
        tempPart.Life = partSystem.AvgLife + (myValue/10)
    else
        tempPart.Life = partSystem.AvgLife - (myValue/10)
    end
    myValue = math.random(1, partSystem.XVariance)
    if math.random(1,100) > 50 then
```

```
        tempPart.X = partSystem.X + myValue
    else
        tempPart.X = partSystem.X - myValue
    end
    myValue = math.random(1, partSystem.YVariance)
    if math.random(1,100) > 50 then
        tempPart.Y = partSystem.Y + myValue
    else
        tempPart.Y = partSystem.Y - myValue
    end
    myValue = math.random(1,partSystem.ScaleVariance)
    if math.random(1,100) > 50 then
        tempPart.Scale = partSystem.Scale + myValue
    else
        tempPart.Scale = partSystem.Scale - myValue
    end
    tempPart.ID = partSystem.BaseID + idCounter
    table.insert(particles, tempPart)
    print("new particle created")
end
```

This process simply walks through the creation of a temporary table with all of the values that are tracked for an individual particle, and it's here that we calculate the variance values for each of the parameters. We then insert a new entry at the end of the particles table (which holds all active particles) with the temporary table values we've just populated.

Back in the ProcessParticles() function, we now walk through, via the ipairs() iterator, all of the active particles and adjust their runtime values. Finally, we check on the age of the particle. If the particle is older than its life span, we delete it (we delete only one item per cycle); otherwise, we render the sprite to the screen. Finally, we remove the last particle that was tagged with the removeMe variable from the particles master table.

This basic system can be expanded and optimized easily. You can use a quick particle system, instead of an animation, to simulate an explosion. You can use a longer-duration particle system to indicate burning rubble and such. In this example, the particles move from left to right, but you can make them move in any direction—even spread out uniformly or collapse back to a central point. It's also easy to add additional behavior to your system. Consider for a moment how you might add a random sprite rotation to the particles.

3D Sidebar

Although this chapter deals exclusively with sprite graphics in the context of our sample code base, Lua is also a great tool with which to control 3D graphics. In our games that we've developed at Magic Lantern, we created a 3D system to provide us the flexibility to develop many 3D games. See Figure 14.7 for an example.

FIGURE 14.7 In this screenshot, we see a 3D game powered by Lua, not only for the GUI elements but also to manage the 3D objects and animations on screen.

We use our own internal system for managing, rendering, and animating 3D models, but we use Lua almost exclusively to control our 3D environments. The following list of functions is our core LuaGlue library that we developed to enable script programmers to control our dynamic and static 3D assets:

StartCamera(): Positions the camera and looks at point in 3D world.

SlewCamera(): Slides the camera to a new position and looks at point with nice acceleration and dampening during the stop. →

StartCamera(): Positions the camera and looks at point in 3D world.

SlewCamera(): Slides the camera to a new position and looks at point with nice acceleration and dampening during the stop.

AddEnvironmentObject(): Adds a 3D object to the world. We can also capture its entity ID, which allows us to modify the object's behavior at run time.

AddLight(): Adds an ambient or directional light to the 3D world.

AttachParticleEffect(): Attaches a 3D particle effect (also defined in Lua) to a node on an entity.

AttachChildEntity(): Attaches a 3D object to a node on an entity. If the parent is moved, the child moves with it.

PositionChildEntity(): Places a 3D object in relation to a node on an existing entity. If the existing entity is moved, this entity remains.

TintEntity(): Tints an entity with an indicated ambient color.

SetEntityAnimation(): Sets an animation for an entity.

StartAnimSequence(): Starts an animation for an entity.

This list just gives a taste of how a 3D system can be controlled via a library of custom-created LuaGlue functions. With a fairly limited set of 3D control functions—but the power of a full scripting language and event system—we have been able to manage and control dynamic 3D assets in more than a dozen published games to date.

SUMMARY

In this chapter, we explored a myriad of examples of using Lua to control graphical screen elements in 2D. Although 3D is certainly becoming the dominant form of gaming these days, the 2D world is still a viable platform for game development, and it's a great environment in which to learn core game-development processes.

By coupling together the *Take Away* game and the examples from the last two chapters, you now have the foundation on which to build your very own game. If you don't want to dive under the hood and write your own LuaGlue functions, the *Take Away* executable, together with Lua, gives you a robust toolbox to create numerous games, from simple board games to complex RTS games with intelligent enemies controlled by finite state machines.

If you do want to dive in deeper and write your own LuaGlue functions, one place to start is in creating a system to allow Lua to interface with 3D objects. This system would grow your arsenal to cover most major aspects of game development with the Lua scripting language.

No matter what path you take, you now have the tools to press forward with your own unique creations. In the final portion of this book, we'll cover debugging your Lua programs, working with compiled scripts, and distributing Lua in your games.

15 Final Things to Consider

In This Chapter

- Adding Sound and Music
- Working with an Editor
- Debugging Lua Scripts
- Managing Assets
- Delivering Lua Code
- License Issues
- Next Steps

Throughout this book, we've grown in our understanding of Lua as a scripting language tool that can help us craft an exciting and addictive game. We began from square one, with an introduction to scripting languages themselves, and have worked our way through the language and through our own game project, *Take Away*. We now have nearly all the tools we need to work with Lua, both with our current codebase and as a component of your own from-the-ground-up game project.

We've come a long way, but we still have a few issues to cover before we set you out on your own course. In this chapter, we'll take a look at adding sound and music to your games (and controlling playback from Lua), debugging your scripts, deploying your scripts, and where you might go from here.

ADDING SOUND AND MUSIC

Sound and music can add another dimension to your game and make it feel far more complete. Many sophisticated systems for integrating sound effects and multichannel music to a game project are available, but we're going to cover the bare essentials here.

First, let's look at adding some simple sound effects to an interface. In most game programs, we hear some sort of click or other aural indication that we've clicked a button in the game. Because we are capturing that event already, it's quite simple to add a sound effect. An example from our *Take Away* game follows:

```
if id == GUI_MAIN_MENU + 300 then
    PlaySound(1, "button.wav")
    RunGUI("GUI_InGame.lua")
end
```

In this example, the 1 argument is an ID value that we are assigning to the sound. In our codebase, a Lua sound will stop by itself when it is finished, but if you want to stop a sound manually, you will need the ID number, as shown in the next example:

```
StopSound(1)
```

PlaySound LuaGlue

Sound effects are sounds that play one time and are in the WAV format. The sound is loaded and played using DirectSound. When started, the DX9 library loads the DirectSound system. The code that handles the internal workings of DirectSound is taken directly from the Microsoft sample library. The files are dsutil.cpp and dsutil.h. The Sound LuaGlue follows:

```
extern "C" int _PlaySound(lua_State *L)
{
    int argNum = 1;
    cLua *lua = g_pBase->GetLua();

    int  soundID       = lua->GetNumberArgument(argNum++);
    const char *soundName   = lua->GetStringArgument(argNum++);
    if(soundName && (soundID != 0))
    {
        DXContext::GetInstance()->PlaySound(soundID, soundName);
    }
    return 0;
}
```

The PlaySound LuaGlue creates an object much like GUI ID. An ID is assigned to allow the user to reference it later, and the filename of the WAV file to be played is passed. The sound is played and then stops when the sound is complete or the LuaGlue function StopSound is called.

```
extern "C" int _StopSound(lua_State *L)
{
    int argNum = 1;
    cLua *lua      = g_pBase->GetLua();
    int  soundID   = lua->GetNumberArgument(argNum++);
    if(soundID != 0)
    {
        DXContext::GetInstance()->StopSound(soundID);
    }
    return 0;
```

```
}
```

The Lua code can stop any sound in progress by passing the ID into the StopSound LuaGlue.

Music

Music functionality is provided by the ogg/vorbis library. Ogg/vorbis, a free library that is also patent free, gives similar compression to other formats that are available for a license fee. You can learn more about the format in the Internet at *www.vorbis.com/*. The library is hooked into the existing DirectSound functionality. The Music LuaGlue follows:

```
extern "C" int _PlayMusic(lua_State *L)
{
    int argNum = 1;
    cLua *lua = g_pBase->GetLua();
    int  musicID        = lua->GetNumberArgument(argNum++);
    const char *musicName    = lua->GetStringArgument(argNum++);
    if(musicName && (musicID != 0))
    {
        DXContext::GetInstance()->PlayMusic(musicID, musicName);
    }

    return 0;
}
```

PlayMusic is similar to PlaySound except it takes an OGG file as input. See the next example:

```
extern "C" int _StopMusic(lua_State *L)
{
    int argNum = 1;
    cLua *lua = g_pBase->GetLua();
    int  musicID = lua->GetNumberArgument(argNum++);
    if(musicID != 0)
    {
        DXContext::GetInstance()->StopMusic(musicID);
    }
    return 0;
}
```

Calling the StopMusic LuaGlue with the ID of the music stops the music.

■ Everyone that develops games has his own standard set of advice to give anyone that asks about game programming. Most of this sage advice boils down to two things: keep all your assets organized, and secure the gameplay of your game.

WORKING WITH AN EDITOR

Lua files are text files that can be edited within any program that can manage text files, from Microsoft Word all the way down to Notepad. Because Lua reports errors in files by line numbers, you'll be best served by using an editor that displays line numbers. Beyond that, the choice is really up to you.

ON THE CD

A number of programmer editors out there can offer you more bells and whistles, but the key is to find one that fits your style. The editor included on the CD-ROM is Zeus (see Figure 15.1), the program editor we use in-house. It has all the features we use regularly, plus it allows us to write macros for file and function headers, has some great tools for quickly searching for function names in a project, and allows you to actually write macros for the editor in Lua. One feature that is really useful is the ability to set up your own colors for keywords. That way, you can use one color to indicate Lua keywords and another color to indicate your LuaGlue functions.

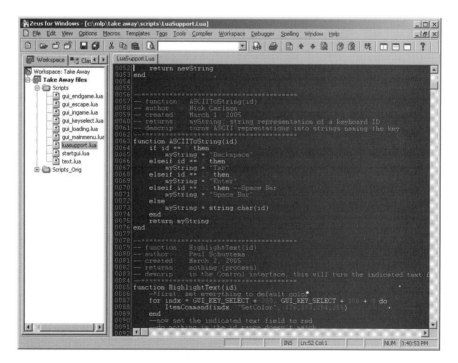

FIGURE 15.1 The Zeus program editor is the tool we use in-house to compose and edit Lua scripts.

DEBUGGING LUA SCRIPTS

Lua isn't a language that you can debug in the same manner that you do for C++ within a full-featured development environment such as Microsoft Visual Studio®. We can't, within a text editor, step through our Lua script a line at a time or set up a variable to watch within a window.

Just because we don't have an IDE (Integrated Development Environment) for Lua doesn't mean we can't debug our complex Lua scripts effectively. In the pages that follow, we'll explore some ways in which we can decipher what is happening in our scripts so that we can more easily debug our games.

General Principles

Our goal, as game developers who use Lua to create games, is the same as any other game developer: we want to create a fun and addictive play experience. We hear that a lot: "fun and addictive." What we don't hear so often—but is often even more important—"we want to create a game that is bug-free."

Bugs are errors in the program code of a game. In a game, a bug can either crash a game or simply foul up the data in some way so the game logic doesn't perform properly. The bottom line is that we want to deliver our games free from errors, because nothing spoils a game experience for the player more than a program that crashes or a game that "cheats" the player due to erroneous logic. A game done well will immerse the player—a bug will immediately throw our player out of that immersion and remind him that he's operating a computer program (and a faulty one at that!) rather than actually flying a spaceship through the depths of the solar system.

Removing errors (bugs) from our game is a process called "debugging" (odd, because removing bugs from our house is called "extermination"), and we often hear programmers use the phrase "I squashed that bug." Game developers come from two camps when we discuss the subject of debugging a game. Some liken it to a trip to the dentist's office: no fun, but it has to be done. Others relish the opportunity to become Sherlock Holmes and track down the clues to find and fix each bug.

The first step in debugging your game is to find a bug. Often, as soon as you go looking, you'll find many, many bugs lurking in the dark corners of your code. When you find a bug, you need to document it in some way. If you are a one-man-shop, the first step might be to just jot it down on a piece of paper. If you are part of a larger team, you may need some sort of defect-tracking document or system to list all of the bugs found and if they were fixed.

Many, many defect-tracking software packages are out there for use from small teams to giant multisite operations. In-house, we like to keep things as simple as possible, so we utilize the Mantis system, which is a free Web-based system (*www.mantisbt.org*). See Figure 15.2.

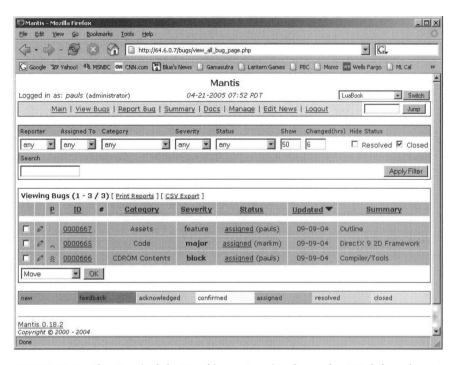

FIGURE 15.2   The Mantis defect-tracking system is a free, robust Web-based system.

Of course, probably the very first step you need to take, even before documenting a bug, is to apply the scientific method and *repeat the experiment*. A bug is virtually impossible to fix if it can't be duplicated, so this is clearly your first step. If you are working with multiple developers (or are lucky enough to have a tester on your team), you need to get the bug reporter in the habit of writing up a clear and easy "steps to reproduce" statement for every bug found. Determining what situation causes the bug offers the best first clues for tracking down and fixing a program error.

Once you have found a bug, and can create a situation in which it will repeat (this is another great reason for using Lua to save your game data—you can create a save-game file that can restore your game world to the moment just before the error occurs), your next step is to simplify the problem. Often, a fully featured game will have many things happening at once. Even in our simple *Take Away* game, we simultaneously track multiple enemies, projectiles, and targets.

You job is to peel away as much extra stuff as possible so that you can just focus on the problem at hand. In this respect, using block comments is a great approach, because you can take large chunks of code "out of play" easily. With some work and simplification, you should be able to isolate the potential candidates for trouble in your code and then fix the problem. Of course, you'll find a good handful of bugs that are simple typos (you capitalized a variable name here but not over there) or obvious errors in logic. These types of errors will make up 70 to 80 percent of your bugs and will only take 5 percent of the time to fix. It's the logic bugs or data overflow bugs deep in your scripts that will take the most time and detective work.

Once you've set the foundation, you are ready to dive in and search for your bug. One of the most important things you need to know is where you are in the flow of the program and what values variables have at certain times. In an IDE, you have the option of setting breakpoints, stepping through code, and viewing variable values at any time. We have to be a little more creative in Lua, because we don't work within an IDE. Some suggestions that will allow you to track progress through your scripts and view variable values follow. With this information, you should be able to find the cause of the error easily and correct it.

Although Lua doesn't give us the full-featured debugging controls of a development environment, we do have some advantages in our camp. We can easily edit and rerun a script without recompiling anything. This ability allows us to use trial-and-error methods quickly and effectively. We can also use capabilities like a runtime command prompt (see the next section) to edit, view, and change our game values right at runtime.

DoFile

A simple first-pass brute-force method of making sure that your Lua script is a legal script is to try to load your file with the `dofile()` function. When the Lua interpreter parses and compiles your file, it will fail and return the first uncompilable error it finds (not logic errors, though).

Lua Error Messages

The Lua command interpreter processes Lua chunks at runtime. If it encounters an error (something that it cannot process), it will generate an error message to the controlling C++ program. In the codebase that we have developed throughout this book, we pass that error message out to the debug window (see the next section) so that you can read it. Lua attempts to deliver as much information about the error as possible, such as the filename and the line number within which it occurred (which is why it's vital to work with an editor that gives you line numbers). Lua will even report line numbers with compiled scripts.

These error messages are your primary tool for fixing errors that cause Lua itself to fail, but remember that an error in line 165 might not actually be an error there at all, but an error somewhere else in your script where you set the variable that was passed to a function in line 165.

Using the Runtime Debug Window

You'll notice that the base executable we use in this book (not the console program we introduced at the start) launches with a second window—a debug window. This is your most powerful tool with which to debug Lua, because it is a full Lua command-line interpreter that operates within the same Lua environment as your game (and at the same time). You can use the debug window exactly like we used the stand-alone console in the earlier chapters, and this, in and of itself, will be quite useful. But consider that while your game is running, the debug window console has access to all of the variables and functions in your entire game. If you are running the game and need to see the value of a variable, you could simply enter the following script:

```
print(curDistance)
```

Within your scripts, you can also make use of the `print()` function. The output of this function will be sent to the debug window. If you want to determine if you hit a certain function during the running of your game, you could add a `print()` call as follows:

```
function HardMath(myValue)
    print("running HardMath()")
    return myValue * 2
end
```

Other examples of ways to utilize the debug window during runtime follow:

- You can move interface items to preview layout positioning:

```
SetItemPosition(GUI_MAIN_MENU + 200, 498, 292, 0, 0)
```

- You can run complete GUIs when script loading is not yet in place:

```
RunGUI("GUI_MainMenu.lua")
```

- You can reload changes in a just-edited script by recalling the file while the program is running:

```
dofile("Scripts\\GUI_DamageFire.Lua")
```

- You can run game functions directly:

```
ClearGUI(GUI_INGAME)
```

- You can print out mathematic calculations using the Lua functions:

```
print(math.cos(math.pi/3))
```

- You can view table values (helpful in determining which parameters are filled):

```
print(myEnemies[1].X)
```

- You can determine value returned by a function you have written:

```
var1 = GetState()
print (var1)
```

- You can "force" a GUI event to happen by simply running the event handler manually:

```
InGameEvent(gThrustKey, GUI_KEY_PRESS)
```

- You can also use the debug window to copy and paste lines from a function you are trying to debug right into the prompt. In this way, you can "step" through a function a line at a time. Add some print statements, and you can really get a look at what's going on step by step.
- You can also use the built-in debug function to see the functions that are currently on the Lua Stack. This ability isn't that useful to a scripter, but if you are trying to fix an unfixable error, using this function with the help of a C++ programmer (who can help decode the memory locations) might give you the extra ammunition you need:

```
print(debug.traceback())
```

Using Text Fields

Another simple tool is to set up several text fields in your main game display that are, by default, turned off. You can then map to a GUI_KEY_PRESS event to enable those fields and populate them with the values you with to track, as in the next example:

```
if eventCode == GUI_KEY_PRESS then
    if id == 118 then -- v key
        if gDebugVisible == false then
            EnableObject(100, 1, 1)
            EnableObject(101, 1, 1)
            ItemCommand(100, "SetString", string.format("%s%d",
            "Current Thurst value: ", curThurst))
            ItemCommand(101, "SetString", string.format("%s%d",
            "Current Rotation value: ", curRot))
            gDebugVisible = true
        else
            EnableObject(100, 1, 1)
            EnableObject(101, 1, 1)
            gDebugVisible = false
        end
    end
end
```

With this little "debug monitor", you can toggle your display on or off, and see the values at any time during gameplay.

Using File Output

When you are dealing with rapid data processing or simply a huge amount of data that you need to debug, printing to the debug window may not be practical.

You can create a simple debug file-output system with the following three functions that you would place in your LuaSupport.lua file:

```
function StartDebugOutput()
    debugFile = io.open("debug_data.txt", "w")
    if debugFile ~= nil then
        debugFile:write("-- Auto-generated debug report")
        debugFile:write(string.char (10))
        debugFile:write(string.char (10))
        debugFile:write(string.format("%s%s", "-- File created on: ",
        os.date()))
        debugFile:write(string.char (10))
        debugFile:write(string.char (10))
    end
end
```

In this first function, you open a file for output and write out some header information. You would put the call to this file somewhere during the initialization of your game (perhaps even in StartGUI.lua, after you run your LuaSupport script). We then need to close the file when we are finished. We just use this function, which we can call right before we quit the program, as follows:

```
function EndDebugOutput()
    io.close(debugFile)
end
```

Finally, we have the function that allows us to output our information, as follows:

```
function DebugMsg(myString)
    if debugFile ~= nil then
        debugFile:write(myString)
        debugFile:write(string.char (10))
    end
end
```

This function will receive a string as a parameter and write it out as a line in a file. Remember, you can use string.format() to build a string comprising text and numbers. This function can be called anywhere in your program, but it's a good idea to add some sort of identifier to the line that is written out so you know what the value is and where the message came from. For example:

```
DebugMsg(string.format("%s%d","function: CalculateRange(), curRange: ",
curRange))
```

This script will print out not only the function but the value you want to tracking. If you hit this function over a tenth of a second, you'll get too much data for the debug window, but you can simply review this file to see where your value started heading off track.

If you write regular updates to this file, indicating where your program is, and you stumble into an error that either gives you a hard crash or an endless loop, this tool is also valuable. In a hard crash, you can open this file (which wasn't neatly closed by your program, but it crashed anyway) to see where the program was when it crashed. If you are caught in an endless loop, you can press Alt + F4 to get out of your program and, again, see where it was when you bailed by looking at this file.

MANAGING ASSETS

Assets are anything that is of value in the game-development process. Examples of assets are source code, 2D and 3D art, tools, and music. In complex games there can be a lot of files to keep track of. These files are usually updated regularly, so you have the additional problem of making sure the latest and greatest assets make it into the game. When you add people to the team, the assets can get out of hand very quickly. You also must consider the runtime organization of assets. Do you just deliver a pile of files to the user, or are they organized in some way? What are the names of the files? Where do they live on the disk? How does the game code find the assets?

Asset Organization

Assets are the components of your game, from Lua scripts, to C++ header and code files, to bitmap interface images, to sound and music files. Your game needs to access certain assets during runtime, but so does your development team during the creation of your game.

Source Control

Assets that are used during development must be kept up to date and accessible by all team members. The tools that provide this function are called source-control tools or configuration-management tools. A very good tool for organizing these assets is CVS, or Concurrent Versions System (*www.cvshome.org/*). Other good tools available are SourceSafe from Microsoft (*http://msdn.microsoft.com/ vstudio/previous/ssafe/*) and Perforce (*www.perforce.com/*). CVS has the advantage of being open source (that is, free) and well supported across many platforms. CVS is also in general use all across the Internet. If you choose CVS and are using Windows, a wonderful add-in tool is TortoiseCVS (*www.tortoisecvs.org/*), which plugs into the Windows desktop and makes using CVS a snap.

Whichever tool you choose, the benefits will be many. Use the system to store and track all source assets like source code, Lua scripts, source artwork, 3D models, and so on. Make sure you also include a completely up-to-date build or a process to obtain the latest build by gathering all the assets from the repository. This brings us to the organization of the runtime data. All the examples in the book use a simple directory structure. The main file in the root of the game directory is the game program. Other files can be there, but the program does not usually use them. Other runtime assets are grouped together into folders. The folders are Scripts, Textures, Sounds, and Music. If 3D models were on the asset list, there would also be a Models directory. You could also pack the files in each directory into an archive file, like a ZIP file, and modify the C++ code to read the archives. Doing so would reduce the runtime disk footprint and set up the code for systems that had poor or nonexistent file systems.

Runtime Folders

Of course, all the organization in the world will not help if the game doesn't understand the system. The sample code automatically uses the folder organization laid out in the previous section. The C++ code looks for Lua code in the Scripts folder, bitmap files in the Textures directory, sounds (.wav files) in the Sounds directory, and music (.ogg files) in the Music directory.

DELIVERING LUA CODE

You can send out your Lua code as text files like the ones you use during development. This ability can be very cool for people in the "modding" community and it allows great access to the end user. If you don't want your users modifying your Lua code or you don't want to give away the secrets of the system you have put together, you do have another method for distributing Lua code. The final text files can be run through a program that the Lua authors have provided in the standard distribution. This program, called luac.exe, "compiles" the Lua text files into a binary format. Delivering compiled Lua code makes it much harder for cheaters and hackers to see what your game does and what technology you use.

The Lua Compiler

The source for luac.exe can be found in the original distribution of Lua in the directory lua-5.0.2\src\luac. The sample workspace has a Visual C++ project to build the program. The program is a command-line application, which means it takes parameters on the command line from a command prompt (DOS prompt). A typical compile command would be as follows:

```
Luac —o StartGUI.lub StartGUI.lua
```

This line would compile the file StartGUI.lua and place the binary data in a file called StartGUI.lub. One way to make this process easier is to make a batch file. This is a text file with command-prompt commands in it. The file must have the .bat extension for Windows to recognize it as a batch file. You can put a compile command (like the one mentioned earlier) in the file for each of the Lua files you wish to compile. Once the file is built, all you would have to do is double-click it from the Windows desktop to compile all your files.

LuaGlue: RunScript

Lua can read code in numerous places and formats. In all the examples, Lua code is always in the Scripts directory. It can be the standard text file with the .lua extension or a compiled (with luac.exe) binary file with the .lub extension. The RunScript LuaGlue function simplifies locating code to run. RunScript is a replacement for the Lua do_file function. It searches for the passed script in the Scripts folder, and if that fails it looks in the current directory; if that fails it starts over after changing the script file extension from .lua to .lub.

Using different extensions for text and binary files is a good practice. Use the extension .lua for the Lua code in text format and .lub for the Lua code in the binary format. The Lua interpreter doesn't care if you send it a text file or a binary file or what the extension is, but it is useful for the humans working on the game to know the difference at a glance. The cLua object's RunScript member calls a helper function, findScript, to locate the proper Lua code file to run, listed next (found in cLua.cpp):

```cpp
static std::string findScript(const char *pFname)
{
    FILE *fTest;
    char drive[_MAX_DRIVE];
    char dir[_MAX_DIR];
    char fname[_MAX_FNAME];
    char ext[_MAX_EXT];
    _splitpath( pFname, drive, dir, fname, ext );
    std::string strTestFile = (std::string) drive + dir +
            "Scripts\\" + fname + ".LUB";
    fTest = fopen(strTestFile.c_str(), "r");
    if(fTest == NULL)
    {
        strTestFile = (std::string) drive + dir +
            "Scripts\\" + fname + ".LUA";
    fTest = fopen(strTestFile.c_str(), "r");
    }
    if(fTest == NULL)
    {
        strTestFile = (std::string) drive + dir + fname + ".LUB";
        fTest = fopen(strTestFile.c_str(), "r");
    }
    if(fTest == NULL)
    {
        strTestFile = (std::string) drive + dir + fname + ".LUA";
        fTest = fopen(strTestFile.c_str(), "r");
    }
    if(fTest != NULL)
```

```
    {
        fclose(fTest);
    }
    return strTestFile;
}
```

LICENSE ISSUES

Lua is free software and can be distributed in both not-for-profit or commercial software free of charge and without having to first seek permission from PUC-Rio in Brazil. Lua is open-source software and is licensed under the terms of the MIT license. The text of the license follows:

Copyright © 1994–2004 Tecgraf, PUC-Rio.

Permission is hereby granted, free of charge, to any person obtaining a copy of this software and associated documentation files (the "Software"), to deal in the Software without restriction, including without limitation the rights to use, copy, modify, merge, publish, distribute, sublicense, and/or sell copies of the Software, and to permit persons to whom the Software is furnished to do so, subject to the following conditions:
    The above copyright notice and this permission notice shall be included in all copies or substantial portions of the Software.

THE SOFTWARE IS PROVIDED "AS IS", WITHOUT WARRANTY OF ANY KIND, EXPRESS OR IMPLIED, INCLUDING BUT NOT LIMITED TO THE AND NONINFRINGEMENT. IN NO EVENT SHALL THE AUTHORS OR COPYRIGHT HOLDERS BE LIABLE FOR ANY CLAIM, DAMAGES OR OTHER LIABILITY, WHETHER IN AN ACTION OF CONTRACT, TORT OR OTHERWISE, ARISING FROM, OUT OF OR IN CONNECTION WITH THE SOFTWARE OR THE USE OR OTHER DEALINGS IN THE SOFTWARE.

A file containing this license document (which is found in the "License" folder on the CD-ROM) must be included with any distribution of the software. The Lua team also suggests, but certainly does not mandate, that a Web site that promotes the software have a blue Lua logo displayed somewhere.
    If you develop a project with Lua, it's a great idea to list your project on Lua List of Projects page (*www.lua.org/uses.html*), to let everyone know what you have created.

NEXT STEPS

Now that you have a handle on the Lua scripting language and you've worked with us to explore our first game together, it's time to take a look down the road. What are your next steps as you grow your skills and interest with Lua?

A great place to start is to become part of the Lua community. Stop by the official Lua Web site (*www.lua.org*) and see what's there. Read the documentation, the tutorials, and the discussions. Get involved, and post your questions and your discoveries. Although Lua has been around for several years, it is only just making headway into the games industry in a big way, so this is your chance to become part of a grassroots movement in our industry.

Another great next step is to write your own game from the *Take Away* codebase provided with this book. You'll notice, as you flip back through the LuaGlue documentation, that none of the LuaGlue functions are specific to our *Take Away* game—they are all general-purpose function on which we built the game with Lua. That means that you have in your hands a simple game development environment and all the tools you need to craft your own game, even if you don't know how to program C++.

Think through a game that you would like to develop—something simple, but perhaps more advanced than our *Take Away* game. Look through the tools and examples, from collision detection to sprite rotation to pathfinding—what kind of game can you create that uses these tools? Working through an entire project, in which all of the game play is controlled by Lua, will give you great experience with the language and will also allow you to experience the many aspects of game development, from interface design to game design to programming to sound and music.

Once you have a game under your belt, get online—see if there are any collaborative projects out there (*www.garagegames.com* is a great place to locate collaborative projects) already using Lua or that might be able to take advantage of a Lua implementation. Working with a collaborative team is a great way to learn about shared workloads, documenting your scripts, and working together to create a shared vision for your game. If you can't find a collaborative project online, start one yourself.

If you are already working in a development team, share the Lua language with them and let them see its capabilities, advantages, and disadvantages. See if it could become another tool to add to your team's development arsenal for future projects.

In-house we never set out to become Lua experts, but Lua seemed to fit our needs for a general-purpose scripting language after we developed our own language that was both limiting and expensive to debug and maintain. We've now created more than 17 projects with Lua, and we learn more with each project (and we even learned quite a bit writing this book!). It's a great component of our development arsenal, so I would recommend that any serious development team with scripting needs at least to review what Lua can do.

Finally, you can learn even more about the language and how to use the language in your applications. Lua wasn't created as a game-scripting language (the fit just happens to be great, and it is now a key part of what Lua will be in the future), so there are many other applications that can be served by Lua. Look at the Lua and Tecgraf Web sites, and you'll see Lua used in many contexts—even as an HTML preprocessing language like PHP.

There are also other aspects of Lua, such as the patterning system for string processing, that we didn't cover fully in this book. Co-routines are another example. Review the Lua documentation and the other books out there (including the essential *Programming in Lua* by one of Lua's creators Roberto Ierusalimschy, now available online at *www.lua.org*) and grow your knowledge of this small but fascinating language.

SUMMARY

We have now completed our portion of the journey together, and it is time for you to take what you have learned, expand on it, and make your own great games using Lua. We started from scratch and learned much along the way, from how to write our first function to how to navigate our way through an arbitrarily complex maze of obstacles.

You have learned the technical aspects of integrating Lua into your own C++ projects and how to write and interface your own LuaGlue functions with the scripting language. You have learned how to build the foundations of an event-driven system and how to create a GUI system on top of that.

You have learned how to work through a simple game design and then turn that game into a reality using Lua as your primary tool. From there, you learned many other tools and tracks, from artificial intelligence to distance vectors to particles systems. You now have the tools and the knowledge to sally forth and create your own play experiences.

We certainly hope that you have enjoyed the journey—we certainly have. It has been our pleasure to share our knowledge of Lua with you and hopefully grow the Lua community one reader at a time—because as the community grows, so do the chances too for those great moments of collaborative creativity. So go forth and make a great game—Lua style!

About the CD-ROM

In This Chapter

- System Requirements
- Contents
- Important Note

T his book features a companion CD-ROM that provides the source code for everything covered in this book, plus a number of useful tools and utilities.

SYSTEM REQUIREMENTS

- P450 or better processor
- Windows 2000/XP
- 32MB of RAM

- For the demos:
  - DirectX 9 (included on CD-ROM)
  - DX-compatible 3D video accelerator
- For the DirectX SDK:
  - OS: Microsoft Windows(r) 98, Windows Millennium Edition (Windows Me), or Windows 2000, Windows Server 2003, Windows XP
  - Approximately 65 megabytes (MB) of available space for installation (Once installed, you can delete the installation files. The remaining DirectX files use approximately 18 MB of hard drive space. If you had an earlier version of DirectX installed on your computer, you will see little difference in used space on your hard drive. DirectX 9.0 will overwrite the earlier versions.)
- For Lua:
  - Lua runs on most any system that can compile standard C code.
- For Ogg Vorbis:
  - Microsoft Windows 95, 98, Me, NT, 2000 or XP
  - A soundcard
  - Processor: Pentium 200 mhz or more
  - 32 Mb of RAM
- For Zeus:
  - Microsoft Windows 95, 98, Me, NT, 2000 or XP
  - 4 MB RAM
  - 4.5 MB available disk space

CONTENTS

The contents of the CD-ROM are organized within the following folders:

C++ Code: this folder contains the Visual Studio projects and all C++ source code for the Take Away game and other examples found in the book (for use with the .NET version of Visual Studio). There is also a companion folder, VS6_C++ Code, that contains the code for use with Visual Studio 6.

Chapters: this folder contains sub-folders (named for the chapters they support) that contains the Lua scripts and executable programs used within the book.

Documents: this folder contains the Take Away design document and a Lua scripting style guide.

DX9.0c: This folder contains the DirectX 9 SDK plus the latest runtime distributable package.

Figures: This folder contains all of the figures from the book, organized in folders by chapter.

License: This folder contains the distribution license documents for both Lua and Ogg Vorbis.

Lua: This contains the Lua console, the Lua manual and the source code for Lua 5.0

OggVorbis: This contains the source code to the Ogg Vorbis music system.

Take Away: this is the complete version of the Take Away game discussed in the book (partial versions appear in the chapter folders as well)

Zeus: This is the shareware version of the Zeus program editor—a great tool for editing Lua scripts.

IMPORTANT NOTE

We are currently in a transition time between the older architecture of Visual Studio and the .NET approach. The primary code in the book, plus the included DirectX SDK, are designed to work with the .NET version of Visual Studio.

We realize that many programmers are still working within Visual Studio 6, and we've included the game projects for that version of Visual Studio as well. It is important to note that the DirectX SDK included on this CD will not work with Visual Studio 6-you will need the Summer 2004 build of the DirectX SDK, which can be found at this link:

http://www.microsoft.com/downloads/details.aspx?FamilyId=FD044A42-9912-42A3-9A9E-D857199F888E&displaylang=en

Index